Camping!
Northern California

Dennis J. Oliver

The Complete
Guide to Public
Campgrounds for
RVs and Tents

SASQUATCH BOOKS
SEATTLE

Printed in the United State of America.
Distributed in Canada by Raincoast Books, Ltd.
07 06 05 04 03 02   5 4 3 2

Cover photograph: Stone/Rich La Salle
Cover design: Karen Schober
Interior design: Kate Basart
Interior composition: Andrea Reider
Maps: GreenEye Design
Interior photographs: Dennis Oliver

Library of Congress Cataloging in Publication Data
Oliver, Dennis
        Camping! Northern California : the complete guide to public
campgrounds for RVs and tents / by Dennis J. Oliver.
        p. cm.
        Includes indexes.
        ISBN 1-57061-262-5
        1. Camp sites, facilities, etc.--California, Northern--Guidebooks. 2. Camping--California, Northern--Guidebooks. 3. California, Northern--Guidebooks. I. Title.
        GV191.42.C2 O45 2001
        647.94795'09--dc21   00-068023

Disclaimer: Please use common sense. No guidebook can act as a substitute for careful planning and appropriate training. Know your personal limits; it is incumbent upon any user of this guide to assess his or her own skills, experience, fitness, and equipment. Readers must assume responsibility for their own actions and safety. Changing or unfavorable conditions in weather, roads, trails, waterways, etc. cannot be anticipated by the author or publisher, but should be considered by any outdoor participants. Likewise, be aware of any changes in public jurisdiction. Do not camp on private property without permission. The author and the publisher will not be responsible or liable for your safety or the consequences of using this guide.

        The information in this edition is based on facts available at press time and is subject to change. The author and publisher welcome information or updates conveyed by users of this book.

SASQUATCH BOOKS
615 Second Avenue
Seattle, Washington 98104
206/467-4300
books@SasquatchBooks.com
www.SasquatchBooks.com

Camping!
Northern California

State Park Reservations
ReserveAmerica
800-444-7275

Contents

Redwood Coast / 1

Wine Country / 35

Bay Area / 67

Big Sur Region / 101

Northern Mountains / 119

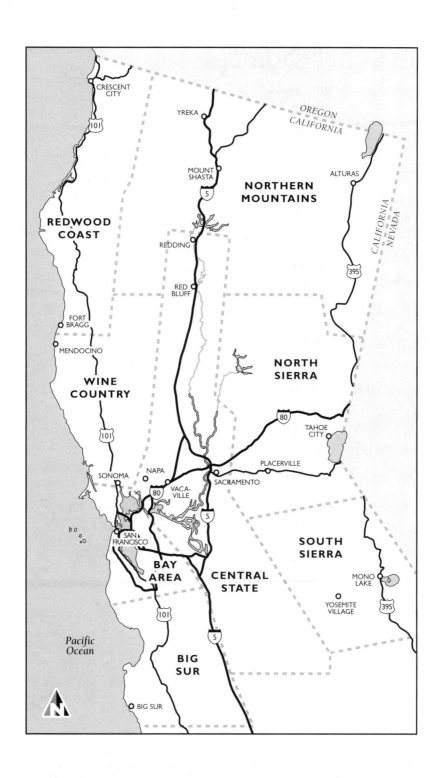

Acknowledgments

Researching a camping guidebook is a lot like going on a hundred 24-hour vacations; you hit the road, unfurl the sleeping pad, pack it up, and move on endlessly. Thanks are due Michael Carr, who rode shotgun on most of the road trips taken to research this book. But equal thanks are also due the manufacturers of my laptop computer (I won't name the brand), which is equipped with a battery that holds a charge for an amazing amount of time. (Still, every little hole-in-the-wall diner or tavern where I was allowed to charge the battery back up deserves some kudos as well!) This book is dedicated to Nellie, the jackass I rode during my last trip into the Marble Mountains Wilderness; I do hope that stomach gas problem worked itself out. To the great staff at Sasquatch Books, namely senior editor Kate Rogers and her production staff, thanks for another successful project.

Introduction

We were supposed to be afraid of Bigfoot. The man-ape stalked us behind every tree and lurked in secret corners during childhood campouts. Each broken twig and windblown tree branch was a sign that he had been nearby, or soon would be. But, of course, we all survived the taunts of this vivid legend etched into our imaginations by B-grade horror flicks and exaggerated stories around the campfire—a rite of passage for young campers throughout Northern California. Bigfoot was indeed the Blair Witch incarnate.

I also survived classic scouting initiation pranks: walking from campsite to campsite during the annual jamboree in search of a "left-handed smoke shifter," or stomping through the forest in search of a flightless bird we would have to capture and eat for dinner (if only it had existed). Sure, my cheeks turned crimson when stuff like this happened, but as a boy, it was thrilling to be out in the wilderness, building fires, sleeping in tents, and vacationing from parents, siblings, and everyday life.

There is more to all of this than monsters and memories, however. To grow up camping in Northern California means experiencing the redwood forests, the blue mountain lakes, the granite peaks of Yosemite National Park, the snowcapped summit of Mount Shasta, and the golden sunsets over the Pacific Ocean. The landscape of the region becomes woven into the fabric of our lives.

The state wasn't quite as crowded a few decades ago as it is today, and there are many here who are reluctant to share their most treasured secret places with others, especially newcomers. (As a matter of fact, I was warned not to disclose a few that did actually get mentioned in this book.) But, generally, Californians love to introduce novices and visitors to the outdoor treasures we have grown to love, enjoy, and perhaps take for granted. Look at this book as the best advice you can get from locals on where to camp and what to expect when you choose a location.

The information contained in this book is the result of a lifetime exploring the vast system of state and national parks, the endless network of national forest roads, and the long, winding coastal highways of Northern California. Beyond that, it is also the result of countless inquiries and interviews with fellow campers and hikers who were kind enough to share their trials and triumphs exploring the northern half of the Golden State.

But let's get one thing out of the way before you begin using this guide: Many of the campground descriptions are quite opinionated! This is a guidebook, not a directory, and the author has his biases. First, if given the choice, I prefer to camp as far away from highways, large groups of people, and concrete slabs as possible. This means most of the campgrounds I ranked high are going to be on the quiet and out-of-the-way side, but not all of them.

Second, I believe exploring the outdoors is one of the most important keys to understanding California history; therefore, many high-ranked campgrounds are in places of historical significance.

I also believe the national forests are underappreciated, and for this reason a significant percentage of highly ranked campgrounds found in this book are in portions of national forests that you may never have heard of. Often, I advise outdoor adventurers to camp in forests near the more popular tourist attractions, such as Lake Tahoe or Yosemite National Park, to avoid the crush.

And, I have to admit, I am not a fisherman. While you will find no shortage of places to camp in this book that are suitable for fishing trips, campgrounds along California's Central Valley rivers, or near some of the reservoirs where the best bass fishing in the world can be found have been rated lower by me than they might have been by a person whose rod and reel are an extension of his forearm. So don't be afraid to plan a fishing trip.

With these caveats in mind, use *Camping! Northern California* as a friend and travel companion, whether you're on vacation or just hitting the road for the weekend. We designed this book to fit in the glove compartment or door pocket of your vehicle; it is a road map to the wonderful place I call home, and a guide for the best way to see Northern California. Hope to see you out there somewhere.

How to Use This Book

The easy-to-read format of this guide should make using *Camping! Northern California* fairly self-explanatory. But a few notes on its construction, as well as on our philosophies in describing and rating each campground, should make it even more helpful. Here's a look at how each campground listing is set up.

Sample Listing:

② Manchester State Beach

Alder and Brush Creeks cut through this area's more than 700 acres of meadows, wild dunes, and beach. Both creeks have good steelhead and salmon runs in the winter season. This is a great place to find interesting samples of driftwood on the shore, as the topography of this section of coast makes it a magnet for debris from the ocean. Of course, that isn't always a good thing: There is also plenty of junk washed up on this beach if you catch it at the wrong time. But all in all, this is a pleasant and pristine section of coast—suitable for bird-watching, spring wildflower walks, and creekside hikes. Look for flocks of brown pelicans at the freshwater lagoons formed by the creeks. Most of the campground is in the direct line of fire for strong ocean winds, so be prepared to tie down and bundle up if necessary. The Point Arena Lighthouse is visible from the beachfront.

sites	*46*
	46
	46, no hookups, RVs to 32 feet
open	*All year*
reservations	*Up to 8 weeks in advance; California State Parks, 800/444-7275*
contact	*Manchester State Beach, 707/882-2437*

Facilities: Each site has a picnic table and a fire grill. Running water and outhouse toilets are available nearby, as is an RV disposal station.

Getting there: From Point Arena, drive north on US 101 for 7 miles. Drive through the town of Manchester and then beyond for 1 mile to the beach entrance on the left side of the road.

Ratings

Sites are rated according to activities and attractions found nearby, but the ratings are also based on highly subjective criteria. Following is a key to the campground ratings you will find throughout this book.

🌲🌲🌲🌲🌲: If this were a hotel, you would find the bed turned down at night and a wonderful assortment of chocolates and mints spread across a newly fluffed pillow. There are no screaming kids or barking dogs. The hand of God himself reached down from the clouds and carved this place out. It's perfect, so don't mess with it. If you can land a site here, guard it with your life. It's a keeper.

🌲🌲🌲🌲: You can see the "light in the trees" that Annie Dillard wrote about so eloquently from here. Afternoons are for napping, in places reminiscent of a warm down comforter that smells like your favorite perfume. These sites may well be the highlight of your trip, but you have other exploring to do.

🌲🌲🌲: The place is a little rough but it's all worth it because you're in the area you need to be in, near the attraction you want to see, and the place is clean. There are a few hidden corners of the campground where tents rule. The sound of the river lulls you to sleep. These are great places to leave your camp set up during a long hike.

🌲🌲: There is an Irish setter chained to a post in the campsite next to yours and it wants to play, whether you're in the mood or not. Its owners are a gang of children whose shouts echo through the canyons at 7 a.m. Still, there are occasional moments of serenity here, and it's good enough for a night or two.

🌲: This campground is good to know about if you're desperate, but if you have a choice, pass it by.

No trees means that if this were a hotel room, the towels would be slightly damp from the previous guest's morning shower, and there would be no toilet paper. Also, the door would only lock sometimes, and the manager's name would be Norman. Run for your life.

Sites

The campground descriptions in this book are structured in such a way that the reader can easily find a place to unfurl the bedroll without having to lower standards or put up with unpleasant surprises. For each campground, we have indicated the total number of sites, as well as the number of sites designed for use by RVs and the number designed for tents only. Obviously, tent-only campgrounds are for just that—tents only. Campgrounds with a lot of RV spaces, especially those with full or partial hookups, are more likely to feature some pavement, though tents are usually still welcome.

Tent and RV symbols

The tent and RV symbols provide an easy guide to what kinds of sites you can find at a given campground. The tent symbol means there are sites suitable for tents; the RV icon indicates there are sites that can accommodate RVs and trailers. Next to the symbols you'll find details on RV hookups and length, or number of tent-only or walk-in sites. These symbols will help you quickly determine your options; a campground with fifty RV sites, for example, might be a bit more chaotic than a campground with only ten.

Open (the camping season)

While the official outdoor season runs from Memorial Day to Labor Day, in many parts of the state the camping season actually begins in April and doesn't end until November. And in some places, it's always camping season (particularly if you're a snow camper). Each site listing indicates whether the site is open year-round or between certain dates only, but this information comes with a big footnote: seasonal dates apply only under normal circumstances. For example, a high mountain site that normally might be open by June 1 can quite conceivably be buried in snow well into July. Likewise, flooding, fires, and environmental regulations can affect actual opening dates. It's also often permissible to camp outside of the official season in some cases, particularly at some national forest sites. It is critical that you check with ranger stations and park offices to make sure campgrounds are in working order before just dropping in. Another good idea is to check current weather conditions in the area of interest. Go to www.nws.mbay.net for up-to-date information about California weather.

Reservations

Despite advances in technology that make it possible to reserve a campground using your digital hand-held pocket computer with built-in cellular modem, the best way to do it still involves picking up the telephone.

California State Park campsites can be reserved up to eight weeks in advance in most cases. The phone number to call is 800/444-7275, the state parks reservations system. Go to www.parks.ca.gov for basics.

In **national parks**, sites can be reserved up to five months in advance. The phone number for ParkNet, the national park system, is 800/436-7275. Yosemite National Park sites are wildly popular, so be sure to call five months to the day of when you want to make your trip, and use a phone with a redial button. Go to http://reservations.nps.gov for more information.

With **national forest** sites, reservations can be made 240 days in advance. Call the forest service reservations system, 877/444-6777. Go to www.reserveusa.com/camping/ for more particulars.

Local and regional park districts will have their own reservations policies and fees, and these are described with individual campground listings.

One special trick to finding a site during peak times is to look for forest locations where campgrounds are awarded on a first-come, first-served basis. It is also sometimes prudent to check desired parks for cancellations the day of arrival.

Contact

In addition to the reservation phone number, we have included contact information for campgrounds that have numbers for general information and current conditions. There are a number of other resources, however, that may be of use. The California State Parks web site is a good place to go to get an idea of what different regions of the state have to offer, at www.parks.ca.gov. Likewise, the national forest service officially recommends campers use www.reserveusa.com/camping/ for basic information about camping opportunities in its facilities. The aforementioned national park service reservations site, at http://reservations.nps.gov/ also includes a wealth of information about campgrounds and attractions in general. What this book will provide that none of these sites can duplicate, however, is an honest and completely subjective assessment of whether specific campgrounds are worth your time. And always check in with ranger stations and visitor centers when using public campgrounds and parks, where updated information on road and campground conditions, along with other news you may need to know, is available. Other good resources for this are the major outdoor retailers, such as REI, and local chambers of commerce and tourist bureaus.

Campground descriptions

Each campground description is structured so that the reader not only has a good idea of the amenities and ambience of the each spot, but also can tell what major attractions and activities can be enjoyed nearby. By reading the detailed campground descriptions, adventurers will know whether to bring the hiking boots, birding scope, or fly rod and reel, and which sites are situated near put-ins for rafters and kayakers. Also in these descriptions, travelers will find a detailed account of campground amenities and the general topography, climate, and vegetation of the area, along with wildlife notes.

Facilities

With each campground description, a full accounting of the facilities is included. This gives the reader a quick and easy way to tell where a hot shower will be available, which campgrounds have flush toilets, and how primitive or fully developed sites are.

Getting there

There are specific directions for how to reach each campground, as well as regional maps at the beginning of each chapter, which show the general location of the campgrounds listed and their proximity to major attractions and highways. I strongly encourage you to use official park and forest maps, however, particularly if traveling within national forests. Forest service roads can be labyrinthine and complicated—it's easy to get lost! In the case of state and national parks, official maps will better outline road restrictions and accessibility.

Other Details:

Fees

Camping fees are subject to change at any time. At press time, fees in state parks had just been lowered to a range of $8 to $12; national park sites are currently $15 per night. The cost of national forest sites varies. Some sites are free, others are $9 or $10, and still others are $16 to $17. And to make it even more confusing, those that do have fees sometimes don't, depending on current conditions and the time of season. For example, at some campgrounds, self-registration is allowed before the official camping season starts and there is no charge.

Rules and regulations

Each government agency has its own set of rules and regulations, and it's your responsibility not only to find out what they are but also to abide by them. Fires, for example, are never allowed in national forest wilderness areas and dogs are not allowed outside of campgrounds and parking areas in national parks (unless, of course, they are guide dogs for the disabled). Dispersed camping outside of designated campgrounds is not allowed in state parks, but it's encouraged in national forests. Some forest service roads are closed to all-terrain vehicle action during specific parts of the year, while others never are. In Yosemite National Park, fishing is not allowed in the Merced, for example. The best plan for sorting out the myriad rules and regulations is to make sure you stop in at visitor centers and ranger stations to pick up official handouts.

Safety

Don't feed the bears, don't stomp through an avalanche-prone canyon in the snow; carry a first aid kit and a cell phone, and use proper gear. Don't camp alone unless you know what you're doing. Safety amounts to common sense and seeking out the correct information. Do it. Your life may depend on it.

Redwood Coast

Still wondering if that waterproofing you applied to the seams of the new tent actually works? California's Redwood Coast is the place you are sure to find out. You see, the farther north you trek in the Golden State, the wetter everything gets. Even during the summer, you will find out sooner or later just how winter-proof you are with all your fancy gear. If it turns out you leak, though, resist the temptation to move to a comfortable, dry spot (like the nearest cheap motel). You can shower and powder up some other time. For now, just towel off and enjoy the cold, wet, nights and drizzly, foggy mornings that help make redwood country one of the most remarkable places on Earth.

Step for the first time into an ancient virgin grove of redwoods or watch a sunset over the Pacific at the mouth of the Mattole River and you will immediately understand. Put in on the unrestrained Smith River or the rabid Klamath and the wild currents will take you on a turbo tour. Gold Rush history, the abandoned nineteenth-century military town of Fort Jones, the Native American settlements of Hoopa Valley, and the legendary man-ape known as Bigfoot add to this area's potpourri of all things California.

Perhaps the best campsites in the north coast region are those found on the banks of the Smith River in Jedediah Smith Redwoods State Park, the longest free-flowing river in the state and one of six major rivers crisscrossing the coastal mountains. There are also the misty forests of Humboldt County's oceanfront parks, the hidden corners of Smith River National Recreation Area, the serenity of the Van Duzen River canyon, or the lazy comfort of Benbow Lake.

In this part of California myths get debunked—especially that one about all the biggest, best stuff being in Texas. Here you will find the tallest trees, the heftiest salmon and steelhead, the longest free-flowing river, the highest sand dunes, the thickest fog, the coldest wind, and the steepest and most winding Forest Service roads leading to some of the most well-hidden campgrounds. The cold salt breezes, the majestic Roosevelt elk, the freak snow storms in summer, the shady creek beds lined with perfect gravel—these are the superlative reasons you won't care how wet or cold or scruffy you feel when the elements get the best of you.

Redwood Coast

1. Jedediah Smith Redwoods State Park
2. Big Flat Camp
3. Panther Flat Camp
4. Grassy Flat Camp
5. Patrick Creek Camp
6. Boise Creek Camp
7. Lakes Earl and Tolowa
8. Nickel Creek Camp
9. Mill Creek Campground, Del Norte Coast Redwoods State Park
10. De Marin Camp
11. Flint Ridge Camp
12. Elk Prairie Campground
13. Gold Bluffs Campground
14. Patrick Point State Park
15. Grays Falls Camp
16. East Fork Trinity Camp
17. Aikens Creek Camp
18. Pearch Creek Camp
19. Fish Lake Camp
20. Grizzly Creek Redwoods State Park
21. Albee Creek Campground
22. Burlington Campground
23. Hidden Springs Campground
24. Benbow State Recreation Area
25. Oak Flat Campground
26. Sinkyone Wilderness State Park
27. MacKerricher State Park
28. Wages Creek Campground
29. Union Landing State Beach
30. Jackson State Demonstration Forest

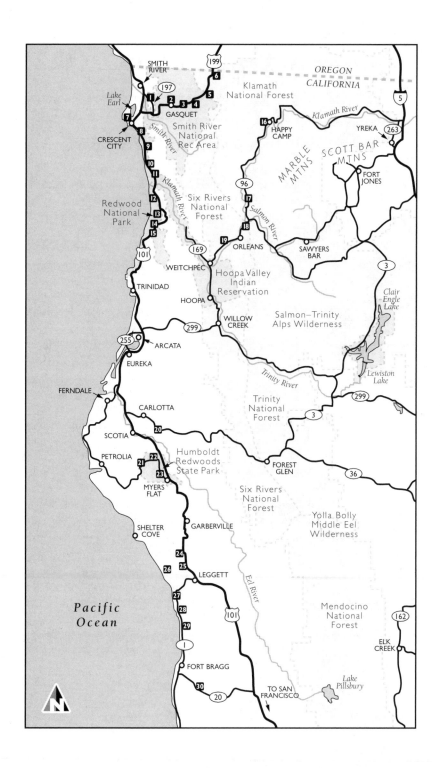

Del Norte Coast and Redwood National Park

① Jedediah Smith Redwoods State Park 🌲🌲🌲🌲🌲

This is where it all comes together. Because the Smith River is the last major free-flowing river in the state, it is as much an attraction here as are the ancient redwood trees found in this 10,000-acre preserve east of Crescent City. The campsites are arranged near the river's edge in a lovely old-growth forest. Aside from the main access road, there is very little pavement in the camp area. Don't worry about being surrounded by concrete slabs here. The trees in this park are so big around and so tall you'll be blown away the minute you enter. The timeless beauty of this forest is overpowering.

sites	*108*
🏕️🚐	*No hookups, RVs to 30 feet*
open	*All year*
reservations	*Up to 8 weeks in advance; California State Parks, 800/444-7275*
contact	*Jedediah Smith Redwoods State Park, 707/464-6101*

Just as entrancing and interesting as the forest are the river and its banks. In California, we have become so accustomed to rivers whose flows are controlled by dam operators that when we come across a wild river like this one, we aren't sure what to think of it. The Smith is indeed unique. Its banks are strewn with rocks carried hundreds of miles along its banks. Salmon need gravel like this, distributed by the river's flows, to spawn. The Smith presents a rare opportunity not just for flyfishing but also to witness the spectacle of nature that makes the salmon an amazing creature.

Camping in a place like Jedediah can be a challenge for those who are accustomed to the more mild climate found in other parts of California. Even during the summer, be prepared for WET weather here. If it's not raining, the morning fog can be dense. Long after the fog burns off, moisture drips from the trees. Redwood forests are almost always damp; this is what makes them interesting, and why it is home to things like banana slugs, mushrooms, and moss.

Adjacent to the main camping area here is one of the nicest nature trails you will find in any redwood preserve. Jedediah is also a good staging point for longer day hikes not only in the state park but also in the adjacent Smith River National Recreation Area. There is good swimming during the summer in the river's numerous coved areas, a few of which are very near the campground. Those who

The nature trail at Jedediah Smith Redwoods State Park is one of the best old-growth forest walks you will find on the north coast, and easy to access.

want to enjoy the redwoods without RVs or as many fellow campers should consider dispersed camping in the national forest areas or smaller backpack camps described elsewhere in this section.

Facilities: Each site has a picnic table and a fire pit. Piped water, flush toilets, and showers are available nearby. Those wishing to fish in the river must show up with gear and bait; there is no tackle shop in the park. The best services are in Crescent City, 9 miles west.

Getting there: From Crescent City, head 9 miles east on US 199. The park entrance is on the right side of the road.

The entrance to the Jedediah Smith Redwoods State Park nature loop is adjacent to the campground on the banks of the Smith River.

❷ Big Flat Camp 🌲🌲🌲🌲

Don't forget the iron skillet. In the late spring and early fall, Hurdy-Gurdy Creek comes to life with healthy runs of steelhead and chinook salmon. This is also a good tubing creek during high water when the weather is warm. The campground is a find because it is right in the middle of redwood country, has easy access to a decent segment of the Smith River, but is small enough and sufficiently out of the way that it is never overrun during the peak season. Sites are large, and those along the creek offer the best ambience and privacy. Trying to avoid big RVs and the trappings of main tourist areas? Camp here and take day trips to the river and the more popular parks, such as nearby Jedediah Smith Redwoods State Park. Unfortunately, the size of this campground has one drawback—it can fill up quickly on summer and holiday weekends. Enough people know about it that the sites are aggressively sought out.

sites	28
🏕️🚐	No hookups, RVs to 22 feet
open	May to September
reservations	None
contact	Gasquet Ranger Station, 707/280-2267

Facilities: Each site has a picnic table and a fire pit. Outhouse toilets are available nearby. There is no running water, so be sure to pack in enough to last your entire stay.

Getting there: From Crescent City, drive east 10 miles on US 199 to South Fork Road. Turn right, and then continue another 15 miles. The camp entrance is on the left side of the road.

❸ Panther Flat Camp 🌲🌲🌲🌲

Get away from the hordes. Fall and winter flyfishing expeditions along the unimpeded Smith River lead many away from the more popular state redwood parks for the quiet reserve of this smaller and lesser-known national forest campground. It is as if the fish that are largest and most willing to bite are attracted to this lovely stretch of the Smith. During the summer, the camp makes a terrific jump-in spot for water sports such as rafting and kayaking, or just plain tubing and swimming. Do be careful, however, as the Smith can change character rapidly and without warning. Jedediah Smith Redwoods State Park is nearby.

sites	39
🏕️🚐	No hookups, RVs to 22 feet
open	All year
reservations	National Forest Reservations, 800/280 2267
contact	Gasquet Ranger District, 707/457-3131

Those who want to see the big trees without having to pack into the larger and more popular campground at Jedediah Smith can't go wrong if there is space at

The Smith River is the longest free-flowing river in the state.

Panther Flat. Still, it is a good idea to make a reservation in advance, particularly on nice summer weekends and during the fishing season. The campsites here are spacious and reasonably private. All are near enough the river that the sound of rushing water will serenade you through the night no matter what site you are assigned to.

Facilities: Each site has a picnic table and a fire pit. Flush toilets, running water, and showers are available nearby.

Getting there: From Crescent City, drive 20 miles east on US 199. At mile marker 16.75, look for the campground entrance to your left. The campground is clearly marked with Forest Service signs.

④ Grassy Flat Camp 🌲🌲🌲

The small band of mostly Douglas-fir and Jeffrey pine forest separating US 199 from this small camp on the banks of the Smith River isn't enough to shelter some sites adequately from highway noise. If you end up here, try to secure a site nearest the river. On a positive note, the salmon and steelhead runs along this section of the Smith are impressive, and the camp serves as a good put-in for kayakers. For less pass-through traffic from day visitors, consider other campgrounds farther north on 199.

sites	19
🏕️🚐	No hookups, RVs to 22 feet
open	May to September
reservations	National Forest Reservations, 800/280-2267
contact	Gasquet Ranger Station, 707/457-3131

Facilities: Each site has a picnic table and a fire pit. Running water and outhouse toilets are available nearby.

Getting there: From Crescent City, drive 25 miles northeast on US 199 to mile marker 18.87. The clearly marked campground entrance is on the right side of the road.

⑤ Patrick Creek Camp 🌲🌲🌲🌲

Day hikers who want easy access to the stunningly beautiful Siskiyou Wilderness Area can use Patrick Creek Camp as a staging point. The campground offers the best of both worlds. Not only are hiking areas in Siskiyou prime, but some of the best winter-run salmon and steelhead fishing is found where Patrick Creek dumps into the wild and scenic Smith River. A weekend at Patrick Creek should most certainly include one full day of hiking and one full day of fishing creekside or on the river. Because the campground is small and reasonably secluded, it doesn't get overrun even on popular holiday and summer weekends. That's because most day-trippers looking for a decent fishing spot will typically decide to stop on the riverbanks along US 199 long before they get this far northeast. An extra 15 minutes of driving can make all the difference in the world if it's privacy and quiet you're looking for.

sites	13
🏕️🚐	No hookups, RVs to 22 feet
open	May to September
reservations	National Forest Reservations, 800/280-2267
contact	Gasquet Ranger Station, 707/457-3131

Facilities: Each site has a picnic table and a fire pit. Running water and flush toilets are available nearby.

Getting there: From Crescent City, drive northeast for 25 miles on US 199 to mile marker 22. The clearly marked campground is on the right side of the road.

Salmon spawn in the perfect gravel banks of the Smith River.

⑥ Boise Creek Camp 🌲🌲🌲

It's all downhill from here. Highway 299 follows the Trinity River through some of the best Class II and Class III rafting runs found anywhere in the state. These are ideal for beginning and intermediate rafters who like the security of a river with controlled flows. This is more of a rafting and flyfishing experience than a pristine nature experience, however. Along 299 you will not get away from the sound of the highway or the flurry of activity that accompanies river sports—shuttle buses, life jackets, overturned rafts, and general carrying on. The Trinity is rafting central. Those looking for more of a nature experience should consider continuing north to the Marble Mountains Wilderness Area section of Klamath National Forest or the Trinity Alps. Rafting is best here in the late spring and early summer, but flows can remain adequate well into the summer during good snowmelt years. If you're into the busy river scene, this campground is not too shabby. What sets this campground apart from some of the others is that some sites along the creek bed are a fair walking distance from the main river. The tent-only sites are prime real estate.

sites	20
🏕️🚐	3 tent-only No hookups, RVs to 40 feet
open	May to September
reservations	None
contact	Lower Trinity Ranger District, 530/629-2118

Facilities: Each site has a picnic table and a fire pit. Running water and outhouse toilets are available nearby.

Getting there: From US 101 at Arcata, drive east on Highway 299 for 39 miles. The campground entrance is on the left side of the road.

⑦ Lakes Earl and Tolowa 🌲🌲🌲🌲🌲

This is one of those special places where the river meets the sea. Pulses of fresh water from the Smith River drainage created two conjoined lagoons in a large basin on the Pacific oceanfront. The result is 10,000 acres of marshes, wetlands, and meadows adjacent to wild sand dunes. Bird-watchers flock to this area to view hundreds of species of songbirds and waterfowl, including the Canada Aleutian goose. What makes this a prime camping spot, however, is its seclusion. While competition for the scarce campsites here can be fierce, they are always a sure bet for those determined enough to be first in line to snatch them up when the park office opens.

sites	22
🏕️	6 tent-only, 16 horse campsites
open	All year
reservations	None. Call 707/464-9533 for current conditions.
contact	California State Parks, 800/444-7275

Jedediah Smith Redwoods State Park is a great place to see the light in the trees.

The reward for such persistence is a rarity for California parklands: beautiful, secluded, private campsites nestled in the thick of a thriving wilderness. Looking to leave the Winnebagos and hordes of day-trippers out of sight for a while? This is one of the best places on the entire north coast to do so, not only because of its seclusion but because it is situated close to a number of popular attractions, including the Smith River and Jedediah Smith Redwoods State Park. The campsites are sheltered from ocean winds and are out of the way of through trails. Beach access is a short walk from the camping area through the dunes. In high water flow months, the two lagoons seem more like one kidney-shaped body of water and connect directly to the ocean like the mouth of a river. During these times, salmon and steelhead can be seen migrating from the ocean into the lagoons and up the tributaries feeding into them.

Facilities: Each hike-in site has a picnic table, a fire pit, and a food locker. Pack in enough water for your stay. The horse camp has picnic tables, fire pits, corrals, and nonpotable water. Water for campers also must be packed in.

Getting there: The two camps are in different parts of the preserve. To reach the tent camp, from Crescent City drive south for 2 miles on US 101 and take the Elk Valley Road exit west. Continue 1.5 miles to Lower Lake Road. Turn left and follow Lower Lake 2.5 miles to Kellogg Road. Turn left on Kellogg and proceed 1 mile to the camp parking area on the right side of the road. To reach the horse camp, follow the same directions but instead of turning on Kellogg Road continue another half a mile to Palo Road. Turn left on Palo and follow the signs to the camp staging area.

⑧ Nickel Creek Camp 🌲🌲🌲🌲🌲

Just south of Crescent City where the Redwood Highway departs the coastline, is a 5-mile stretch of beachfront property that will blow you away. Even better, a small primitive backpack camp is located right in the heart of this area on bluffs overlooking the beach and ocean. This is a fantastic spot to lay on your back in a grassy meadow and watch cloud formations float by while the crash of ocean waves and the wind in the trees create perfect music. Redwood National Park does a great job of regulating the number of visitors here so that those with reservations are ensured a peaceful time. One negative thing that can be said about this campground is that because it is so small getting in can be a challenge—especially since it has officially been "discovered" by the hordes. Those savvy enough to work the

sites	5
🏕	5 walk-in only
open	All year
reservations	Redwood National Park, 707/464-6101
contact	Enders Beach, 707/464-9533

system will be rewarded with a great night or two under the stars, or by invigorating mornings with thick fog blowing over them off the Pacific. Expect a little wind and wet, but relish in the fact that the interplay between land and sea is the key to making the redwood forest ecosystem behave the way it does.

The camp is midway between wonderful old-growth redwood groves and the beach. Enderts Beach is about half a mile away. Those visiting in the summer will find some of the best tidepooling on the north coast at Enderts. Interpretive walks are hosted by the park service.

Facilities: These sites are quite primitive, but unlike those found at Flint Ridge, they do have picnic tables and cooking grills. There are outhouses nearby, but there is no running water. Enough water must be packed in for your stay.

Getting there: From Crescent City, drive south on US 101 for 2 miles to Enderts Beach Road, and go west for 1 mile to the Nickel Creek Camp trailhead on the south side of the road.

⑨ Mill Creek Campground, Del Norte Coast Redwoods State Park 🌲🌲🌲🌲

While most of the redwood forest found in this 6,400-acre preserve is made up of second-growth trees, this is a very nice place to camp, particularly for those who are able to nab one of the prized walk-in sites. In addition to redwoods, you will find oaks, madrones, red alders, bays, and big leaf maples scattered throughout the forest here. The highest peak is just under 1,300 feet, with cliffs overlooking the Pacific Ocean. Wilson Beach and False Klamath Cove are below, but these areas are not safe for swimming. Beach access is by Damnation Trail and Footsteps Rock Trail.

sites	145
🏕️🚐	35 tent-only No hookups, RVs to 31 feet, trailers to 27 feet
open	April 1 to October 1
reservations	Up to 8 weeks in advance; California State Parks, 800/444-7275
contact	Del Norte Coast Redwoods State Park, 707/464-6101 ext. 5120

Facilities: Each site has a fire pit and a picnic table. Running water, flush toilets, and showers are available nearby.

Getting there: From Crescent City, take US 101 south 7 miles. The entrance to the park is clearly marked on the left side of the highway.

⑩ De Marin Camp 🌲🌲🌲

This is a no-frills campground. Those looking for flushing toilets or a place to plug in the RV will be disappointed here. What it lacks in modern conveniences, however, it makes up for in simple primitiveness; this is a good place to escape concrete slabs and out-houses. Backpackers making their way along the California Coastal Trail make use of this camp more than campers just looking for a quick place to unroll the sleeping pad, but if you're lucky a few sites will be open and available. Be prepared for a moderate hike of almost 3 miles.

sites	*10*
open	*All year*
reservations	*None*
contact	*Redwood National Park, 707/464-6101*

Facilities: Running water and food lockers are available nearby, but other than that there are no amenities or creature comforts at this bare-bones campground.

Getting there: From Crescent City, take US 101 20 miles south to the Wilson Creek Road exit. From there, head east. The trailhead to the camp is at the end of the road.

⑪ Flint Ridge Camp 🌲🌲🌲

For what you get—a secluded spot on a bluff overlooking the Pacific—this small walk-in camp is amazingly easy to reach. Set on the cliffs overlooking the mouth of the Klamath River, this is a great spot for those trying to catch a glimpse of the California gray whales migrating between Alaska and their birthing waters in Baja California. This is also a great spot for those who would like to combine a fishing trip with a little backpacking. Because the walk to the campsites is relatively short, there is no need to worry about hauling a lot of fishing gear through some steep back-country trail. The Klamath is one of the largest rivers in the state and a popular fishing area for salmon and steelhead. Be mindful of the fact that this camp is on the California Coastal Trail route; long-distance backpackers are likely to have sites sewn up during summer and holiday weekends.

sites	*10*
	10 walk-in only
open	*All year*
reservations	*Up to 8 weeks in advance; Redwood National Park, 707/464-6101*
contact	*Redwood National Park, 707/464-6101*

Facilities: These are primitive, undeveloped sites with few improvements. Running water and outhouses are available nearby. All cooking must be done on a camp stove. There are no tables. Bait and tackle shops and boat rentals are available along the riverfront.

Getting there: From Crescent City, drive south on US 101 for 15 miles to the Coastal Drive exit at the Klamath River. The parking area for the camp is 3 miles up the road on the left side. The camp is an easy quarter-mile walk from the parking area.

Humboldt Coast

⑫ Elk Prairie Campground ▲▲▲▲

This is the larger of two campgrounds at Prairie Creek Redwoods State Park, and is a bit less desirable than the other. Be sure to ask for a site as far away from the highway as possible, as some are susceptible to traffic noise. The campground is smack dab in the middle of one of the more popular scenic routes in redwood

The canopy of Prairie Creek Redwoods State Park keeps the forest floor damp and brimming with life.

sites	75

	No hookups, RVs to 27 feet, trailer limit 24 feet
open	All year
reservations	Up to 8 weeks in advance; California State Parks, 800/444-7275
contact	Prairie Creek Redwoods State Park, 707/488-2171

country, so expect to see plenty of people whose mission for the day is to take in the magic and beauty of the redwoods without actually having to get out of the car. Still, this is a good spot to see the magnificent Roosevelt elk. Stick around after the day crowds thin out (or even before) and chances are you'll see a few—maybe even get to photograph them. This is also a good staging point for redwood hikes and bike rides, as several key trailheads are nearby.

Facilities: Each site has a picnic table and a fire pit. Running water and flush toilets are available nearby.

Getting there: From Eureka drive north on US 101 north for 50 miles to Newton B. Drury Scenic Parkway in Orick. Take Drury about 1 mile to the park entrance.

13 Gold Bluffs Campground 🌲🌲🌲🌲

How surreal it is to wake up in the morning and look out over the fog-shrouded beaches, meadows, and redwood forests to find a herd of majestic 1,000-pound Roosevelt elk staring back at you through the mist. Despite their intimidating size, these creatures can literally sneak up on you! They move silently and deliberately and stand so still that in the cool mist of the north coast they blend in with their surrounding.

sites	25

	No hookups, RVs to 24 feet
open	All year
reservations	None; call California State Parks, 800/444-7275, for current conditions
contact	Prairie Creek Redwoods State Park, 707/488-2171

Gold Bluffs is one of the most spectacular spots on the California coast to camp out. The spacious sites are just a short walk from both the Pacific Ocean and magnificent redwood groves. Don't, however, expect a pristine nature experience here, as there is not only RV access but also ample beachcombing and hiking available for day visitors, who quickly overrun the place on nice weekends and holidays. Also keep in mind that this is not a perfect Southern California *Baywatch* scene; the beach is windblown, overcast, and cold most of the time, except during the late summer months. Be prepared with tie-downs, rain gear, and warm clothing to bundle up in. Also be sure to keep your distance should the elk happen by. If calves are present, adults can be aggressive.

Facilities: Each site has a picnic table, a fire pit, and a food storage locker. Running water, showers, and flush toilets are available nearby.

Getting there: From Orick on US 101, go 6 miles west on Davidson Road to the campground entrance. Note that Davidson Road is unpaved in sections. High-clearance vehicles should be used when the road is wet, just as a precaution. Call ahead to check on road conditions.

⑭ Patrick Point State Park 🌲🌲🌲🌲

For a large car-camping spot like this one, the sites are spaced well enough to give the illusion of privacy and the forest is surprisingly quiet. Several attractions are found nearby, including a 2-mile-long hiking trail along bluffs situated 600 feet above the Pacific Ocean. Native American sites are found here, along with one of the best museums in Northern California focusing on California's original inhabitants. There are the obvious drawbacks here; to enjoy the good stuff you will most likely have to put up with kids, dogs, and concrete.

sites	124
	No hookups, RVs to 31 feet
open	All year
reservations	Up to 8 weeks in advance; California State Parks, 800/444-7275
contact	Patrick Point State Park, 707/677-3570

Facilities: Each site has a picnic table and a fire pit. Running water and flush toilets are available nearby.

Getting there: From Trinidad drive north on US 101 for 4 miles, then follow the entrance road half a mile west to the campground.

⑮ Grays Falls Camp 🌲🌲🌲🌲

Waterplay areas like this one at Grays Falls are not just for rafting during the high water runoff in the late spring and early summer. Late summer draws hordes of swimmers once the river calms down. Rowboats or canoes are not an uncommon sight. Because of its proximity to the highway, the waterfront is sure to be inhabited by day visitors as well as campers on hot sunny weekends and holidays. This is also a particularly popular place for families with children, and because large RVs are also allowed, just about anything is fair game. If you want to cool off and

sites	32
	No hookups, RVs to 35 feet
open	May to September
reservations	None
contact	Lower Trinity Ranger District, 530/629-2118

The Humboldt coast boasts some of the tallest trees in the world.

need a campsite by the river, Grays Falls may work for you. But those in search of a quiet spot to commune with nature should consider hiking up to a lake in one of the wilderness areas instead.

Facilities: Each site has a picnic table and a fire pit. Running water and flush toilets are available nearby.

Getting there: From Willow Creek, drive east on Highway 299 for 12 miles to the campground entrance on the right side of the road.

16 East Fork Trinity Camp 🌲🌲🌲

Sometimes a little smart planning makes all the difference. What makes this small out-of-the-way campground a score for rafters is that, because it is downstream from the runs, your rafting trip will end at the very place you have your food, belongings, Therm-a-Rest, and dry clothing. Outfitters and guides will be able to calculate how long and how far to take the river in the late morning so that your afternoon is spent at the camp.

sites	*8*
🏕️ 🚐	*No hookups, RVs to 22 feet*
open	*All year*
reservations	*None*
contact	*Lower Trinity Ranger District, 530/629-2118*

Facilities: Each site has a picnic table and a fire grill. Outhouse toilets and running water are available nearby. There are put-ins for rafting on the Trinity River.

Getting there: From Willow Creek, drive north on Highway 96 for 8 miles. The campground entrance is on the right side of the road.

Smith River National Recreation Area and Six Rivers National Forest

⑰ Aikens Creek Camp 🌲🌲🌲⚶

Get ready for a wild ride. Put-ins for decent Class II and Class III runs on the Klamath River are close to Aikens Creek Campground. Rafting gear is a staple here during the late spring and early summer meltoff, which is usually the best time to take a spill down the mighty Klamath. The popular Somes Bar put-in is a few miles north of the campground on Highway 96. Please note that the longer run from up north is a Class IV run. Novices should not attempt it on their own. The tent-only sites are nicely segregated from the rest of the campground; if you're staying in a tent, try to get one of them. The campground gets a fair amount of highway noise and because of its size is not always necessarily the most peaceful in the area. Sites away from the highway and nearer the creek are your best bet.

sites	29
🏕 🚐	10 tent-only No hookups, RVs to 35 feet
open	All year
reservations	National Forest Reservations, 800/280-2267
contact	Orleans Ranger District, 530/627-3291

Facilities: Each site has a picnic table and a fire pit. Flush toilets and running water are available nearby.

Getting there: From the town of Orleans, drive 5 miles north on Highway 96 to the clearly marked campground entrance on the right side of the road.

⑱ Pearch Creek Camp 🌲🌲🌲🌲🌲

The Klamath River has one of the state's best salmon and steelhead fish runs, and the stretch of waterway where Pearch Creek and the main river intersect is a prime flyfishing spot in the late summer and early fall. What makes Pearch Creek a prime place to unfurl the bedroll, however, is not just the great fishing nearby but the seclusion and quiet that come with it. Because only two sites accommodate trailers or RVs, much of the time you will find neither here;

sites	10
🏕 🚐	8 tent-only No hookups, RVs to 22 feet
open	May to November
reservations	None
contact	Orleans Ranger District, 530/627-3291

Looking skyward at the Smith River National Recreation Area.

count on listening to the sound of the creek rushing rather than the sound of an RV generator.

Follow the creek bed about half a mile to where it meets the Klamath. This is a pleasant and easy walk from the camp. When the water is high enough and it's the right time of the season, fishing in the creek yields good results. During the summer before the fish runs begin in earnest, use Pearch Creek as a summer swimming spot. Birders also will enjoy Pearch, as the Klamath River and its tributaries attract more than 250 different varieties of birds. Among the grasslands, juniper, pines, and oak are found flycatchers, nighthawks, starlings, wrens, doves, owls, terns, swans and geese, hawks, quail, coots, and sandpipers. Because the campground is so small, you can fill half of it up with friends for an intimate outing relatively free of outsiders. Timing is everything, however, so if you are going to try this be sure to have an alternative plan just in case.

This trail near Fish Lake Camp is a favorite day hike.

Facilities: Each site has a picnic table and a fire pit. Outhouse toilets are available nearby. There is no running water, so be sure to bring enough to last your entire stay.

Getting there: From the town of Orleans, go 1 mile north on Highway 96 to the clearly marked campground entrance on the right side of the road.

⑲ Fish Lake Camp 🌲🌲🌲

Unfold the lounge chair. While this part of the state is known more for its fly-fishing and Class IV rapids, that doesn't mean it isn't possible to be sleepy at lakeside once in a while. Fish Lake has that good ole-fashioned fishin' hole feel. This nicely appointed campground makes an excellent place to drop out for the weekend during the heat of the summer for some lazy afternoons casting a reel or bobbing around on an inflated tube. The pine and fir forests in this area give way to craggy rock peaks and meadows of wildflowers. The lake looks like it's been dropped into the midst of it out of nowhere. Tent-only sites are the best fare. Expect plenty of aluminum fishing boats, trailers, RVs, and camper rigs, however, as this is a popular trout fishing spot during the midsummer—and that means plenty of activity. Looking for perfect privacy? Look elsewhere.

sites	23
🏕 🚐	10 tent-only
	No hookups, RVs to 35 feet
open	May to September
reservations	National Forest Reservations, 800/280-2267
contact	530/627-3291

Facilities: Each site has a picnic table and a fire pit. Outhouse toilets and running water are available nearby.

⑳ Grizzly Creek Redwoods State Park 🌲🌲🌲🌲

Talk about vision! Owen R. Cheatham, founder of Georgia-Pacific Corporation, saw to it that this small forest complex on the banks of the Van Duzen River was never logged—and was ultimately donated to the state as a park. This small park is very lovely—and quiet, being so far from the main highway corridor of US 101. Visitors to redwood country who want the convenience of car camping but crave peace and quiet will be a lot happier here than at some of the larger and easier

sites	30
🏕 🚐	10 tent-only
	No hookups, RVs to 31 feet, trailers to 24 feet
open	All year
reservations	Up to 8 weeks in advance; California State Parks, 800/444-7275
contact	Grizzly Creek Redwoods State Park, 707/777-3683

to reach campgrounds closer to the Avenue of the Giants. Stop here instead, and relax. The tent sites are particularly nice. And there's a bonus: This is a key put-in spot for canoes and kayaks, so if you're combining a camping trip with some water sports, you'll be in heaven here. Of course, flyfishers will also feel right at home on the banks of the Van Duzen, which boasts healthy wintertime runs of steelhead. Grizzly Creek is not nearly as large as some of the other redwood preserves in the area, but the old-growth groves are as stunningly beautiful as any. Interpretive nature walks are held during the summer.

Facilities: Each site has a picnic table and a fire pit. Running water, flush toilets, and showers are available nearby. Load up on supplies before leaving the US 101 corridor, as there are few services out this way.

Getting there: From Eureka, drive south on US 101 for 20 miles, then head 17 miles east on Highway 36 to the park entrance.

21 Albee Creek Campground 🌲🌲🌲

Some of the best hiking in Humboldt Redwoods State Park is not on the trails but rather along the creek beds. Albee Creek is set in a pretty old-growth grove

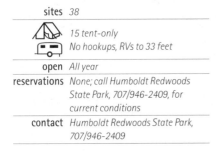

sites	38
	15 tent-only
	No hookups, RVs to 33 feet
open	All year
reservations	None; call Humboldt Redwoods State Park, 707/946-2409, for current conditions
contact	Humboldt Redwoods State Park, 707/946-2409

right dab in the middle of one of the most amazing public redwood preserves you can find. Despite the popularity of the park, this particular camp can be quite serene even at peak times; it has something to do with the acoustics of the place. The sites are spacious and nice. Try to get a tent-only spot and you may be spared the sound of an RV generator next door.

Albee is one of hundreds of small creeks meandering through this forest complex. Following the creeks instead of trails to explore ensures you a more personal nature experience and increases your chances of running into some of the abundant wildlife found here. Just don't try it when the creek is flowing too high, unless you're prepared to contend with some mud.

Facilities: Each site has a picnic table and a fire pit. Running water is available nearby, as are pit toilets.

Getting there: From Myers Flat, drive north on US 101 for 2 miles to the state park headquarters. This is where you try to pick up a camping pass for the night. The campground is 5 miles west of US 101 on Bull Creek Road, which is an amazing route to the ocean through the Mattole River Canyons.

Burlington Campground 🌲🌲🌲

Ever wonder what an ancient forest would look like with a major highway slicing it down the middle? That's pretty much what you'll find here: big trees, but also lots of pavement, cars, minivans, and RVs. Camping here isn't a complete loss, however. While the campground is noisy and a little crowded, the section of forest in which it is located is conveniently near good canoeing and fishing spots on the Eel River. This location is also no slouch if you plan to set up camp and then head out to explore the rest of redwood country. Just be prepared to share space.

sites	58
🏕️ 🚐	No hookups, RVs to 24 feet
open	All year
reservations	Up to 8 weeks in advance; California State Parks, 800/444-7275
contact	Humboldt Redwoods State Park, 707/946-2409

This view from atop Mattole Road shows the Humboldt Redwoods State Park tree line and a meadow tucked into the coastal mountains.

Facilities: Each site has a picnic table with fire pit. Running water, flush toilets, and showers are available. Because this campground is located so near US 101, services are easily had in nearby towns.

Getting there: From US 101, take the Newton Road exit near Weott and continue a short distance to the intersection with the ever-popular Avenue of the Giants. The campground entrance is at the intersection.

㉓ Hidden Springs Campground 🌲🌲

The one thing that doesn't make this crowded, noisy campground at the edge of an obnoxiously busy stretch of highway a complete loss is that it is situated among some of the most amazing and easily accessed giant trees you'll find anywhere. The Avenue of the Giants is a 32-mile stretch of scenic highway, along which you will find the world-famous Dyerville Giant, along with the Federation and Williams Groves. This is also one of those places you can drive your car through a hollowed-out redwood, which can be a thrill for children. Don't camp out here, however, if tour buses and camcorders aren't your cup of tea, as this is hardly the far reaches.

sites	154
	No hookups, RVs to 24 feet
open	All year
reservations	Up to 8 weeks in advance; California State Parks 800/444-7275
contact	Humboldt Redwoods State Park, 707/946-2409

Facilities: Each site has a picnic table and a fire pit. Running water, flush toilets, and showers are available nearby, as is a disposal site.

Getting there: This campground is at ground zero for those wishing to visit the big trees. To find it, take the ever-popular Avenue of the Giants half a mile south from Myers Flat. You can't miss it.

㉔ Benbow State Recreation Area 🌲🌲🌲

A small hydroelectric dam on the south fork of the Eel River isn't used to generate power anymore, but it creates a wonderfully pleasant shallow lake for those looking for a place to take a dip during those hot summer months. Some of the campgrounds are arranged along the lake's edge, while others are closer to the riverbank below the dam. If you have a choice, get as close to the river as possible—it's better to listen to rushing water than to children splashing around and shouting "Marco Polo." Swimming

sites	75
	No hookups, RVs to 30 feet
open	All year
reservations	Up to 8 weeks in advance; California State Parks, 800/444-7275
contact	Benbow State Recreation Area, 707/923-3238

in the lake during the summer and fishing in the river below the lake during the winter are both worthwhile. The lake is a popular summer camping destination for families during the peak outdoor season between Memorial Day and Labor Day. During winter fishing season, camping spots are easier to come by; drop-ins are typically able to find space here.

Facilities: Each site has a picnic table and a fire pit. Running water, flush toilets, and showers are nearby, as is an RV disposal site.

Getting there: From Garberville, drive south on US 101 for 2 miles to the park entrance, which is on the west side of the highway.

25 Oak Flat Campground 🌲🌲🌲

Because it is at ground zero, where northbound US 101 first meets the redwood forests of Humboldt County, this is also the spot where thousands upon thousands of road-weary tourists are sure to pull over to look a the big trees and take their first photographs. For that reason, this is one of the most visited spots on the north coast, with 250,000 people passing through annually. Thus, as you would expect, the campground tends to be a bit crowded. Some sites are far too close to the highway. If you end up having to unroll the sleeping pad here, try to get as far away from the highway and as close to the Eel River as possible. Summer weekends are typically booked.

sites	95
🏕️🚐	Electric and water hookups, RVs to 30 feet, trailers to 24 feet
open	Mid-June to mid-September
reservations	Up to 8 weeks in advance; California State Parks, 800/444-7275
contact	Richardson Grove State Park, 707/247-3318

Facilities: Each site has a picnic table and a cooking grill. Running water, flush toilets, and showers are available nearby, as is an RV disposal site. The park has a visitor center and a small store with limited supplies on hand, but services are available along US 101. The park lodge has cabins for rent also.

Getting there: You can't miss Richardson Grove—US 101 bisects both the park and the campground. From Garberville, drive south on US 101 for 7 miles. This is the gateway to redwood country for those heading north out of Mendocino County.

Northern Mendocino Coast

㉖ Sinkyone Wilderness State Park 🌲🌲🌲🌲🌲

Pin a note on yourself with your name and address written clearly—they don't call this the "Lost Coast" for nothing. More than 7,300 acres of wild-running creeks, black sand beaches, alder and eucalyptus forest, fields of wildflowers, and dramatically eroded 1,000-foot bluffs looking over the ocean are found here. There are waterfalls dropping directly into the Pacific, vast stretches of beach where you won't see a soul, and a rugged, naked, natural beauty from the wild rushes of wind and water to the night skies blanketed with stars. The weather can be a bit intense here between November and May, so those not prepared for the extremes should consider visiting in the late summer. Spring is probably the best time to come here, preferably on a weekend before the Memorial Day kickoff for the official outdoor season.

sites	40
open	All year
reservations	None
contact	Sinkyone Wilderness State Park, 707/986-7711

Sinkyone is named for the Sinkyone Indians, who occupied this section of the Mendocino coast for thousands of years before European settlers arrived. In many ways, this area has changed little since that time despite years of logging in the region and pressure from land speculators to build a highway through and promote development. The Sinkyone villages were established along the network of creeks found throughout the preserve. The main food source was the steelhead and salmon. The once-abundant fish runs have dwindled in recent decades, but bring your gear anyway if flyfishing is on the agenda.

Winter months are a good time to watch spawning in the creeks. Watch out for Roosevelt elk, mule deer, black bears, and more than a hundred species of bird. There are few creature comforts here. While some camps are reachable without much hiking, you're still out in the middle of nowhere; thus, your stay is going to have the feel of a backpacking trip. Backpackers wishing to move on from here will find easy trail connections to the adjacent King Range National Conservation Area, which is run by the Bureau of Land Management.

Facilities: Picnic tables and cooking grills are found at 15 sites at Usal Beach; there are outhouses nearby. There is no running water. The other 25 sites are more primitive, have few amenities, and are more difficult to reach. Either pack water in, or bring a water purifier so you can use creek water.

Getting there: There are two ways to reach the Sinkyone Wilderness. Those planning to camp at Usal Beach should enter the park from Usal Road. From Fort

Bragg drive north on Highway 1 for 40 miles. Where the highway veers to the east away from the coast, turn left on Usal Road (gravel) and continue to the beach area. Note that low-clearance vehicles, RVs, and trailers should not be driven here. The more primitive sites can be reached most easily from US 101. From Redway on 101, drive west on Briceland Road for 25 miles to a gravel road leading south toward Needle Rock. A ranger station is located a short distance down the road. Call ahead to check on road and weather conditions before using either of these routes.

27 MacKerricher State Park 🌲🌲🌲🌲🌲

If you want it all, this may be the best spot on the Mendocino coast to get it. Forest, sand dunes, beaches, bluffs, a freshwater lake, bluffs overlooking the ocean, meadows, tidepools—you name it, it's here! MacKerricher covers not only 7 miles of serene oceanfront but a sample platter of every type of terrain found in the region. Because of this, a campsite here doubles as a staging point for very imaginable outdoor activity. Bring your fishing gear, bicycle, birding equipment, and kayak. Go beachcombing, hiking, tidepooling—the possibilities are boundless. Wildlife here also runs the gamut: Harbor seals sun themselves on the rocky shores, while bluebirds, warblers, shorebirds, swallows, and jays are found in the woods and marshes. In the spring, a full range of coastal wildflowers blooms here.

sites	152
🏕️	10 tent-only No hookups, RVs to 35 feet
open	All year
reservations	Up to 8 weeks in advance; California State Parks, 800/444-7275
contact	MacKerricher State Park, 707/865-2391

The campgrounds are spacious, well-maintained, and partitioned out so that they seem reasonably private. Note, however, that this park attracts its share of day visitors. Particularly on sunny weekends, most sections of the camping area are going to get a fair amount of pass-through foot traffic, particularly those nearest the beach. Weather can be a bit nasty along this section of coast as well. Watch out for strong ocean winds and persistent overcast, sometimes even at the height of summer.

Facilities: Each site has a picnic table and a fire pit. Running water, flush toilets, and showers are available nearby. Because this campground is just a few miles from Fort Bragg, there are services close by; don't fret about forgetting something.

Getting there: From Fort Bragg, drive north on Highway 1 for 3 miles. The park entrance is on the west side of the road.

28 Wages Creek Campground ▲▲▲▲

Those planning to backpack through the Lost Coast (or those ending a backpacking trip) can use the beach and campground at Wages Creek as a meeting point or a place to unwind once the high-country adventures are concluded. This is a particularly good meeting point if members of your hiking party are coming from different areas to group up. Wages Creek should not, however, be looked upon as just a staging point for something more glorious. The sites are sizable and reasonably private considering the size of the campground. There are no good ocean views, but if you're lucky you will score a site on the banks of the creek. The beach is a short hike away. Winter runs of salmon and steelhead make Wages Creek a suitable place for rainy season camp-outs with rod and reel.

sites	175
	No hookups, RVs to 31 feet
open	All year
reservations	Up to 8 weeks in advance; California State Parks, 800/444-7275
contact	Wages Creek State Beach, 707/964-2964

Facilities: Each site has a picnic table and a fire pit. Running water, flush toilets, and showers are available nearby. The nearest services are found a mile south on Highway 1, but save money by picking up supplies in Fort Bragg instead.

Getting there: From Fort Bragg, drive north on Highway 1 for 30 miles to the beach and campground entrance on the left (west) side of the highway.

29 Union Landing State Beach ▲▲▲▲

Pack up the binoculars and spotting scope—this stretch of the northern Mendocino coast is a prime birding and whale-watching location. Union Landing is a great place to set up camp and watch for gray whales making their annual migration south to Baja California for the winter and north to their Alaskan feeding waters in the summer. Yes, it's true: You don't need a boat to go whale-watching. You can actually see these giant mammals without getting your feet wet. The campsites are situated along a bluff overlooking the ocean. Sites are protected from the strong ocean breezes, so you don't have to worry too much about tying down. This is also a good spotting location for shorebirds of all varieties, warblers, jays, and a long list of other favorites. During peak season, the sites go fast. Get there early.

sites	100
	No hookups, RVs to 35 feet
open	All year
reservations	None
contact	California State Parks, 800/444-7275; Union Landing State Beach, 707/937-5804

Facilities: Each site has a picnic table and a fire grill. Running water and outhouse toilets are available nearby. There are few other improvements.

Getting there: From Fort Bragg, drive north on Highway 1 for 28 miles. The campground entrance is on the west side of the highway.

㉚ Jackson State Demonstration Forest 🌲🌲🌲

Those who stop here may just learn something. If you can forget for a moment that logging has been taking place among these 50,000 acres of redwoods, Douglas-fir, Bishop pine, and alder for the past 150 years, camping here can actually be a pleasant experience. Sites are in a quiet section of forest at streamside. Mountain bikers love it. There are many miles of logging roads open to bikers, some reaching the headwaters of the Noyo River at 2,000 feet. Also enjoy swimming, horseback riding, hiking, and bird-watching in areas where logging and deer hunting

sites	*44*
🏕	*26 tent-only*
🚐	*No hookups, RVs to any length*
open	*All year*
reservations	*Jackson State Demonstration Forest, 707/964-5674*
contact	*Jackson State Demonstration Forest, 707/964-5674*

aren't going on. There are two nice old-growth groves of redwoods. One section of the river has a 50-foot waterfall. Learn about sustained yield logging on self-guided interpretive nature walks.

Facilities: Each site has a picnic table and a fire pit. Outhouses are available nearby. There is no running water, so be sure to bring enough for your stay.

Getting there: From Fort Bragg, drive 10 miles east on Highway 20 to the park entrance, which is on the north side of the road. You will need a forest map to find your campsite, as logging roads within the forest complex are unmarked and confusing to navigate. Pick up your map at the park office in Fort Bragg, 802 North Main Street.

Wine Country

The aluminum fishing boat was obviously invented for a reason. What you might not expect is that you will find that reason in Northern California's wine region. The answer—and you need to pronounce it correctly if the crowd around here is going to have any idea of what you're talking about—is good old-fashioned feeshin'.

That's right. Forget all those visions you had about pinky-in-the air dining at patio cafes and winery restaurants. Most of the seafood consumed in this part of California comes right out of the black skillet and onto a paper plate—with head, eyes, and skin still intact. Ignore what you've heard about the finer points of Napa, and meet us at the cleaning station next to the campground on the shores of Clear Lake, one of the best bass fishing spots in the nation and the second largest natural lake in the state of California.

The range of outdoor experiences at your fingertips in the valleys, foothills, and coastal mountains north and west of Napa are enough to keep every variety of outdoorsperson happy. Indian Valley Reservoir in the foothills east of Clear Lake has the sleepy feel of a country pond, while the Snow Mountain Wilderness area of Mendocino National Forest contains small campgrounds in hidden pockets where nobody will find you. Camp beneath the redwoods in the forested hills of the Sonoma Coast, or join rafters and kayakers camped out on the banks of Cache Creek to listen to the valley breezes through the oak woodlands after an exciting day chasing rapids.

The Wine Country has more than vineyards and bed and breakfast inns to offer. But don't rule the wine out completely. The central Napa region is ideally suited for RV camping, while the wine valleys make a wonderful day trip for those camping out in the perimeter—and that means the best of both worlds.

Wine Country

1. Russian Gulch State Park
2. Manchester State Beach
3. Gualala River Campground
4. Salt Point State Park
5. Stillwater Cove
6. Fort Ross State Historic Park
7. Sonoma Coast State Beach
8. Doran Beach
9. Austin Creek State Recreation Area
10. Spring Lake Regional Park
11. Sugarloaf Ridge State Park
12. Napa Valley State Park
13. Napa County Fairgrounds
14. Clear Lake State Park
15. Blue Oak Camp
16. Boggs Mountain Demonstration Forest
17. Cache Creek Regional Park
18. Lake Solano County Park
19. Plaskett Meadows Campground
20. Little Doe Campground
21. Eel River Campground
22. Wells Cabin Campground
23. Hammerhorn Lake Campground
24. Sunset Campground
25. Lower Nye Campground
26. Oak Flat Campground
27. Pogie Point Campground
28. Bear Creek Campground
29. Fuller Grove Campground
30. Deer Valley Campground
31. Middle Creek Campground
32. Letts Lake Campground
33. Lily Pond/Mill Valley Campground
34. South Fork Campground
35. Mill Creek Campground
36. Davis Flat Campground
37. Fouts Campground
38. Cedar Camp
39. Whitlock Campground

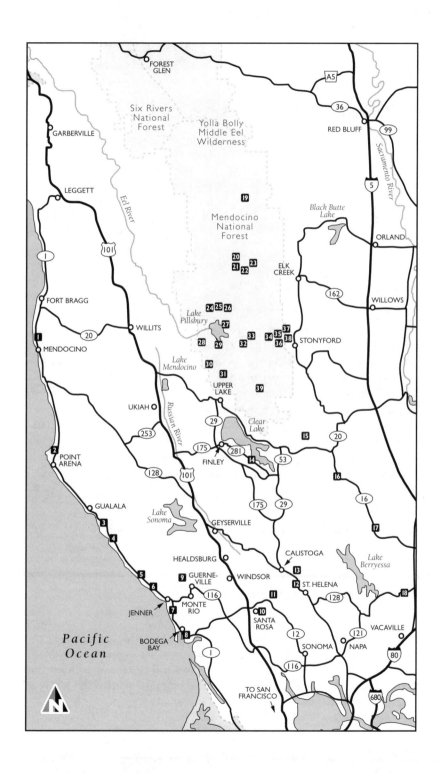

Sonoma Valley / Napa Valley

① Russian Gulch State Park 🌲🌲🌲🌲🌲

Break out the geology textbooks. The sites at this state park are a short hike away from the Devil's Punch Bowl, a sea cave that over the years has been so relentlessly pounded by the churning Pacific that it has collapsed into a large expanse of rocks open to the tide. The result of this geologic turn of events is one of the largest and most productive tide-pooling spots you will find. Naturalist programs are available during the summer for those who want to explore.

sites	30
	No hookups, RVs to 27 feet
open	All year
reservations	Up to 8 weeks in advance; California State Parks, 800/444-7275
contact	Russian Gulch State Park, 707/937-4296

The campground is not on the beach, but rather near Russian Gulch Creek, which cuts a narrow, wooded canyon through the 1,100-acre preserve on its path to the ocean. Fishing is best from the shore in midsummer. Those who don't mind the chilly water in this part of the state also should pack up the skin diving gear. Other amenities include a 3-mile cycling trail, a visitor center where the history of the Mendocino coast lumber industry is outlined, and a recreation hall. Be sure not to miss the main attraction: a sea cave with a blow hole that jettisons water dozens of feet into the air when the waves crash in. Waterfalls, blow holes, expansive tidepools, and extensive riparian areas loaded with wildlife make this a great stopover for those who want to see nature's very own sideshow. The campground is small enough to be reasonably quiet, and is arranged so that sites have a fair amount of privacy.

Facilities: Each site has a picnic table and a fire pit. Running water and flush toilets are available nearby.

Getting there: From Mendocino, drive north on Highway 1 for 2.5 miles to the park entrance on the left side of the road at the beach.

② Manchester State Beach 🌲🌲🌲🌲

Alder and Brush Creeks cut through this area's more than 700 acres of meadows, wild dunes, and beach. Both creeks have good steelhead and salmon runs in the winter season. This is a great place to find interesting samples of driftwood on the shore, as the topography of this section of coast makes it a magnet for debris from the ocean. Of course, that isn't always a good thing: There is also plenty of

sites	46
	No hookups, RVs to 32 feet
open	All year
reservations	Up to 8 weeks in advance; California State Parks, 800/444-7275
contact	Manchester State Beach, 707/882-2437

junk washed up on this beach if you catch it at the wrong time. But all in all, this is a pleasant and pristine section of coast—suitable for bird-watching, spring wildflower walks, and creekside hikes. Look for flocks of brown pelicans at the freshwater lagoons formed by the creeks. Most of the campground is in the direct line of fire for strong ocean winds, so be prepared to tie down and bundle up if necessary. The Point Arena Lighthouse is visible from the beachfront.

Facilities: Each site has a picnic table and a fire grill. Running water and outhouse toilets are available nearby, as is an RV disposal station.

Getting there: From Point Arena, drive north on US 101 for 7 miles. Drive through the town of Manchester and then beyond for 1 mile to the beach entrance on the left side of the road.

③ Gualala River Campground 🌲🌲🌲🌲

Soak your lazy bones. By the time summer comes around the Gualala River is transformed from a moving torrent of fresh water meeting the ocean very near this campground to a long, serene lake very suitable for kayaking and canoeing.

sites	25
	7 tent-only
	No hookups, RVs to 30 feet
open	All year
reservations	Sonoma County Parks, 707/785-2377
contact	Gualala River Park, 707/884-3533

This is because a sandbar forms each year at the mouth of the river. When runoff from the river's headwaters slows down to summer levels, the result is a peaceful lake-like setting. Fishing, swimming, beachcombing, tidepooling, and bird-watching are also good here. The mouth of the river creates a marshy riparian habitat that attracts ample shorebirds and migrating waterfowl. Also count on seeing plenty of sea lions and seals, along with the occasional migrating gray whale (from a distance). The campground is actually quite nice, as is often the case with regional park agencies in this part of the state. If you're a tenter, try to avoid, if at all possible, the section of the campground that allows RVs—but if you get stuck in it, you won't mind. The sites are spacious and have a fair share of privacy.

Facilities: Each site has a picnic table and a fire pit. Running water, flush toilets, and showers are available nearby, as is a disposal station for RVs.

Getting there: The camp is on the west side of Highway 1 at the Sonoma/Mendocino County line.

④ Salt Point State Park 🌲🌲🌲🌲

There are two campgrounds at this expansive 6-mile state beach complex, one closer to the water and the other nestled nearer the park's most unusual feature: a pygmy forest where coastal pines and firs have been stunted by the odd composition of this area's ground and soil. The park has a good cross-section of opportunities to offer outdoor enthusiasts. There is an underwater reserve for divers, a long stretch of beach for walking and tidepooling, high bluffs for whale-watching, and cliffs of sand-

sites	110
🏕️🚐	No hookups, RVs to 31 feet
open	All year
reservations	Up to 8 weeks in advance, March 2 to November 30 only; California State Parks, 800/444-7275; first come, first served rest of the year
contact	Salt Point State Park, 707/847-3221

stone for climbing practice. There are 30 sites near the beach at Gerstle Cove. The beach sites lack adequate protection from strong sea breezes, however, so if you don't have tie downs and aren't prepared for a little chill, one of the 80 sites at Woodside a short distance inland would probably work out best for tenters. Watch out for wild pigs in this area.

Facilities: Each site has a picnic table and a fire pit. Drinking water and flush toilets are available nearby. Showers are available at the campground nearest the beach but can be used by guests at both campgrounds.

Getting there: From Jenner, drive north on US 101 for 20 miles. The park entrance is on the left (west/beach) side of the road.

⑤ Stillwater Cove 🌲🌲🌲🌲

Dive for your dinner. As the name would suggest, the ocean waters tend to be far more tame in this rocky cove than in other areas of the Sonoma coast. For this reason, many a newbie diver has chosen this as the first place to put his face in the water. Sometimes there are so many novice divers splashing around in the surf here that it looks like an invasion. This is a great place, nonetheless, to break in a new wet suit and set of fins. During the abalone season, this tends to be one of the more popular spots, since the absence of strong currents makes harvesting abalone less of a challenge than in other areas.

sites	23
🏕️🚐	No hookups, RVs to 35 feet
open	All year
reservations	Stillwater Cove Regional Park, 707/847-3245
contact	Stillwater Cove Regional Park, 707/847-3245

The campground, run by the county parks department, is quite nice, and often oddly quiet. It can sometimes be the only game in town when more obvious accommodations are booked up. Note that the day-use area here is quite popular, however. If you choose to camp here, you will be sharing the cove with many more people than those who have pitched tents or rolled up in their RVs.

Facilities: Each site has a picnic table and a fire grill. Nearby are running water, flush toilets, and showers. There is also an RV disposal site.

Getting there: From Jenner, drive north on Highway 1 for 15 miles. The clearly marked park entrance is on the left side of the road.

⑥ Fort Ross State Historic Park 🎄🎄🎄

You can almost breathe the history here. This small campground is tucked away in a small canyon among 3,300 acres of meadows, bluffs, and forests of fir, redwood, and pine. The state park gets its name from an early-nineteenth-century Russian settlement established here by a small group of immigrants who set up their homes and businesses along a rocky, desolate, windswept stretch of the coast. In addition to taking in the history here, plan on keeping busy beachcombing, diving in an underwater park, bird-watching for abundant waterfowl and songbirds, and surf fishing. While the park does not have a developed trail system, the varied terrain and easy beach access make this one a winner. There is no RV access to the sites, which are well sheltered from the sea breezes and the rest of the park. The campground often gets overlooked by those cramming into the Sonoma coast area for big weekends.

sites	20
open	March 15 to December 1
reservations	None
contact	Fort Ross State Historic Park, 707/847-3286

Facilities: Each site has a picnic table and a cooking grill. Running water and vault toilets are available nearby.

Getting there: From Jenner, drive north on Highway 1 for 11 miles. The park visitor center is on your left.

⑦ Sonoma Coast State Beach 🎄🎄🎄🎄🎄

It's time to bundle up. Be prepared to survive ocean winds and cold foggy mornings while camping along this stunningly beautiful stretch of California coast. Waiting for you here are endless sandy beaches, rocky shorelines, dramatically eroded cliffs, tidepools, coastal marshes, meadows of wildflowers and native grasses, wild dunes, and a whip of salt and sand on the cold breeze. Naturally there are also hot summer days when the beaches here are more like a Southern California or Hawaii sun lover's paradise, but don't count on it unless the weather man is in an especially good mood. This is Northern California: pack a sweater! Rock fishing in the surf is best during the mid- to late summer. Tidepooling is best on the northern portion of this beach complex, near Wrights Beach. Be sure to tie down in case of a heavy wind. The sound of the ocean will lull you to sleep here. The camp-

sites	128
	No hookups, RVs to 27 feet at 30 sites and 31 feet at 98 sites
open	All year
reservations	Up to 8 weeks in advance; California State Parks, 800/444-7275
contact	Sonoma Coast State Beach, 707/875 3483

sites are distributed among two main beaches: Wrights Beach to the north and Bodega Dunes 5 miles to the south. Wrights Beach is the best deal because it is smaller, but this stretch of coast is so primo that even an oversized campground isn't going to spoil the moment.

Facilities: Each site has a picnic table and a fire pit. Running water and flush toilets are available nearby. The nearest town with a decent array of services and good prices on gasoline and supplies is Guerneville, 15 miles east on Highway 116.

Getting there: From Guerneville, drive 15 miles west on Highway 116 to Highway 1. Turn left (south). The first 30 campsites are 3 miles down Highway 1. The other 98 are another 5 miles down.

⑧ Doran Beach 🌲🌲

Okay, so it's not the Hyatt. While Bodega Bay can be a pleasant setting for bird-watching, whale-watching, and some water sports, this campground is more of a fishing trip staging point than a place you'll want to pitch a tent for the night expecting to commune with nature. Especially during the summer and early fall, expect to find the campground overrun with RV rigs, campers, fishing boats, and lots of people drinking beer and cleaning fish. As wondrous as being right on the waterfront might sound, this campground has a little too much pavement and is a bit too noisy to serve as much more than a

sites	114
	10 tent-only
	No hookups, RVs to 31 feet
open	All year
reservations	Doran Regional Park, 707/527-2041
contact	Doran Regional Park, 707/527-2041

place to ditch the boat trailer. Tent campers would do best to continue north to the Sonoma and Mendocino coasts, or east to Mendocino National Forest.

Facilities: Each site has a picnic table and a fire pit. Running water, showers, and flush toilets are available nearby. There is a full-service marina and public boat ramp in the park. Bodega Bay, just a mile away, is the best place to get supplies.

Getting there: From Bodega Bay, drive south on Highway 1 for 1 mile. The park entrance is on your right.

⑨ Austin Creek State Recreation Area 🌲🌲🌲🌲

Gribbit. The campsites are arranged very near Bull Frog Pond—and the pond didn't get its name by accident. This is one place where you're guaranteed to be serenaded to sleep at night by legions of croaking amphibians. The terrain is unique and varied. There are gorgeous redwood groves at the adjacent Armstrong Redwoods State Park, but here look also for oak woodlands, meadows, riparian habitat at creekside, and open ridgelands. Marble Mine Ridge stands 1,900 feet above the preserve, which has more than 20 miles of hiking trails. Wildflowers in the spring, scads of interesting birdlife, and even the occasional feral pig or mountain lion keep things interesting. The campground is well maintained and well equipped. The number of sites is small enough to keep crowds down, but what really makes this a great place is that because no reservations are taken, the campers here tend to be real outdoorspeople who are on the move. Because the access road is somewhat treacherous, you won't see many big RVs.

sites	24
🏕️🚐	No hookups, RVs to 20 feet
open	All year
reservations	None
contact	Austin Creek State Recreation Area, 707/865-2391

Facilities: Each site has a picnic table and a fire ring. Running water, flush toilets, and showers are available nearby. The nearest services are in Guerneville 6 miles away.

Getting there: From Guerneville, drive 2.5 miles north on Armstrong Woods Road to the entrance to Armstrong Redwoods State Reserve, and then continue through Armstrong another 3.5 miles to the Austin Creek entrance. The road is very narrow and winding; vehicles over 20 feet and all trailers are prohibited!

⑩ Spring Lake Regional Park ♣♣♣

Locals from Santa Rosa and the surrounding area tend to use this shoreline campsite for simple weekend outings with their children, so don't head out to Spring Lake expecting to find Lake Woebegone. Good summer trout action and safe swimming conditions make Spring Lake a suitable place to cool off and cast a line. The sites are at the waterfront, but some lack privacy. For this reason, the sites at either end of the campground offer the best ambience. Also found here are nice hiking trails along the water's edge, but this is more a place for an afternoon stroll than a major workout in the backcountry.

sites	30
🏕️🚐	No hookups, RVs to 30 feet
open	All year
reservations	Sonoma County Parks, 707/539-8082
contact	Spring Lake Regional Park, 707/539-8082

Facilities: Each site has a picnic table and a fire pit. Running water, showers, and flush toilets are available nearby, as are a public boat launch, a marina, boat rentals, and a general store.

Getting there: From Santa Rosa at US 101, drive east on Highway 12 for 0.75 mile. Turn right at Hoen Avenue and continue half a mile to Newanga Avenue. Turn left and continue another half a mile to the park entrance.

⑪ Sugarloaf Ridge State Park ♣♣♣

Redwood forests, oak woodlands, a waterfall on Sonoma Creek dropping 30 feet into a deep, cold pool: These are some of the characteristics that make Sugarloaf Ridge a superb place to camp out in Sonoma County. The campground is in a pretty wooded area in the shadows of 2,700-foot Bald Mountain. Scores of trails for mountain biking, hiking, and horseback riding are found here. Hiking to the Bald Mountain summit is a workout; during the summer do it in the morning before the weather gets too warm. Because the campground is not visible from the main Highway 12 and US 101 corridors, Sugarloaf tends to get less drop-in traffic than other state parks in this region. This can work to your advantage. The park is in a prime location and is quiet lovely, yet there are peak weekends when it doesn't fill up. Enjoy that while it lasts!

sites	50
🏕️🚐	No hookups, RVs to 27 feet
open	All year
reservations	California State Parks, 800/444-7275
contact	Sugarloaf Ridge State Park, 707/833-5712

Sugarloaf Ridge State Park is near Sonoma Creek, on the edges of redwood forestlands and oak woodlands.

Facilities: Each site has a picnic table and a fire pit. Running water and flush toilets are available nearby. Day-use facilities are adjacent to the campground for those who prefer to not spend the night.

Getting there: From Santa Rosa, drive east on Highway 12 for 8 miles. Turn north on Adobe Canyon Road and continue 2.5 miles to the park entrance.

⑫ Napa Valley State Park 🌲🌲

Nestled in the heart of wine country, the campground at Napa Valley State Park is most certainly a unique alternative to the frilly resorts and inns more commonly associated with wine tasting. The camp is little more than a series of concrete slabs with a patch of ground for pitching a tent. But this isn't exactly roughing it. There is a swimming pool (during the summer months) for those who wouldn't dream of submerging themselves in a lake or stream, a parking lot with lots of trees around it, and way too much noise from motorhome gizmos. If

sites	*50*
🏕️🚐	*No hookups, RVs to 31 feet*
open	*All year*
reservations	*California State Parks, 800/444-7275*
contact	*Napa Valley State Park, 707/924-4575*

you're in wine country and this is a good alternative for you to shelling out for fancy and expensive accommodations, this campground will do. But don't come here expecting to hear the sound of birds and running creeks over the sound of televisions, radios, barking dogs, and RV doors slamming.

Facilities: Each site has a picnic table and a fire grill. Running water, flush toilets, and showers are available nearby.

Getting there: From St. Helena, drive 5.5 miles north on Highway 29. The park entrance on the west (left) side of the road.

⑬ Napa County Fairgrounds 🌲

Don't even think of pitching a tent here: This is little more than a place to park an RV overnight while visiting wine country. Concrete, pavement, full electric hookups, and every imaginable modern convenience is to be had here. The RV set can have at it any time except when the county fair is going on during the summer; those who want to rough it at least a little bit will have to move on to another gig.

sites	50
🚐	Full hookups, RVs to 35 feet
open	August through May (closed June/July)
reservations	None
contact	Napa County Fairgrounds, 707/942-5111

Facilities: Each site has a picnic table and a cooking grill. Hot showers, flush toilets, running water, a small store for supplies, a laundry center, and a disposal station are available nearby.

Getting there: From Napa, drive north on Highway 29 for 31 miles to Calistoga. Make a right turn on Lincoln Avenue and follow the signs to the fairgrounds entrance at Fairway Drive.

⑭ Clear Lake State Park 🌲🌲

The sign on the trailer door reads, GONE FISHIN'. The campground is large and quite noisy during the summer—more of a parking lot for RV rigs and trailers than a place to pitch a tent and feel like you're getting away from the hustle and bustle of civilization. Granted, Clear Lake is an interesting geologic feature. The lake is the second largest freshwater lake in California, and the largest whose area is entirely within the state. The bass fishing at Clear Lake is considered to be the best in the nation by the U.S. Bass and other

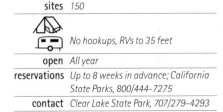

sites	150
⛺ 🚐	No hookups, RVs to 35 feet
open	All year
reservations	Up to 8 weeks in advance; California State Parks, 800/444-7275
contact	Clear Lake State Park, 707/279-4293

organizations. The campground is mostly used as a staging point for fishing trips, especially during the summer. Just about everyone has a fishing boat and spends a good chunk of time on the lake. There is other stuff to do here, however. Hiking trails encircle the lake and surrounding uplands. There are nice coved areas to swim, cycling trails, and places to view wildlife. All in all, however, this is probably not the best place to camp out unless you're planning to spend a lot of time bobbing in the water waiting for a nibble.

Facilities: Each site has a picnic table and a fire grill. Restrooms, flush toilets, and showers are available nearby. There is an RV disposal site and a fish cleaning area as well. Public boat launches and bait shops are also available nearby.

Getting there: From Kelseyville, drive 3.5 miles north on Soda Bay Road to the park entrance.

The Napa County Fairgrounds camp facility is hardly a glamorous place to unfurl the bed roll; tenters are best off skipping it.

⑮ Blue Oak Camp 🌲🌲🌲🌲🌲

One of the few universal truths is demonstrated right here, among the sprawling oak woodlands and valleys along Cache Creek east of Clear Lake: If you want to get away from the hordes of people crowding into a popular outdoor recreation area all you have to do is brave a few miles of dirt road or trail to find your privacy.

sites	6
🏕️🚐	No hookups, RVs to 24 feet
open	All year
reservations	None
contact	U.S. Bureau of Land Management, 707/468-4000

Blue Oak Camp is just such a place; it's difficult to get to and so most don't even bother to try. Your reward for taking the extra effort is an astoundingly private and pristine campground setting among not just the blue oaks the camp is named for but also among white oaks, bays, laurel, willows, and California Sycamore. The Indian Valley Reservoir is a little more than a mile away from the camp, but don't let that deter you from planning a midsummer or early spring fishing trip here. The walk to the reservoir is a pleasant one. Fishing in the late afternoon and then walking back in the cool evening is a sure way to press that reset button in the soul. This is what "dropping out" for a while is all about. To some, Blue Oak may seem a little too far off the beaten path, but that's just what makes it a perfect place to get away from the hustle. No highway noise, and few fellow campers.

If fishing isn't your bag, there is plenty else to do here. Bird-watchers enjoy spotting grebes, herons, coots, swallows, woodpeckers, juncos, sparrows, and more than 100 other documented species know to frequent the area. The coyote brush, mahogany, and manzanita attract small animals such as jackrabbits, ground squirrels, and foxes. Naturally, birds of prey also are found here, at the top of the food chain. The campground has a few conveniences such as running water, but don't expect to find extra amenities or services here: This is not the kind of camp-out where if you forget an essential you can just drop into the general store or easily drive to the Safeway in the nearest town. The reservoir is best known for its bass and bluegill, but the occasional catfish and crappie are not unheard of. Finally, Blue Oak can be a good place from which to stage a rafting trip on Cache Creek, since a number of good runs are located on the creek below Indian Valley.

Facilities: Each site has a picnic table and a fire pit. Running water and pit toilets are available nearby. There is a public boat ramp and a bait and tackle shop near the campground.

Getting there: From Clearlake Oaks, drive east on Highway 20 for 18 miles. Turn north to Walker Ridge Road. After 4 miles you come to a four-way intersection.

Turn left onto the dirt road and continue another 3 miles to the campground on the right side of the road. The road becomes muddy and rutted during the winter, so be sure to check on conditions and avoid driving on it in low-clearance vehicles.

16 Boggs Mountain Demonstration Forest 🌲🌲🌲

Time heals even the most ghastly wounds. Fifty years ago, this sprawling 3,500-acre forest of pine and fir was so thoroughly picked over by loggers that barely a splinter was left behind. Since being taken over by the state, however, the forest has become a gorgeous second-growth woods complete with ample wildlife. The sites aren't much to look at; the camping experience here is similar to a backpacking trip without the hike. Those who like a primitive experience will fit right in; those who want luxury shouldn't brave it. Note also that logging still takes place in the area, and that deer hunting is allowed from mid-August to September. Watch out for black bears and raccoons. Food must be properly stowed.

sites	15
open	All year
reservations	None
contact	Boggs Mountain, California Department of Forestry, 707/928-4378

Facilities: Each site has a fire ring, but no other improvements have been installed. There is no running water, so be sure to pack enough in to last your entire trip. Pit toilets are available nearby, so at least there is no need to dig a hole in the ground.

Getting there: From Kelseyville, drive south on Highway 16 through the town of Hobergs, and then another 0.75 mile to the Boggs Mountain entrance on the left side of the road. The Forest Service roads and trails can be in disrepair at times, depending on the weather, so be sure to call ahead. Check in at the forest headquarters near the entrance for permits before using the camp, as permits are required.

17 Cache Creek Regional Park 🌲🌲🌲🌲

Cache Creek Regional Park, on the banks of Cache Creek, is a great stopover for beginning rafters and kayakers looking mellow Class I and Class II runs within reasonable proximity of the Bay Area. Indeed, rafting and kayaking are the primary draws here, but don't be deterred from stopping in for a camp-out if you don't plan to put in. There is plenty else to draw you here: clean, spacious campsites, the convenience of being able to drop in without a reservation, and a lovely waterside setting. Fishing, bird-watching, wildlife viewing, and swimming (during the early summer, anyway) will also keep visitors busy here. As with many of the regional parks in this part of the state, Cache Creek is less likely to be overrun with vacationers on peak weekends and holidays than state and federally owned campgrounds. This is a great destination for a spur-of-the-moment trip out of the Bay Area or Sacramento Valley. Oddly, the crowds here tend to be reasonably young and active people, and RVs are rare.

sites	45
	No hookups, RVs to 35 feet
open	All year
reservations	None
contact	Cache Creek Regional Park, 530/666-8115

Facilities: Each site has a picnic table and a cooking grill. Running water and flush toilets are available nearby. Good put-in spots for rafting are adjacent to the campground.

Getting there: From Vacaville, take I-80 east to the I-505 interchange. Drive north for 20 miles on I-505 to the intersection with Highway 16. Turn west on Highway 16 and drive another 60 miles. The park entrance on the left.

⑱ Lake Solano County Park 🌲🌲🌲

This small lake rarely fills up, even on hot and sunny summer weekends, because those out to engage in heavier water sports such as skiing prefer adjacent Lake Berryessa. However, this does not necessarily mean the Lake Solano campground is going to be the quiet alternative. For some reason, an unusual number of campers have brought dogs with them during the times I have visited this park. Dog fights are not uncommon! Additionally, too many sites are located far away

sites	85
	35 with full hookups, RVs to 35 feet
open	All year
reservations	Lake Solano County Park, 530/795-2990
contact	Lake Solano County Park, 530/795-2990

from the water, some are a bit cramped, and many don't offer enough privacy. If you're looking for a lake with less traffic than Berryessa for fishing or swimming, this may be it, but the campground has its own set of problems. A national forest campground is probably going to be a better bet for those who don't have their hearts set on full RV hookups and hot showers.

Facilities: Each site has a picnic table and a fire grill. Running water, flush toilets, and showers are available nearby. Also close by are a marina, a public boat launch, boat rentals, and a small shop for limited fishing gear and other supplies.

Getting there: From I-80 at Vacaville, take I-505 north and drive for 10 miles to the intersection with Highway 128. Go west for 5.5 miles to Pleasant Valley Road. Turn left and continue to the clearly marked park entrance nearby.

Other Sonoma Valley / Napa Valley Campgrounds

Most campgrounds and resorts in the Russian River area are privately owned and operated. Public campgrounds nearest the river are those on the Sonoma coast. One private campground is the Faerie Ring Campground near Armstrong Redwoods State Reserve, 707/869-2746. Another is the Casini Ranch Family Campground on the river near Duncan Mills and Monte Rio. Canoe rentals are available at Casini, which is quite large and packed on peak weekends. Call 707/865-2255 for information.

Mendocino

⑲ Plaskett Meadows Campground 🌲🌲🌲

Tent campers, take refuge. Few RV drivers brave the steep forest roads winding up to 6,000 feet, where this quiet and sparsely used campground is nestled near two high-country lakes. The lakes are stocked with trout, and the fishing is good during the summer. Don't spend all of your time in the water, however. Another wonderful attraction nearby is the strenuous hike to the summit of Black Butte Mountain, which at nearly 7,500 feet is one of the highest peaks in the coastal range. From here you can see seemingly forever on a clear day. In productive years, you may also find some steelhead in Cold Creek just south of Plaskett Meadows. If not, at least use it for a late spring/early summer dip.

sites	32
🏕️🚐	No hookups, RVs to 16 feet
open	June 15 to October 15
reservations	None
contact	Stonyford Ranger District, 530/963-3128

Facilities: Each site has a picnic table and a fire pit. Running water and outhouse toilets are available nearby.

Getting there: From Elk Creek, drive north on Forest Road 7 for 36 miles to the campground entrance, which is clearly marked.

⑳ Little Doe Campground 🌲🌲🌲🌲

You'll feel closer to heaven than the monks at this small, quiet campground in a forested canyon below the 7,000-foot Anthony Peak. This is an easy-to-reach dropout point for those who want to escape RV rigs and trailers without having to hike for miles and miles. The campground's small size and lack of amenities such as running water also keep the experience low-key and primitive. The surrounding forest echoes with the sounds of woodpeckers and scrub jays in the

sites	13
🏕️	
open	June 15 to October 1
reservations	None
contact	Covelo Ranger District, 707/983-6118

morning. Because Howard Creek and Howard Lake are nearby, waterfowl and a host of amphibians such as salamanders and bullfrogs also keep you company. Use Howard Creek for drinking water if you have a filtration system, otherwise pack enough in for the trip. Howard Lake is stocked with trout, and the Eel River's middle fork is not far off to the west.

Facilities: Each site has a picnic table and a fire ring. There are outhouse toilets available nearby. There is no running water here, so be sure to either pack your own or bring a filtration kit to make creek water safe.

Getting there: From Covelo, drive east for 13 miles on Highway 162 to the intersection with Indian Dick Road at the Eel River Bridge. Turn Left on Indian Dick (also marked Forest Road M1) and proceed 12 miles to the campground on the left side of the road.

㉑ Eel River Campground ♠♠♠♠

Considering how near this small, popular campground is to the main highway, it is remarkably quiet and peaceful. Steelhead runs are quite healthy on the middle fork of the Eel, and there are great flyfishing spots within a short hiking distance of the campground. Rose Creek, Bar Creek, and Buck Creek all are found east of the campground. These provide more secluded casting spots, although they are more difficult if the runs are not up to par. The campground is set in a lovely oak woodland frequented by bald eagles, wild turkeys, waterfowl, and owls. Watch out for raccoons here; many an unattended ice chest has been toppled in the night here, as it is a known feeding ground. The highway tends to keep less sociable mammals such as black bears, bobcats, and coyotes away from the campground itself, but surrounding areas, including the creek corridors, are fair game and you should be prepared for anything out there. The main trailhead for Traveler's Home National Recreation Trail is adjacent to the campground. This is a great trail for daylong hikes north along the ridgelines above the Eel. It extends through to Steel Beach, which is a great place to wade in during the summer when flows are gentle enough for swimming.

sites	16
🏕️🚐	No hookups, RVs to 22 feet
open	May 1 to October 1
reservations	None
contact	Covelo Ranger District, 707/983-6118

Facilities: Each site has a picnic table and a fire grill. Running water and outhouse-style toilets are available nearby.

Getting there: From Covelo, drive east on Highway 162 for 13 miles to the campground entrance on the left side of the road.

22 Wells Cabin Campground ♣♠♣

This is as close as you're going to get to high country in the coastal mountains—a sparsely used yet nicely appointed campground set in a red fir forest near the 6,300-foot elevation just north of Cattle Ridge. Steelhead can be found in nearby Burt Creek during the last winter run, but only in productive wet years. The main attraction from here is the mile-long hike to Anthony Peak, which at 6,900 feet offers sweeping views of the Pacific Ocean, Clear Lake to the south, and the Sacramento Valley to the east. While the campground is in a great setting for hiking and views, its location near the main forest road makes it a little less desirable than other spots further off the beaten path. Don't let this deter you, however, as the limited number of sites keeps this area from being overrun, and the elevation tends to keep RV rigs and trailers to a minimum.

sites	25
🏕️🚐	No hookups, RVs to 22 feet
open	July 1 to October 31
reservations	None
contact	Corning Ranger District, 530/824-5196

Facilities: Each site has a picnic table and a fire ring. Running water and outhouse toilets are available nearby.

Getting there: From Paskenta, drive west on Forest Road 23N0 for 33 miles. When you reach Forest Road 23N96, turn right and continue for 3 miles to the campground entrance.

23 Hammerhorn Lake Campground ♣♠♣♦

Talk about a good place to spend a lazy afternoon doing nothing. Hammerhorn is one of hundreds of alpine lakes scattered throughout Mendocino National Forest. It's small, pretty, and in a pleasant setting not far from where Hammerhorn Creek meets the middle fork of the Eel River. The location is key for those who can't make up their minds which they like best: bottom fishing on a small lake stocked with trout, flyfishing on a wild creek, or river swarming with salmon and steelhead. Pack enough fishing gear to fancy any situation and toss a coin. Because of its size, the campground remains relatively peaceful and quiet even in the peak outdoor season. The hike up to Doe

sites	9
🏕️🚐	No hookups, RVs to 16 feet, trailers to 22 feet
open	June 1 to October 1
reservations	None
contact	Covelo Ranger District, 707/983-6118

Ridge or Buck Rock is a good way to work off supper. The mixed conifer forest gives way to several meadows great for wildflowers during the spring. Bird species here run the gamut from roosting owls and birds of prey to waterfowl.

Facilities: Each site has a picnic table and a fire ring. Running water and outhouse toilets are available nearby. There is an unpaved boat launch for small crafts only.

Getting there: From Covelo drive east for 13 miles on Highway 162 to the intersection with Indian Dick Road at the Eel River Bridge. Turn left on Indian Dick (also marked Forest Road M1) and proceed 18 miles to the campground on the left side of the road.

24 Sunset Campground 🌲🌲🌲

Visitors to Lake Pillsbury who want to hike, watch birds, look at wildflowers, or maybe do a bit of horseback riding instead of spending most of their time on

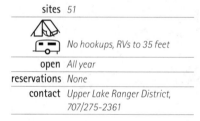

sites	*51*
	No hookups, RVs to 35 feet
open	*All year*
reservations	*None*
contact	*Upper Lake Ranger District, 707/275-2361*

the water will enjoy this nicely situated campground on the lake's northeastern shoreline. Squaw Valley Creek enters the lake just south of the campground. Follow the creek bed for fantastic places to retreat to for a bit of solitude and for the best bird-watching. There is trail access from here to Big Squaw Valley, and those who really want to take advantage of a lakeside setting without getting involved in the boating scene can also safely use Sunset as a staging point for backpacking trips east to the western edge of the Snow Mountain Wilderness area. There is trail access to both the Copper Butte and Crocket Peak areas from here—but be well advised that any hikes leading that far are going to be overnighters, as the amount of ground covered is well over 5 miles round trip, depending on the itinerary.

Facilities: Each site has a picnic table and a fire grill. Running water and vault toilets are available nearby. There is a public boat ramp half a mile away. Pillsbury lake has a whole array of resort facilities and services, including a general store, bait and tackle shops, and lodging.

Getting there: From the Potter Valley/Lake Mendocino area on Highway 20, drive north for 26 miles on Potter Valley/Lake Pillsbury Road. Continue 5 miles past the Forest Service information booth to the campground, which is on the right side of the road.

Lazy days are had on the shores of Lake Pillsbury, near Sunset Campground in Mendocino National Forest.

㉕ Lower Nye Campground 🌲🌲🌲🌲

Bundle up: Snow Mountain Wilderness is one of the wildest severe weather nature spots you're going to find this near the San Francisco Bay Area. It covers nearly 38,000 acres of wildlands made up of oak woodlands, fir, and pine forests. Free-flowing creeks keep virtually all of the wilderness lush and full of life. Lower Nye Campground is a small, little known spot near the northwestern corner of the wilderness area, just outside the wilderness boundaries. It is the closest developed campground to the Snow Mountain Wilderness boundary and therefore makes a more than suitable staging point for backpacking adventures toward the 7,056-foot eastern peak of the mountain. Be sure, however, to check on the

sites	6
🏕️🚐	No hookups, RVs to 22 feet
open	May to September
reservations	None
contact	Upper Lake Ranger District, 707/275-2361

weather before planning all of this out: Snow can persist at the higher elevations here well into the summer. Because Lower Nye is set at a temperate 3,300 feet, snow usually clears out by May or so; at about 6,000 feet, however, hikes may be affected. Be prepared to encounter wild boars, black bears, coyotes, mountain lions, and wild turkeys in this area. More than 150 different birds have been documented here, including the bald eagle and the perigrine falcon. The campground is quiet and secluded—and because the drive in is a bit hairy, there aren't many RVs out here.

Facilities: Each site has a picnic table and a fire grill. Vault toilets are available nearby. There is no running water, so either come prepared to treat creek water or pack enough in to last your entire stay.

Getting there: From the Lake Mendocino junction on Highway 20, drive northeast on Potter Valley/Pillsbury Road for 17 miles. At Bear Creek Road, turn right and continue for 7 miles to the intersection with Forest Road 18N04. From there, turn left and continue another 15 miles to the campground entrance, which is on your right.

26 Oak Flat Campground 🌲🌲🌲🌲

During peak water recreation months, this small well-secluded campground can fill up with RVs, boaters, and dirt bike riders using the lake and off-road vehicle trails. But at other times, particularly in the mid- to late spring months, you stand a pretty good chance of finding it virtually deserted. If water levels in the lake are high enough at the time, this is an absolutely fabulous spot for goofing off all weekend long on the waterfront. The campground is located on a small peninsula at the northernmost shores of the lake, within view of Coyote Rocks. Please note that there is also a small air strip nearby . . . but it is used seldom enough that you won't be serenaded by plane motors all day.

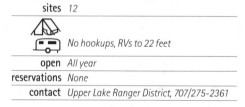

sites	12
	No hookups, RVs to 22 feet
open	All year
reservations	None
contact	Upper Lake Ranger District, 707/275-2361

Facilities: Each site has a picnic table and a fire grill. Vault toilets are available nearby. There is no running water, so come prepared to either filter creek water or pack in enough to last for your entire stay. Boating facilities are available within half a mile, but without vehicle access this is not the camp for those expecting to be able to keep their boats nearby.

Getting there: From Highway 20 near the Lake Mendocino junction, drive east on Potter Valley/Lake Pillsbury Road for 26 miles. The staging point for the campground is 4 miles beyond the Forest Service information booth, which is on the right side of the road.

㉗ Pogie Point Campground 🌲🌲🌲🌲

Even though it is a bit larger than most of the other campgrounds on Lake Pillsbury, Pogie Point can be a pleasant place to stay for a couple of reasons: It's secluded on the northwest corner of the lake away from more populated day-use areas and resort facilities. The sites are well situated to give the illusion of privacy even though neighbors are awfully close by. Ericson Ridge and Coyote Rocks areas are nearby for hiking and limited climbing. Bird-watchers are more likely to see hawks, eagles, and other birds of pray on this end of the lake, although shorebirds and waterfowl also are plentiful. Launching a boat from this end of the lake can also be a bit less hectic, since there are fewer skiers and the lake is less crowded.

sites	52
	No hookups, RVs to 35 feet
open	All year
reservations	None
contact	Upper Lake Ranger District, 707/275-2361

Facilities: Each site has a fire grill and a picnic table. Vault toilets and running water are available nearby. There is a public boat launch nearby. Lake Pillsbury has a resort area with a general store, bait and tackle, and other services.

Getting there: From the Lake Mendocino/Potter Valley area on Highway 20, drive north on Potter Valley/Lake Pillsbury Road for 26 miles, then drive 2 miles past the Forest Service information booth to the campground, which is on the right side of the road.

㉘ Bear Creek Campground 🌲🌲🌲

The small, quiet, secluded campground near the southwestern edge of Snow Mountain Wilderness is not only a great place to drop out of sight for a few days but also a perfect staging point for backpacking trips and day hikes into the Snow Mountain area. The campground is set on the banks of Bear Creek, and Blue Slides Ridge and Blue Slides Creek are nearby. This portion of the forest is lush and brimming with wildlife. During heavy flows, the two creeks form a nice mountain wetland that attracts all varieties of waterfowl. This campground is sometimes used by off-road vehicle recreation types, so be prepared for that if you had your heart set on pristine quiet.

sites	18
	No hookups, RVs to 18 feet
open	May to October
reservations	None
contact	Upper Lake Ranger District, 707/275-2361

Facilities: Each site has a picnic table and a fire grill. Vault toilets are available nearby. There is no running water, so come prepared to treat creek water or pack in enough to last your entire stay.

Getting there: From Upper Lake, drive west on Highway 20 for half a mile to Mendenhall Avenue. Turn left and drive 17 miles to the intersection with Bear Creek Road. Here, turn right and continue 8.5 miles to the campground entrance, which is on the right side of the road.

㉙ Fuller Grove Campground 🌲🌲🌲

During the summer, the Lake Pillsbury Recreation Area is the most heavily used part of the forest, so this is a place for fishing, boating, waterskiing, and long summer nights by the campfire resting up for more waterplay. As much as this lake is a far cry from the secluded nature experience found in more remote sections of the forest and wilderness areas, it is indeed one of the nicest watersports spots in this section of the state. Along the 2,200-acre lake's 31 miles of shoreline are a million hidden corners. If you're determined, you'll be able to find some privacy during your stay. Summer is best for striped bass, crappie, bluegill, and catfish action. Fuller Grove is pretty much a boater's campground because the lake access from here is easily had—don't hesitate, however, to cover a few more miles to find something a little more low key. The sites here are oriented largely around the camping boater. Don't expect a lot of tree cover—you will meet your neighbors whether you want to or not! The terrain is mostly oak woodlands and mixed forest, with intermittent meadows.

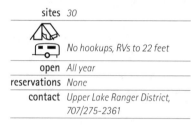

sites	*30*
	No hookups, RVs to 22 feet
open	*All year*
reservations	*None*
contact	*Upper Lake Ranger District, 707/275-2361*

Facilities: Each site has a picnic table and a fire ring. There are outhouse toilets and running water available nearby. A public boat launch is adjacent. There is a lake resort nearby, along with a general store and fish and tackle shops.

Getting there: From Highway 20 at Lake Mendocino/Potter Valley, drive north on the Potter Valley/Lake Pillsbury Road for 13 miles along the east fork of the Russian River. The campground is 1 mile past the Forest Service information booth for Lake Pillsbury.

30 Deer Valley Campground 🌲🌲🌲

In the late spring and through the summer, Deer Valley is a great place to enjoy wildflowers, birding, and quiet strolls in largely unoccupied woodlands. Because most of the outdoor season crowds flock to lakes like Pillsbury and Mendocino, far-flung campgrounds like this very small and secluded spot can be just the escape you're looking for. Bring a comfortable lounge chair and something to read, your birding scope, and a new attitude. Important note: This part of the forest is very popular among deer hunters so if you're a defender of Bambi's mother and you don't want to be around rifles and ammo, skip this campground in the fall.

sites	13
	No hookups, RVs to 22 feet
open	April to October
reservations	None
contact	Upper Lake Ranger District, 707/275-2361

Facilities: Each site has a picnic table and a fire grill. Vault toilets are available nearby. There is no running water, so come prepared to treat creek water or pack enough in to last your entire trip.

Getting there: From Highway 20 at Upper Lake, drive north on Elk Mountain Road for 12 miles to the intersection with Forest Road 16N01. Turn right and continue 4 miles to the campground entrance.

31 Middle Creek Campground 🌲🌲🌲

Talk about perfect solitude. This small, secluded campground on the banks of Middle Creek gets few visitors during the height of the water recreation season because it is located too far from some of the more popular lakes. Don't pass it up so fast, though. It is located in a pretty forested area with direct trail access to Pitney Ridge and Youngs Peak. Be aware, however, that there is also access directly from here to the OHV recreation trails, which means off-road vehicles may be in the area. Also keep in mind that because of the campground's location reasonably near the town of Upper Lake and Mendenhall Avenue, a main road, there are likely to be more RVs here than at a campground that is a little more difficult to reach.

sites	13
	No hookups, RVs to 22 feet
open	All year
reservations	None
contact	Upper Lake Ranger District, 707/275-2361

Facilities: Each site has a picnic table and a fire grill. Running water and vault toilets are available nearby. There are some services available in Upper Lake, which is 8 miles away.

Getting there: From Upper Lake, drive west for half a mile on Highway 20 to Mendenhall Avenue and turn right. Drive another 8 miles to the campground, which is on the right side of the road.

㉜ Letts Lake Campground 🌲🌲🌲🌲

Scrape the barnacles off the old fishing boat. Letts Lake is a popular summer spot to fish for trout, bass, and catfish or for canoeing, boating, and swimming. There are three campgrounds on the east side of the 34-acre lake, each positioned far

sites	42
	No hookups, RVs to 24 feet
open	April to November
reservations	None
contact	Stonyford Ranger District, 530/963-3128

enough apart that they don't seem like one big camping complex. That prevents the "parking lot" effect that can result in campgrounds where visitors are packed in too tightly with their vehicles. The south fork of Letts Creek enters the north end of the lake. Miner and Mills Creeks are to the southeast, a short walk from the camp. All three creeks can provide suitable steelhead runs in productive years. The trailhead for Box Spring Loop Trail, which connects to the 7,000-foot summit of Snow Mountain 2 miles north of Letts Lake, is nearby. This is an excellent staging point for day trips into the Snow Mountain Wilderness for those who prefer the convenience of a developed campground over backpacking. Note that to reach Box Spring Loop, you have a choice between driving north to the trailhead or doing a long hike on the Bathhouse and Trout Creek trails toward the Snow Mountain area.

Facilities: Each site has a picnic table and a fire grill. Running water and vault toilets are available nearby. There is a public boat ramp and a fishing pier near the campground for lake access. Do not launch motorboats.

Getting there: From Stonyford, drive west on Fouts Springs Road for 17 miles to the campground entrance on the east side of the lake.

㉝ Lily Pond/Mill Valley Campground 🌲🌲🌲🌲

Lily Pond is north of Letts Lake and about half its size. Because the campground is also significantly smaller than those found at Letts Lake and because it is also more difficult for RV rigs to park here, Lily Pond and the Mill Valley area can be much more quiet and peaceful. There are also fewer boats here since the pond is not stocked, making this a more suitable stop for those interested in kayaking or canoeing while viewing wildlife. At 4,500 feet, the pond attracts an eclectic mix of waterfowl and foraging birds. Juncos, scrub jays, sparrows, and woodpeckers frequent this area of oak and pine forest with intermittent meadows. Hiking access to the Snow Mountain Wilderness is easily had from here, making this a good staging point for day hikes to the peaks to the north.

sites	15
	No hookups, RVs to 18 feet
open	April to November
reservations	None
contact	Stonyford Ranger District, 530/963-3128

Facilities: Each site has a picnic table and a fire grill. Running water and vault toilets are available nearby.

Getting there: From Stonyford, drive west on Fouts Springs Road for 17 miles to the intersection with Forest Road 17N02. Turn left and continue half a mile to the campground entrance.

㉞ South Fork Campground 🌲🌲

On the surface, this campground looks as if it might be a peaceful weekend getaway spot; don't be fooled, however. For some reason, off-road vehicle riders flock here—often in numbers larger than the campground is designed to accommodate. That means two-stroke motors revving enough to drown out the sounds of the forest. One smart move could be to check ahead to see if road restrictions are affecting the off-roading. If that is the case, South Fork will do. If it isn't, however, chances are your best bet is to skip it and search out more peaceful surroundings.

sites	5
open	All year
reservations	None
contact	Stonyford Ranger District, 530/963-3128

Facilities: Each site has a picnic table and a fire grill. Vault toilets are available nearby. There is no running water here, so be sure to either pack enough to last your entire trip or come prepared to filter and treat creek water for drinking.

Getting there: From Stonyford, drive west on Fouts Spring Road for 8 miles to Forest Road 18N03. Turn right and continue 1 mile to the campground, which is on the north side of the road.

35 Mill Creek Campground ▲▲▲▲

Go ahead, meditate. This small, little-known camp is a godsend for those who want to enjoy the Letts Lake section of the forest and have easy access to the Snow Mountain Wilderness Area trailheads without having to use the larger, more congested campgrounds. The camp is near the banks of Fouts Spring Creek less than a mile from the Bathhouse Trail and Trout Creek Trail trailheads into the Snow Mountain area. This camp can be used as a staging point for day hikes into Snow Mountain. The camp also, however, is known to off-road vehicle users who like it for its proximity to approved roads. Mill Creek is set in a mixed pine forest at 1,700 feet. The creek isn't your best steelhead or salmon run, but it's good for early summer dips. While the campsites offer privacy and quiet, keep in mind that there are several other camps nearby, including one used by youth groups.

sites	6
open	April to October
reservations	None
contact	Stonyford Ranger District, 530/963-3128

Facilities: Each site has a picnic table and a fire grill. Vault toilets are available nearby. There is no running water, so be sure to either bring enough to last your entire stay or be prepared to treat creek water for drinking.

Getting there: From Stonyford, drive west on Fouts Spring Road for 9 miles to the campground entrance. which is on the right side of the road.

36 Davis Flat Campground ▲▲▲

A small lake, suitable for swimming, is within walking distance of this pleasant campground set in a mixed pine forest at 1,700 feet in the shadows of Snow Mountain. Despite the size of the campground, sites are nicely arranged and well kept; you have the illusion of privacy even though you're surrounded by other campers. The campground is also popular with off-roaders, so it may be a good idea to check to see if approved roads are in use during your visit to avoid a run-in with a

sites	28
	No hookups, RVs to 35 feet
open	All year
reservations	None
contact	Stonyford Ranger District, 530/963-3128

gaggle of screaming motors. Like many of the other campsites in this part of the forest, Davis Flat serves as a very good staging point for day trips into the Snow Mountain area. Another thing that could spoil a visit here is that the camp is terribly near recreation areas frequented by day visitors.

Facilities: Each site has a picnic table and a fire pit. Running water and vault toilets are available nearby. There are no services in the forest itself, so stock up on any necessities in Stonyford.

Getting there: From Stonyford, drive west on Fouts Spring Road for 8 miles to the intersection with Forest Road 18N03.

37 Fouts Campground 🌲🌲🌲

This is a pretty but well-traveled section of forest because of its proximity to Snow Mountain. Because Fouts Campground is one of the first you come to when heading into the forest from the town of Stonyford, it often fills up first. While the camp, located on the banks of Fouts Spring Creek and within a stones throw of the main Snow Mountain trailheads, is indeed pleasant, we advise you to not settle here without at least driving another mile west to see whether Mill Creek, a much quieter camp about half the size, is available. This is another site which makes a good staging point for day trips into Snow Mountain.

sites	*11*
🏕️🚐	*No hookups, RVs to 16 feet*
open	*All year*
reservations	*None*
contact	*Stonyford Ranger District, 530/963-3128*

Facilities: Each site has a picnic table and a fire grill. Running water and vault toilets are available nearby.

Getting there: From Stonyford, drive west on Fouts Springs Road for 8 miles to the intersection with Forest Road 18N03. Turn right and continue for 1 mile to the campground entrance, which is on the right side of the road.

38 Cedar Camp 🌲🌲🌲🌲

Because it is so much more difficult to get to than other campgrounds in the Stonyford area of the forest, Cedar Camp can be quite a score during the peak season. If you're the kind of road warrior who doesn't mind a long drive on windy Forest Service roads in exchange a bit of solitude, try to check in here. The camp is at 4,300 feet and so is often quite a bit chillier than some of your other options. Your reward for braving the elements, however, is a fabulous setting in the

sites	*5*
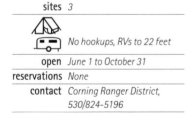	*No hookups, RVs to 16 feet*
open	*May to October*
reservations	*None*
contact	*Stonyford Ranger District, 530/963-3118*

foothills of 6,100-foot Goat Mountain, on Trough Spring Ridge. A creek runs nearby, and there is a small lake for swimming just a short walk away. Note that while other camps in this portion of the forest are good staging points for day hikes to Snow Mountain, that is not the case here, as the trailheads are several miles away and 2,000 feet down.

Facilities: Each site has a picnic table and a fire ring. Vault toilets are available nearby. Pack in your own water or come prepared to treat creek water for drinking. The camp is a windy climb away from Stonyford and there are no stores or other services in the forest—don't forget anything.

Getting there: From Stonyford, drive west on Fouts Spring Road for 6 miles, turn south on Trough Springs Road, and continue 13 miles to the campground entrance, which is on the right.

㊴ Whitlock Campground 🌲

For as far as the eye can see. This small, little-known campground is in an area of oak and pine forest just west of the summit of Round Mountain. Round Mountain offers nice views of the spectacular Elder Creek canyon to the northeast. As wonderful as a campground with so few sites can be, however, it is important to note that the surrounding terrain is not the perfectly pristine wilderness most of us are looking for when we delve deep into the national forests. Radio towers and satellite dishes are visible from Road Mountain. If that spoils things for you, a little distance will fix it. The campground and the summit are at about the same elevation—4,300 feet.

sites	*3*
	No hookups, RVs to 22 feet
open	*June 1 to October 31*
reservations	*None*
contact	*Corning Ranger District, 530/824-5196*

Facilities: Each site has a picnic table and a fire ring. Running water and outhouse toilets are available nearby.

Getting there: From Paskenta, drive west on Forest Road 23N01 for 16 miles to the intersection with Forest Road 24N41. From there, go north a short distance to the campground entrance, which is clearly marked.

Other Mendocino National Forest Campgrounds

There are numerous group camps in the Mendocino National Forest.

The Fuller Group Campground contains 60 sites on the banks of Lake Pillsbury (no hookups, RVs to 22 feet). The campground has piped water, vault toilets, and picnic tables along with fire pits for large groups to enjoy the camaraderie of communal cooking and campfire stories. Contact the Upper Lake Ranger District at 707/275-2361.

Equestrians looking to explore the Snow Mountain Wilderness area on horseback will find the Dixie Glade Group Horse Campground to be much to their liking (14 sites for tents or RVs, no hookups, RVs to 22 feet). There are feeding and water troughs here, along with corrals. Each campsite has a picnic table and a fire grill, and vault toilets are available nearby. It is open only April to October. For more information, contact the Stonyford Ranger District, 530/963-3128.

Bay Area

Under ordinary circumstances, waking up in the morning to see an oil tanker gliding past your tent after a night of sleeping under the stars would be cause for alarm. These are not, however, ordinary circumstances. Mount Livermore forms the 700-foot summit of Angel Island State Park in the middle of San Francisco Bay. Unzip your sleeping bag and go for a midnight stroll and you may discover the TransAmerica Pyramid glimmering at you from across the water through the night fog. In the Bay Area, the definition of "getting away from it all" can be a bit skewed.

This is not to say there aren't places to camp in Northern California's largest urban center that are legitimately primitive. On Mount Diablo, for example, you'd swear you were in the backcountry—instead of just a 15-minute drive from the burgeoning suburb of Walnut Creek. The secluded creeks and canyons of the East Bay, the wild Marin shoreline, the San Francisco peninsula oceanfront, and the remote wilderness of the South Bay's San Antone Mountains also belie the fact that more than 6 million people call this region of the state home.

All this results in some excellent, and surprisingly convenient, weekend camping opportunities of which Bay Area outdoorspeople know how to take advantage. No self-respecting native is going to encourage the wayward Yosemite or Tahoe tourist to staying here instead. We want to keep the home-spun treasures to ourselves as much as possible and quickly learn that not every SUV loaded with gear needs to make the hours-long trek east on Friday afternoon.

So, consider skipping the busier spots and explore these underutilized state, federal, and regional parklands. Just don't tell them who sent you—and by all means let's keep this our little secret.

Bay Area

1. Glen Camp
2. Sky Camp
3. Coast Camp
4. Wildcat Camp
5. Rocky Point/Steep Ravine Environmental Campground
6. Bicentennial Campground
7. Haypress Backpack Camp
8. Kirby Cove
9. China Camp State Park
10. Angel Island State Park
11. Samuel P. Taylor State Park
12. Half Moon Bay State Beaches
13. Butano State Park
14. Memorial County Park
15. Portola State Park
16. Anthony Chabot Regional Park
17. Mount Diablo State Park
18. Stewartville Backpack Camp
19. Sunol Regional Wilderness
20. Del Valle Regional Park
21. Henry W. Coe State Park

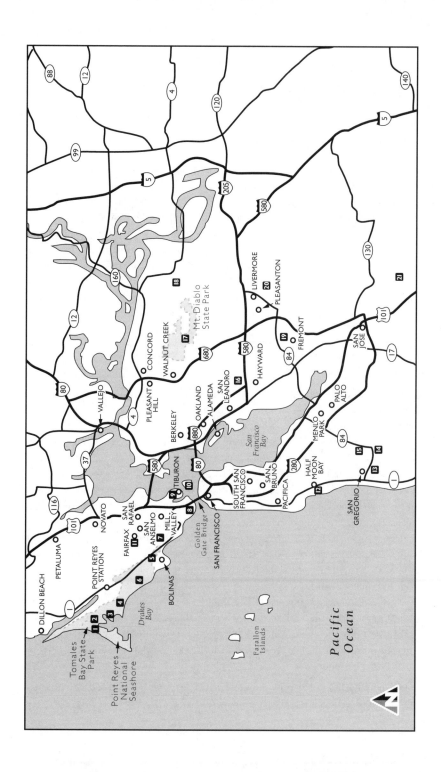

West Marin / Point Reyes National Seashore

❶ Glen Camp 🌲🌲🌲🌲🌲

Even though it's not a dramatic setting on a bluff overlooking the ocean like those Point Reyes National Seashore is famous for, Glen Camp is arguably the best campground of the four in the preserve. The camp is situated in a picturesque forested canyon east of Wildcat Beach. While the hike to the beach is 2 miles, there are a few things that make the extra walking worth it for those who crave silence and serenity in the woods. First, Glen Camp is the only camp at Point Reyes that does not have a group site; this means no jamborees to worry about. And just as important, horses and other pack animals are not allowed in this camp. A common complaint among backpackers who visit Point Reyes is that horses and pack animals can spoil their outdoor experience by creating noise and making a mess. In Glen Camp, you will find none of that. This is also the most recently rehabilitated campground, with all new facilities installed in 1998.

sites	*12*
🏕️	
open	*All year*
reservations	*Up to 3 months in advance; Bear Valley Visitor Center, 415/663-8054*
contact	*Point Reyes National Seashore, 415/663-1092*

To make the most of a backpacking trip to Point Reyes, we suggest the following: See if you can stay at Glen Camp for at least the first and last nights of your visit, and on one or more other nights move to the Wildcat Camp for easier access to the ocean and the beach. This way, if the group camps at Wildcat (or any of the two other camps) are occupied, you are at least guaranteed a few night's peace at Glen. The important thing is to work flexibility and mobility into your itinerary. Again, note that the better you are at packing and setting up an efficient camp, the easier it will be to visit two or more camps at Point Reyes. However your visit is structured, if you decide to stay in more than one camp, make sure Glen Camp is one of them!

There are two ways to reach Glen Camp by foot. One is a 4.5 mile trek along Bear Valley Trail, the easiest route because there are no steep grades. Those wanting to take the scenic route and break a sweat will instead want to approach the camp on Steward Trail from the Five Brooks Trailhead, a 5-mile hike with steep elevation gains.

Facilities: Each site has a picnic table, a fire grill, and a food locker. Running water and pit toilets are available nearby.

Getting there: To reach Point Reyes from San Francisco, drive north on US 101 to San Rafael and exit at Sir Francis Drake Boulevard. Follow Sir Francis Drake for 21 miles until you enter the small town of Olema. Just north of Olema is the park's main entrance and the Bear Valley Visitor Center, where all campers must pick up their wilderness permits and be directed to the proper spot to leave their cars during their stay.

❷ Sky Camp 🌲🌲🌲🌲

There is more to Point Reyes than the beaches and bluffs overlooking the ocean; Mount Wittenberg and Mount Vision each stand over 1,400 feet above the peninsula, and each give sweeping views of the beaches, Drakes Bay, and Drakes Estero below. Sky Camp is located on the western flanks of Mount Wittenberg. While

To reach Sky Camp within Point Reyes National Seashore requires a 1.5-mile hike—but it's a strenuous one, so be prepared.

the walk to this camp is reasonably short, at just more than 1.5 miles from the Sky Trailhead on Limantour Road, keep in mind that there are a few sections of the walk with steep elevation gains. Small children may have difficulty completing this hike, particularly if they pack too much. (A mistake we have seen people make!) Like the Wildcat and Coast Camps, Sky has group camping—but here there is only one group site, meaning while you won't be camping right on the ocean there is less of a chance of a full-scale scout invasion of the campground and trails.

sites	12 individual, 1 group
open	All year
reservations	Up to 3 months in advance; Bear Valley Visitor Center, 415/663-8054
contact	Point Reyes National Seashore, 415/663-1092

Facilities: Each site has a picnic table, a fire grill, and a food locker. Running water and pit toilets are available nearby.

Getting there: To reach Point Reyes from San Francisco, drive north on US 101 to San Rafael and exit at Sir Francis Drake Boulevard. Follow Sir Francis Drake for 21 miles until you enter the small town of Olema. Just north of Olema is the park's main entrance and the Bear Valley Visitor Center, where all campers must pick up their wilderness permits and be directed to the proper spot to leave their cars during their stay.

❸ Coast Camp 🌲🌲🌲🌲

Sometimes, easier is better. Because the hike involved is less than half that required to reach Wildcat, many backpackers visiting Point Reyes National Seashore choose this camp. Like Wildcat, it is also set on 200-foot high bluffs overlooking the Pacific Ocean near Limantour Beach and about a 1.5-mile hike from Sculptured Beach, an interesting place to go tidepooling and view the unusual sculptured rocks along the shore visible at low tide. Because this particular campground is in the northern part of Point Reyes, the weather off the ocean can be just a tad

sites	12 individual, 2 group
open	All year
reservations	Up to 3 months in advance; Bear Valley Visitor Center, 415/663-8054
contact	Point Reyes National Seashore, 415/663-1092

colder and wetter than at other camps. When making a reservation here, but sure to specifically request a site which is well protected from ocean winds. About half of the sites are shielded by brush; the others are more out in the open. As with Wildcat Camp, there is a chance of encountering large scouts or other large groups at this camp, probably more likely since the hike in is the shortest of all backpacking camps here. Be sure to specifically ask if group camps have been reserved on the days you choose.

Facilities: These are primitive camp sites with no amenities. Running water and vault toilets are available nearby. Fires at not allowed, so all cooking should be done on a stove.

Getting there: To reach Point Reyes from San Francisco, drive north on US 101 to San Rafael and exit at Sir Francis Drake Boulevard. Follow Sir Francis Drake for 21 miles until you enter the small town of Olema. Just north of Olema is the park's main entrance and the Bear Valley Visitor Center, where all campers must pick up their wilderness permits and be directed to the proper spot to leave their cars during their stay.

④ Wildcat Camp 🌲🌲🌲

You've got a front row seat. . . . This small backpacking camp in a meadow situated on bluffs overlooking the Pacific Ocean is a perfect place to drop out of sight for a while. Point Reyes is 70,000 acres of pristine and rugged wilderness covering 30 miles of undeveloped coastline. This is one of the best spots along the entire coast of California to see what the shoreline looked like before European settlers arrived in the late eighteenth century. Your adventure begins with a 6.5-mile hike across some of the most stunning coastal countryside remaining in this part of the state. The hike route changes from thick forests of Douglas-fir to coastal plains and flowery meadows. Several small ponds and lakes are found along the way as well. The last leg of the hike follows the coast closely.

sites	5 individual, 3 group
open	All year
reservations	Up to 3 months in advance; Bear Valley Visitor Center, 415/663-8054
contact	Point Reyes National Seashore, 415/663-1092

Be sure to plan smart; one sure way to ruin both the hike and the camp-out is to overpack. Pack in only what you need. Also, don't head out to the Point Reyes oceanfront expecting to have perfect sunny weather. Because the peninsula extends farther into the ocean than the rest of the California coast, Point Reyes can be particularly foggy. In fact, even on summer days don't be surprised if there are only a few hours during which you can see the sky. A little bit of overcast isn't going to be enough to spoil the amazing beauty of Wildcat Camp and its surroundings. There is access from here to the beach, a great place to build a fire and take in the ocean views. There is also a piece of Fantasy Island here; a waterfall drops almost 40 feet directly into the ocean. Another thing to be aware of is that because there are group camps here, you run the danger of having to share the campground with scout troops or other large groups. It is better to ask if the group camps have been reserved when choosing a date for your own camp-out, but even that doesn't give you any guarantees. This is also a popular area among equestrians, and they have a bad habit of bringing their horses into the camp area to take care of business. Should your visit coincide with a scouting event or a group ride, be confident that there is at least enough room for everyone to spread out.

Facilities: Each site has a cooking grill, running water, and vault toilets are available nearby.

Getting there: To reach Point Reyes from San Francisco, drive north on US Highway 101 to San Rafael and exit at Sir Francis Drake Boulevard. Follow Sir Francis Drake for 21 miles until you enter the small town of Olema. Just north of Olema is the park's main entrance and the Bear Valley Visitor Center, where all campers must pick up their wilderness permits and be directed to the proper spot to leave their cars during their stay.

Marin County

⑤ Rocky Point/Steep Ravine Environmental Campground 🌲🌲🌲🌲

This secluded walk-in camp overlooking the Pacific Ocean from high bluffs is arguably one of the most stunning spots on the California Coast to unroll a sleeping bag and fumble with your tent poles. First, let's talk about the setting. The campground is positioned on what seems like the edge of the Earth: a rocky bluff with a blunt drop straight in the Pacific. Looming east of this setting is the 2,517-foot Mount Tamalpais. There is easy trail access to the mountain from here, but be advised that the hikes to the summit are very steep in places; only experienced hikers in good shape should partake if the plan is to venture all the way to the top. A sunrise on a clear morning can be incredibly stunning from this vantage point, as the mountain is silhouetted behind brilliant gold sun bursts. On foggy mornings Tamalpais disappears from view completely. The cold brush of a fog front at the ocean's edge is like wiping your face with a wash cloth that has been dipped in ice water; fog is coldest and wettest when it first hits land. Here it is sure to get your attention. (If you don't like that sort of thing, be sure to have a scarf and head covering on hand). Fall asleep to the sound of the ocean massaging the rocks below; wake to the music of songbirds. This is about as good as it gets, truly, and for that reason the half dozen campsites and 10 cabins fill up quickly.

sites	*6 campsites, 10 rustic cabins*
open	*All year, weather permitting*
reservations	*Up to 12 weeks in advance, 10 a.m. to 2 p.m., Tuesday through Saturday only; Golden Gate National Recreation Area, 415/561-4304*
contact	*GGNRA, 415/331-1540*

Facilities: Each campsite has a tent pad, a food locker, a picnic table, and a fire pit. Cabins are equipped with picnic tables, bunks, wood stoves, and barbecues. Running water and vault toilets are available nearby.

Getting there: From US Highway 101, take the Stinson Beach turnoff and head northwest for 10.5 miles. The clearly marked entrance to the campground is on the west side of the road.

View from Mount Tamalpais.

❻ Bicentennial Campground 🌲🌲🌲

This is a nice and reasonably well-secluded walk-in camp on a forested bluff overlooking the Pacific Ocean at Bonita Cove. The campground is small, and with three sites restricted to two people each there is no chance of encountering big crowds here. There is one potential drawback, however: The Point Bonita Lighthouse is nearby, meaning that on nights when visibility on the ocean isn't good, the fog horn will be sounding all night long. Sure, the sound of a fog horn in the distance can be charming and add to the ambience of an oceanfront setting. This, however, can be a little too close

sites	*3*
🏕	
open	*All year*
reservations	*Up to 12 weeks in advance, 10 a.m. to 2 p.m., Tuesday through Saturday only; Golden Gate National Recreation Area, 415/561-4304*
contact	*GGNRA, 415/331-1540*

and too loud for some people to tolerate. In fact, if the fog horn is going all night long there's a chance you won't get much sleep. It's all about tradeoffs; sure you're on the ocean and there are no crowds, but is a foghorn blasting all night any better than a rowdy crowd of partiers?

Facilities: Each site has a picnic table. Chemical toilets and running water are available nearby. No fires are allowed.

Getting there: From San Francisco, cross the Golden Gate Bridge into Marin County and take the second off-ramp to Fort Baker. Turn left on Conzelman Road and follow it 3 miles west to Bonita Cove. The campground is on the west side of the road; parking is allowed on the road shoulder.

⑦ Haypress Backpack Camp 🌲🌲🌲

Because it is just a short (about two-thirds of a mile) hike from the staging area in the northern Marin Headlands near Tennessee Valley, this compact walk-in camp is an ideal place for families introducing their children to the outdoors. For this reason, those expecting a quiet nature experience without small children to listen to are taking their chances camping at Haypress—always remember that the more walking you have to do to get there the less likely you are to have this problem. Those looking for a good place to take that first step away from car camping with the family, however, can't go wrong here. Tennessee Valley cuts through the Marin Wildlands to the Pacific Ocean; its coastal scrub and brush carpeting deep cut streams and wide lagoons. This is a great place to see the interplay between the ocean and the land; fog and storms roll by in the mornings, and the valley is engorged with heavy runoff by afternoon. The camp is situated between Muir and Stinson Beaches; those wishing to take longer hikes out can stage here and visit the ocean via Coyote Ridge Trail. Be prepared for a bare bones camp, however: No fires are allowed here and there is no running water, meaning campers much pack enough in to last for their entire stay. Still, considering the ease with which the camp is accessible, it provides a wonderful seclusion from roads and automobiles. Try real hard, and you might even convince yourself that this is the deep back-country.

sites	5
open	All year, weather permitting
reservations	Up to 12 weeks in advance, 10 a.m. to 2 p.m., Tuesday through Saturday only; Golden Gate National Recreation Area, 415/561-4304
contact	GGNRA, 415/331-1540

Facilities: Don't expect to find anything more than picnic tables with each site. A vault toilet is available nearby. Bring everything else with you, and don't even think about building a fire, as it's not allowed.

Getting there: Take the Stinson Beach exit from US 101 and head west. After about 1.5 miles, turn left on Tennessee Valley Road. Park in the staging area at the end of the road and hike two-thirds of a mile to the camp on Tennessee Valley Trail.

⑧ Kirby Cove 🌲🌲🌲🌲🌲

This is some of the hottest beachfront property found anywhere, and it's amazingly quiet and secluded for its proximity to San Francisco and the Golden Gate Bridge. To camp at Kirby Cove means having a double angled view of both the Pacific Ocean and San Francisco Bay. The beach here is just west of the bridge yet separated from the rest of the coast by steep bluffs. The campground is 50 yards from the beach in a lovely cypress and eucalyptus forest protected from ocean breezes by a sea wall constructed by the Navy for use during World War II. As is the case in throughout the Marin Headlands, facilities built up for the Pacific Coast defense are still intact here. Because vehicle access to the cove from the public road is restricted, this can be an amazingly private stretch of waterfront. Each site can hold a limit of 10 people, which means the most you might ever find camping here at any given time is 40 (and that is hardly ever likely to happen). Typically, a few campers and no more than a dozen or so day visitors can be found inhabiting the cove even on warm summer days; chalk that up to the typical sun worshipper's reluctance to walk the 1 mile downhill to the beach. Because the road is gated, many also just assume there is no public access allowed. All of this works to your advantage if you're lucky enough to nab a campsite here.

sites	4
⛺	
open	April 1 to October 31
reservations	Up to 12 weeks in advance, 10 a.m. to 2 p.m., Tuesday through Saturday only; Golden Gate National Recreation Area, 415/561-4304
contact	GGNRA, 415/331-1540

Facilities: Each site has a picnic table, a fire ring, and a barbecue pit. Pit toilets are available nearby. There is no running water; campers must pack in enough fresh water to last their entire stay.

Getting there: From San Francisco, take the Golden Gate Bridge to Marin County and exit at the Sausalito Lateral Road exit. Turn left at the end of the off-ramp and pass under the freeway. You are now on Conzelman Road. Continue up Conzelman Road about half a mile west to the Kirby Cove entrance on the left side of the road. The parking area is at the bottom of the access road, about 100 yards from the camp sites.

At Kirby Cove, the Golden Gate Bridge is an unlikely backdrop for a truly unique urban camping experience.

⑨ China Camp State Park 🌲🌲🌲

This camp area is a favorite among those seeking a riparian/marsh setting for bird-watching or bay shore access for windsurfing. Because vehicles are left in a parking area 100 yards away from the campground, the open space feel here is for real. There is no getting away from the fact, however, that the campground is just big enough to draw a fair share of noise. Careful planning should mitigate this; avoid this campground on peak season weekends and holidays unless you have no other options. The camp is set in a nice woodland of oak trees and laurel, and there is trail access to the west edge of San Pablo Bay. There are 1,500 acres to explore here, among them remnants of a mid-nineteenth-century Chinese fishing village, a few redwood groves, and meadows that yield impressive wildflower displays in spring.

The San Pablo Baylands Wildlife Area, just north of China Camp, is one of the largest restored wetlands on the bay, making this a premiere birding area.

sites	30
open	All year
reservations	Up to 8 weeks in advance; California State Parks, 800/444-7275
contact	China Camp State Park, 415/456-0575

Facilities: Each site has a picnic table, a food locker, and a fire pit. Piped water, flush toilets, and showers are on site. While RVs cannot enter the campsite, RV parking is permitted in the China Camp lot. There are no RV services.

Getting there: From San Francisco drive north on US 101 for 11 miles to San Rafael. Take the San Pedro Road exit east and drive for 3.5 miles to the park entrance on the right.

⑩ Angel Island State Park 🌲🌲🌲🌲🌲

It may sound like something out of a dream, but this is the honest truth: For the price you would normally pay to rent a small campsite in a crowded park, you can have the exclusive use of a mile-wide island in the middle of San Francisco Bay.

sites	10
	No vehicle access
open	All year
reservations	Up to 8 weeks in advance; California State Parks, 800/444-7275
contact	Angel Island State Park, 415/435-5390

The campground is near the summit of Mount Livermore, which stands 781 feet over San Francisco Bay. From here you have spectacular vistas of the Golden Gate, the city skyline, the East Bay hills, and beyond. Unfolding below the mountain is a potpourri of outdoor treasures: fields of wildflowers, groves of oak and fir, eucalyptus forests (although much of the eucalyptus has been abated for fire danger and replaced by native vegetation), miles of trails and fire roads for hiking and biking, a marina with guest mooring, and more. What really makes this a prime camping experience, however, is that there is so much space on the island compared to the small capacity of the campground itself. Because the park is closed to day visitors every afternoon, overnight campers are left with just about all the privacy they need. In midsummer, that often means more than 4 hours of daylight for private hiking, swimming, bike rides, kayaking, and other activities.

At night the cold breezes of the Pacific coming through the Golden Gate can make the island a bit chilly, so come prepared for abrupt climate changes to avoid being uncomfortable. This minor concern aside, however, what really makes the Angel Island camp-out a sure bet is that it is an unusual opportunity to not just have a nature experience without venturing too far out of the city but to do so while the urban jungle remains visible. Where else can you look across the water at the very thing you're trying to get away from? Nighttime on the island is most

Ocean breezes through the Golden Gate make San Francisco Bay a perfect spot for wind-surfers—and Angel Island State Park a spot for tent tie-downs.

interesting; the city becomes a necklace of lights. The sounds of sea breezes rustling the trees are broken by fog horns and the gurgle of a tug boat's engine. In the morning, the famous San Francisco fog leaves a blanket of dew on the island and the city remains hidden until the fog burns off, sometimes well after noon.

Needless to say, this is among the most popular of all Bay Area campgrounds, so those hoping to sleep on the island during the peak outdoor season are strongly advised to plan well in advance and make reservations. Keep in mind, however, that the off season can be a more rewarding experience because not only are some of the sites likely to be vacant, but the soggy weather is likely to make the island seem more alive with plants and wildlife. There are a few other things to keep in mind if considering a night on the island: There is no ferry service back to the mainland between 4:30 p.m. or so and the early morning. In fact, day visitors who find themselves stuck on the island because they miss the last ferry are escorted to Tiburon by a patrol boat and required to pay a fine. Because you are literally cut off from the rest of the world for as long as 15 hours, it is a good idea to take bring a cellular telephone. Additionally, pay attention to when the sunrise and sunset will be. While the island may not seem large from afar, it can take a couple of hours to walk from one side to the other. It's easier than you think to get lost if you're caught too far away from the campground at sunset—even if you have a flashlight.

Facilities: Each site has a picnic table and a fire grill. Running water and vault toilets are available nearby. There are a number of services available on the island during daytime business hours only; these include a small snack shop, café, and bicycle and kayak rentals.

Getting there: There aren't a whole lot of options for how to get to the island; it is accessible only by boat. If you don't have a private boat to take out there, one of three ferry services will have to do. The shortest ride is from the Tiburon peninsula in Marin. For schedule and fare information from Tiburon, call 415/435-2131. The second best option is the ferry from Pier 41 in San Francisco; call 415/773-1188. The Blue and Gold Fleet, which runs the San Francisco ferry, also has service from Vallejo in the East Bay. Call the Pier 41 number for information on that ferry.

⑪ Samuel P. Taylor State Park 🌲🌲🏕

This will do. This 2,600-acre redwood preserve serves mostly as an overflow camp for the more popular Point Reyes National Seashore 7 miles to the west. Samuel P. Taylor State Park isn't too shabby for a place that is looked at mostly as a stopover. If you find yourself checking in here, be sure to ask for a site as far away from Sir Francis Drake Boulevard and as close to Lagunitas Creek as possible—the best sites are nearest the creek but not too close to the picnic area used by day visitors. This camp

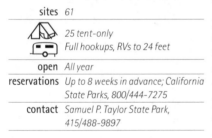

sites	61
🏕	25 tent-only
🚐	Full hookups, RVs to 24 feet
open	All year
reservations	Up to 8 weeks in advance; California State Parks, 800/444-7275
contact	Samuel P. Taylor State Park, 415/488-9897

fills up fast on holidays and peak outdoors season weekends. While the park is certainly pleasant, with well maintained trails and a nice view from a 1,400-foot ridge, it's a little too much asphalt with a roadway cutting right through it and a few too many people.

Facilities: Each site has a picnic table, a fire grill, and a food locker. Running water, flush toilets, and showers are available nearby.

Getting there: From San Francisco drive north on US 101 to Sir Francis Drake Boulevard. Drive west on Sir Francis Drake for 15 miles. The park is bisected by the roadway and has entrances on both sides.

Other Marin County Campgrounds

Another option for the traveler who doesn't have advance reservations is the Pantoll Campground off the Panoramic Highway in Mount Tamalpais State Park. There are 16 walk-in sites here, and they are held for drop-in visitors. Each site has a picnic table, a grill, a food locker, and a tent pad. No reservations are taken. Call the state park ranger station directly for information, 415/388-2070. To reach the campground, take the Stinson Beach exit from US 101 and proceed 4 miles northwest to the entrance on your left.

For RV campers who can't find a spot in the parks, try contacting Marin Park Inc. in San Rafael, a full-service RV park with 89 sites and complete amenities. The phone number is 415/461-5199.

Peninsula and the South Bay

⑫ Half Moon Bay State Beaches 🌲🌲

How can we complain about having a place to camp out right near the beach on the scenic California coast? We hardly can. Let's just say, however, that this 4-mile stretch of beach isn't the best place to drop anchor. Sure the ocean is as stunning as ever, and the state beach is a decent place to body surf, fish, and tidepool.

sites	55
	15 with electrical and water hookups, RVs to 36 feet
open	All year
reservations	Up to 8 weeks in advance; California State Parks, 800/444-7275
contact	Half Moon Bay State Beach, 650-726-8820

Trouble is that this campground is just plain not ideal. First of all, there is so much asphalt here that the campground has an ambience similar to that of a K-Mart parking lot, despite the smattering of lawn and trees here and there. Additionally, facilities such as restrooms have long been in dire need of rehabilitation. Further, this area of coast attracts hordes of people on sunny weekends and holidays, so you run the risk of being overrun with weekend warriors out for the day. Given all of this, the campground's location near the city of Half Moon Bay can be a plus if you're just stopping in on your way to somewhere more off the beaten path.

Facilities: Each site has a picnic table and a cooking grill. Running water and toilets are available nearby. There are also numerous services very near this stretch of beach, including supermarkets, restaurants, and gas stations, making it a good stopping place for those who need a day or two to load up on supplies before moving along.

Getting there: From San Francisco, drive south on I-280 to the intersection with Highway 92; go west on Highway 92 to the end where it meets the Coast Highway. Take the coastal route 1 mile south, turn west on Kelly Avenue, and continue two blocks to the park entrance, which is on the right side of the road.

⑬ Butano State Park 🌲🌲🌲🌲

This 3,200-acre redwood preserve just east of Pescadero State Beach is a godsend for outdoor enthusiasts who want to camp out as close to the ocean as possible without getting sand in their sleeping bags. Butano is just a five-minute drive from the ocean—a perfect spot for those who want it both ways: an ocean setting, but camping far enough off the coast that direct sea breezes don't knock the tent over in the middle of the night. Unfortunately, the campground here is small

Sure you're right at the ocean, but the Half Moon Bay State Beaches campground is a lot of asphalt.

enough and the word about Butano has been spread wide enough that there are hardly ever drop-in sites available on nice weekends or holidays. Because of its proximity to the Bay Area, families with small children and barking dogs tend to congregate here as well; be prepared for a bit of noise. What the campground lacks in these areas, however, it makes up for in other ways: The sites are nicely spaced and situated in a beautiful forest setting with as little pavement as possible. Some are set well away from the access road and out of sight of other sites—get one of these spots and you have it made. Unfortunately, the walk-in camp isn't quite as nice as the drive-

sites	39
	18 tent-only
	No hookups, RVs to 31 feet
open	All year
reservations	Up to 8 weeks in advance; California State Parks, 800/444-7275
contact	Butano State Park, 650/879-2040

in camp because the sites are contained in too small an area. There are a number of fantastic hikes out of Butano; be sure to explore the trails here. Interpretive programs and campfire chats also are conducted by park docents during the summer.

Facilities: Each site has a cooking grill and a picnic table. Running water and restrooms are available nearby. The nearest services are in the town of Pescadero and are expensive, so be sure to load up before driving to this area.

Getting there: From Half Moon Bay, drive south on the Coast Highway for 15 miles to Pescadero Road and then turn left; continue east through the town of Pescadero and then right onto Cloverdale Road to the park entrance, which is on your left.

14 Memorial County Park 🌲🌲🌲🌲

Camping among the redwoods is always a winner, but what makes this little-known county-owned park a real treasure is that early risers are pretty much guaranteed a site here when everyplace else is packed. That's because reservations are not taken. What makes this even more sweet is that this is not a shabby place at all to be exiled to as a punishment for not planning ahead. Because the Midpeninsula Regional Open Space District has not suffered some of the funding problems the state park system has in recent years, this park is much more immaculately cared for than some of the others in the area. The park also has trail connections to other redwood preserves along the San Mateo County coast and Santa Cruz Mountains.

sites	136
	No hookups, RVs to 32 feet
open	All year
reservations	None; call 650/879-0212 for current conditions
contact	Memorial County Park, 650/879-0212

Those who claim sites earliest have pick of those nearest Pescadero Creek—but don't fret if you arrive too late to camp streamside. Despite its size, the campground is very well laid out, meaning everyone will have enough peace, quiet, and space to enjoy the forest. Most of the forest in this area is previously logged, but there are old-growth stands in neighboring parks, such as Butano State Park to the south west. The second-growth stands are mature enough, however, that they have the feel of a pristine setting. Steelhead are being reintroduced to the creek here, and there is no shortage of other wildlife, including more than 100 species of birds, an occasional mule deer, and coyote. It will seem to you, however, that the predominant wildlife here is the raccoon if you make the mistake of leaving food out where these pesky critters can get their paws on it. Raccoons raid the

Skyline Ridge on the San Mateo County coast is visible from points above Butano State Park and Portola State Park, both great places to camp without venturing too far from the urban center.

campground nightly, often turning ice chests over and banging pots and pans together. Lock this stuff in your vehicle at night to avoid being shaken out of sleep by a whole lot of racket.

Facilities: Each site has a picnic table and a fire grill. Running water and showers are available nearby. Be sure to gas up and purchase supplies before heading out here; the few services available nearby are overpriced.

Getting there: From Half Moon Bay, drive south on the Coast Highway for 15 miles to Pescadero Road, then drive east on Pescadero for 10 miles to the park entrance.

⑮ Portola State Park 🌲🌲🌲

In the chain of redwood parks and preserves traversing the Santa Cruz Mountains and San Mateo County coast, Portola State Park is one of the key links. The headwaters to the two main tributaries of Pescadero Creek are found on the adjacent Island Forest Grove. Pescadero flows 20 miles west through Memorial County Park and Butano State Park before it meets the Pacific Ocean in a river of fresh water snaking across the beach. In the creek's path are some of the most beautiful and less visited redwood groves remaining on the California coast. Those in need of a redwood fix should be glad to land in any of these three parks, or those to the south in the Santa Cruz Mountains. Because Portola is a little more difficult to reach than the other parks, fewer RVs come here. The vistas are sweeping at Portola: It is possible to see over the Santa Cruz mountain range to the south and beyond from up here. One of the tallest trees in this region, found in Portola, stands 300 feet. Also found here are fossilized marine deposits from when the area was submerged in ocean.

sites	52
🏕️🚐	No hookups, RVs to 24 feet
open	All year
reservations	Up to 8 weeks in advance; California State Parks, 800/444-7275
contact	Portola State Park, 650/948-9098

Facilities: Each site has a picnic table and a fire grill. Running water, flush toilets, and showers are available nearby. Services nearest the campground are pricey; gas up and purchase supplies in the Bay Area before heading out this way.

Getting there: The easiest approach is on I-280. Head south of I-280 from San Mateo County to the Page Mill Road exit near Mountain View. Head west on Page Mill for 4 miles to the park entrance, which is on the left side of the road. Note that the access road from the entrance is steep and narrow. Large vehicles, RVs, and trailers should enter with care.

East Bay

16 Anthony Chabot Regional Park 🌲🌲🌲

Here is a perfect spot for weekend family outings or quick vacation stopovers. Lake Chabot is a 300-acre water storage facility for the East Bay that is surrounded by eucalyptus forest and grassy hillsides. Nearby are biking and hiking trails and a full-service marina with a restaurant and boat rentals. Trout fishing is best here beginning in fall; during the summer count on reeling in a few nice, fat catfish. The stocking program here is quite aggressive. It's one of those places where anyone can walk away with a big catch of the day, even little kiddies. Who knows how many youngsters have cast their first line here? It is a favorite place to introduce children to all aspects of the outdoors. The campground is in a wooded area a short walk from the lakeshore. For an RV/car camping facility of this size, Chabot is a surprisingly nice campground. Cement slabs are minimal, and the smell of eucalyptus refreshing. Sites in the main campground are a bit too close together, however, so the hike-in sites are your best bet. Keep in mind also that the lake is a popular day-use area; on nice summer and holiday weekends, the place fills up with picnickers, anglers, hikers, cyclists, and equestrians. Thankfully there is plenty of space for everyone to spread out, and the day-use picnic facilities are on the opposite side of the lake from the campground.

sites	75
🏕	10 tent-only
🚐	12 with water and septic hookups, RVs to 24 feet
open	All year
reservations	Up to 12 weeks in advance; East Bay Regional Park District, 510/636-1684
contact	East Bay Regional Park District 510/562-PARK; Anthony Chabot Regional Park, 510/569-4428

Facilities: Each site has a picnic table and a cooking grill. Running water, flush toilets, and showers are available nearby. Horse stables, a marina, and a small coffeeshop/store are also are found here, as is a small bait shop where fishing licenses may be purchased.

Getting there: From Oakland, drive east on I-580 for 3 miles and exit at 35th Avenue. Follow 35th Avenue east a short distance to Redwood Road. Continue east on Redwood another 6 miles to the park entrance on the right.

Anthony Chabot Regional Park is a popular family camping spot in the East Bay.

17 Mount Diablo State Park 🌲🌲🌲🏕️

Ancient native Californians regarded Mount Diablo, at the geographical center of the Bay Area, as the center of human creation. As folklore tells it, Diablo's twin peaks were once the only portion of the mountain visible above a much higher Pacific Ocean and it was from these two islands that life on Earth emerged. Ancient rituals still happen atop the mountain, but the Pacific has long since pulled back to reveal one of the most impressive wilderness areas in this part of Northern California. And what a treasure it is; so much of the terrain around the

3,800-foot mountain is flat that Diablo's silhouette is visible for hundreds of miles in all directions. It's the up-close view of Diablo that is the most impressive, however.

sites *58 in three campgrounds*

50 with full hookups, RVs to 20 feet

open *40 sites all year; 18 sites October through May.*

reservations *Up to 8 weeks in advance, October through May; no reservations in summer; California State Parks, 800/444-7275*

contact *Mount Diablo State Park, 925/837-2525*

While the developed campgrounds are far from quiet (because of their popularity among families with children, dogs, RVs, and portable radios), they are clean and well appointed. The rest of the park makes up for the lack of privacy at the campsites. Explore lush, shaded oak woodlands and evergreen forests; waterfalls and open sandstone outcroppings with caves carved by wind erosion; hundreds of varieties of wildflowers, including some found nowhere else on Earth; black-tailed deer, skunks, bobcats, mountain lions, and red-legged frogs; and tarantulas, which come out in force every fall for mating season. Choosing

Mount Diablo State Park is part of the urban oasis that makes the Bay Area an outdoorperson's dream location.

between the three campsites is a toss-up, but the best deal on balance is the Live Oak Campground, which is located in an area of oak woodlands near the Southgate Road entrance to the park. With 18 sites, Live Oak is much smaller than Juniper Campground, which has 34 sites. Live Oak is also more quiet than the smaller Junction Campground, which has 6 sites but is very near the park's main ranger station. This said, all three campgrounds are worth checking out if it means the difference between not being able to get into the park at all. Mount Diablo has become increasingly popular among locals and vacationers alike; during peak season reservations are strongly recommended. The state parks system does not allow dispersed camping, but there is plenty of room among Diablo's 50,000+ acres to do it and many do it anyway (but you didn't hear it here).

Facilities: All sites have running water nearby and are equipped with picnic tables and cooking grills. Live Oak and Juniper Campgrounds have vault toilets; flush toilets are available near Junction Campground. Juniper Campground is the most RV friendly and has several pull-through sites.

Getting there: From Oakland, drive east on Highway 24 for 14 miles to I-680 south. Continue for 4 miles on I-680 to Diablo Road. Drive east on Diablo Road for 5.5 miles to the park entrance.

⓲ Stewartville Backpack Camp 🌲🌲🌲🌲

The amenities may be a bit rough and there is no running water, but this little-known backpack camp in secluded Stewartville Canyon, in the foothills east of Mount Diablo, is both easy to reach and far enough out of reach. The canyon is flanked by Mount Diablo, whose north peak is visible from near the site. Black Diamond is an interesting place; the 4,000-acre preserve contains five Gold Rush–era ghost towns that were once occupied by coal miners who helped fuel the exploding economy of the Golden State during the mid-nineteenth century. Left behind are old mines, some of which are open for tours or self-exploration, a few town buildings, and a historic cemetery filled with the graves of miners who died in accidents, women who died in childbirth, and children who died of diseases.

sites	1, with room for 20 people
🏕	Walk-in only
open	All year
reservations	Up to 12 weeks in advance; East Bay Regional Park District, 510/636-1684
contact	Black Diamond Regional Preserve, 925/757-2620

Beyond the history, however, Black Diamond is also both a nature lover's paradise and a popular destination for fans of hard sports like mountain biking. The town roads and smaller trails cover 34 miles, and there are many looping combinations. The terrain is rugged and steep in places, but canyons also give way to flat, open meadows. The flora and fauna are similar to that of Mount Diablo; wildflower blooms are impressive in spring. There are rocky outcroppings, forested canyons of mixed evergreen, oak-studded hills, and even rare black locust and pepper trees introduced by the first European settlers. The key to having a good experience at this camp is successful planning. During the winter, trails can be muddy and damaged by cattle. In fact, the park district does a lousy job of keeping cattle under control during the winter months and they can really make a mess of this area. During the summer, temperatures can reach the 90s and 100s out here; since there is no running water (you have to pack your own in) and no swimming holes or lakes, picking the wrong summer weekend can be quite unpleasant. Your best bet may be the late fall—before cattle arrive for the grazing

Mount Diablo State Park

season and after summer hot spells are no longer a danger. The camp is 3.2 miles from the park headquarters and the hike out is more difficult than the hike in.

Facilities: Picnic tables and a pit toilet are located at the camp; there is no running water but water for horses is available. Campers must pack their trash out.

Directions: From Oakland drive east on Highway 24 for 13 miles to I-680 north. Continue 4 miles to Highway 242 and then another 3 miles north to Highway 4 east. Drive 11 miles on Highway 4, exit at Somersville Road, and continue southwest to the park gates.

⑲ Sunol Regional Wilderness 🌲🌲🌲🌲

Nothing compares to waking up in the morning to the sounds of songbirds and a wild running creek in the distance instead of an alarm or a ringing telephone. At Sunol Regional Wilderness, it is possible to have the solitude and solace we all long for without really leaving the metropolitan Bay Area. Sunol Regional Wilderness is hidden away in the far southeastern reaches of Alameda County and is contiguous with two other large open space areas and undeveloped water agency lands. The preserve's grassy hills and oak woodlands are accompanied by deep cut canyons and sandstone outcroppings. One canyon is the renowned "Little Yosemite," named so because the gorge on Alameda Creek cascades into three small waterfalls (Yosemite on a smaller scale if you use your imagination).

sites	4
open	All year
reservations	Up to 12 weeks in advance; East Bay Regional Park District, 510/636-1684
contact	East Bay Regional Park District 510/562-PARK; Sunol Regional Wilderness Area 925/862-2244

While this is certainly a prime spot to catch a quick fix of quiet time, the camp also can serve as a staging point for a backpacking trip along the Ohlone Wilderness Trail. The 28-mile trail connects Mission Peak in Fremont to Sunol Regional Wilderness and then Lake Del Valle to the east. The Sunol camp would be a place to jump in midway for a shorter hike, which is the reason it is highly recommended as a first backpacking experience for young children who are being introduced to the outdoors for the first time. While the four sites are generally well maintained, there are a few things to be aware of. The East Bay Regional Park District allows cattle grazing during winter months as part of its program to control fire danger, so Sunol is one of those parks where you can expect to encounter cattle. For this reason, trails may be rutted and the smell of cow pies may compete with the scent of wildflowers. One positive thing you can say about all of this,

Wildflowers in bloom at Oholone Wilderness Regional Park.

however, is that the cattle seem to keep non-native grasses under control enough that there is still a magnificent spring wildflower display at Sunol. The other thing to keep in mind is that there are two group camps in the same sector of the wilderness area; while this is guaranteed to be a pleasant getaway, be prepared to share. Please also note that if you plan to use this camp as a staging area for the longer hike, you will need a wilderness permit to gain legal access to trail camps found along the way. The park agency does a good job of regulating the number of wilderness permits simultaneously active; this helps reduce the likelihood that someone else will come trouncing through your nature experience.

Facilities: Each site has running water, vault toilets, fire pits, and picnic tables.

Getting there: From Oakland, drive east on I-580 for 23 miles to I-680, then drive south on I-680 for 7.7 miles to the Calaveras Road exit. Drive 4 miles south on Calaveras to Geary Road. Turn left and drive 2 miles on Geary to the park entrance. The camp is north of the road at the foot of Flag Hill Trail.

⓴ Del Valle Regional Park 🌲🌲🌲

Let's make one thing perfectly clear before we even start trying to describe this campground: If you're looking for a quiet escape and a meaningful nature experience, Del Valle Regional Park probably isn't for you. The lake, a state water project reservoir with recreation grounds managed by the East Bay Regional Park District, is most heavily used by families with young children who want a place near the urban center for weekend camping trips. The lake also gets a large number of day visitors, particularly during the summer when the overheated masses descend upon the place to jump in the water. Add to that the anglers who use the lake religiously, and we're talking overflowing parking lots, beaches carpeted with sunbathers, and swimmers, windsurfers, and boaters competing for space on the water. The campground during peak times is as noisy as a grammar school cafeteria during a food fight.

sites	150
🏕️ 🚐	21 with water and septic hookups, RVs to 20 feet
open	All year
reservations	Up to 12 weeks in advance; East Bay Regional Park District, 510/636-1684
contact	Del Valle Regional Park, 925/445-4008

There are, however, good reasons to use this campground. First of all, if you have children and want to give them a good camping experience without having to drive too far away from the Bay Area, this is a perfect choice. The campsites are well-appointed, the park is easy to get to and well managed, and there is plenty for kids to do, especially during the summer swim season. Some campsites are right on the water. There are also five hike-in group campgrounds at Del Valle, a few of them a good distance from the main campground. If camping with a group, consider reserving one of these instead. One attraction of particular interest here is a pair of nesting bald eagles that have taken up residence near the lake. It is best to view them during the midsummer, and special interpretive programs are available both through park naturalists and the Ohlone chapter of the National Audubon Society.

Facilities: Each site has a picnic table and a fire pit. Running water and flush toilets are available nearby. Hot showers are also available. A public boat launch is located near the camp. Note, however, that Jet skis are not allowed on the lake.

Getting there: From Oakland, go east on I-580 for 27.5 miles to North Livermore Avenue. Go south to Mines Road. Make a right turn on Mines and continue 3 miles to the park.

㉑ Henry W. Coe State Park 🌲🌲🌲🌲🌲

To think that there are 81,000 acres of wilderness and open space just a stone's throw from Silicon Valley and the San Francisco metropolitan area is amazing, but to actually spend a little time at Henry W. Coe State Park—the largest in Northern California—is to really get an appreciation for just how real the nature experience is here. This place truly has the look and feel of wilderness; get sucked in and you will swear you are nowhere near a place where more than 2 million people live; it simply does not seem possible.

sites	20
🏕️	15 tent-only
🚐	No hookups, RVs to 24 feet, trailers to 20 feet
open	All year
reservations	Up to 8 weeks in advance; California State Parks, 800/444-7275
contact	Henry W. Coe State Park, 408/779-2728

The RV and car camping/tent sites listed here are on a 2,600-foot hilltop from which surrounding peaks and canyons are visible. These sites are easy to reach, and despite their close proximity to the main park entrance and headquarters they have the feel of a much more private and secluded setting. There is, however, a fair share of activity here since there are an adjacent horse camp and stables. Those with more time to explore and in fair enough shape to tolerate some strenuous hiking will want to spend time at one of the more than 50 backpack camps found farther into the park. A few of these camps can be reached in a couple of miles. Virtually all of the backcountry trails and routes at Coe, however, are steep and rugged; only experienced backpackers should try to head into these more distant camps.

This is one of the premiere outdoor areas of the Bay Area region. Coe has hundreds of lakes and small ponds for swimming during the spring. As this was entire area was once in the hands of cattle ranchers, many of the small swimming holes are actually irrigation ponds developed more than a century ago to keep livestock watered. There also are small creeks and streams for swimming on warm days in the early spring. Coyote Creek runs through the park. China Hole, which can get to 7 feet deep during the winter wet season and spring runoff, is a great place to take a dip—but reaching it entails a rigorous 9-mile hike! Indeed, Coe is built for people who have time on their hands and real experience packing. Again, for those experienced and in great shape, this is also a prime destination for bicycle camping, as about 58,000 acres of the park's trails and most of its camps are open to mountain bikers. The meadows, valleys, rocky peaks, oak woodlands and savannah, pine forests, grassy hills, and brush found here seem to go on forever. It's a perfect place to drop out for a while. As is the case with similar places, campers must take proper care to not interfere with wildlife. Raccoons know the campgrounds and aggressively raid those sites where food is left out. In addition,

Henry W. Coe State Park.

rattlesnakes, wild pigs, and mountain lions are found here. The typical precautions must be taken.

Facilities: Each site has a picnic table and fire rings. Running water and pit toilets are available nearby. Flush toilets are located at the park headquarters 100 yards away. The developed drive-in sites are confined to the main entrance to the park; those who want to see more should hike into the park and use one of the more than 50 backpacking camps. In addition, there are two horse camps in the park, including one adjacent to the car camping and RV spots.

Getting there: From the San Francisco Bay Area, drive south on US 101 to the Morgan Hill area between San Jose and the Salinas Valley. In Morgan Hill, take the East Dunne Avenue exit and head east 13 miles to the park headquarters. The access road is windy and narrow in some places. Two sections just past the Anderson Reservoir bridge had one-way controlled traffic only during our last visit because of recent washouts and mud slides.

Other East Bay Campgrounds

To put it plainly, the pickings are slim in the East Bay if you're looking for a public campground. In addition to those listed above, there are several group camps run by the East Bay Regional Park District. These are found at Redwood Regional Park in the Oakland Hills, Tilden Park in the Oakland/Berkeley hills, and Las Trampas Regional Preserve in the foothills west of Mount Diablo. Call 510/636-1684 to reserve any of these camps for up to 10 days. Reservations may be made up to 12 weeks in advance. Keep in mind, however, that these camps are typically used by scouting organizations and clubs—not by single outdoorspeople or large families.

Big Sur Region

The tourists in Big Sur aren't difficult to spot. They're the ones lined up like crows on a fence along the west shoulder of Highway 1, leaning over rocks, standing on posts, or perched on rear bumpers of the rental cars—whatever it takes—to get that perfect shot of what is perhaps one of the most photographed stretches of oceanfront in the world. The first time you steer your car onto the 90-mile stretch of the Coast Highway between Carmel and San Simeon that curves along the dramatic rocky shore of Big Sur, there is an uncontrollable compulsion to stop at the first sliver of road shoulder, grab the camera, and try to imitate Ansel Adams. It just happens, and it's easy enough to get a great shot. If the first European and Mexican settlers had cameras (and if there had been a highway here in the early nineteenth century), they might have done the same thing.

What isn't always easy in Big Sur, however, is finding a campsite in a public park.

Indeed, there is only one game in town—at Pfeiffer Big Sur State Park along the banks of the Big Sur River—and the sites here are almost always booked up for the full eight weeks allowed. Savvy campers either plan their trips well in advance, make Big Sur a day trip destination from the adjacent Ventana Wilderness or from Monterey and Santa Cruz to the north, or find their way into the prime coastal redwood forest sites by lurking outside the campground kiosk to snap up those freed by last-minute cancellations or no-shows. Just don't roll into town without a plan, or you'll end up paying an awful lot of money for a tiny, marginal motel room.

The long, two-lane stretch of highway connecting Big Sur with the rest of civilization can be harrowing. The road is well maintained but winding and steep, with fog in the mornings and big crowds on nice weekends and holidays. Special care is required.

As stunningly beautiful as the Big Sur coastline is, there are also plenty of alternatives not far away. Many of the small drop-in campgrounds in the Ventana Wilderness are easily reached from Big Sir through Carmel Valley. Inland of the Monterey area, Fremont Peak is one of the most secluded state campgrounds found anywhere, and a great spot for stargazing. Further north in Santa Cruz, you have a rough dilemma: the ancient redwood forests of the Santa Cruz Mountains or one of the state beaches where you can watch golden sunsets over Monterey Bay.

Big Sur Region

1. Big Basin Redwoods State Park
2. Henry Cowell Redwoods State Park
3. Sunset State Beach
4. Manresa Beach State Park
5. Seacliff State Beach
6. New Brighton State Beach
7. Andrew Molera State Park
8. Pfeiffer Big Sur State Park
9. Bottchers Gap
10. White Oaks Campground
11. China Camp
12. Arroyo Seco Campground
13. Escondido Campground
14. Fremont Peak State Park

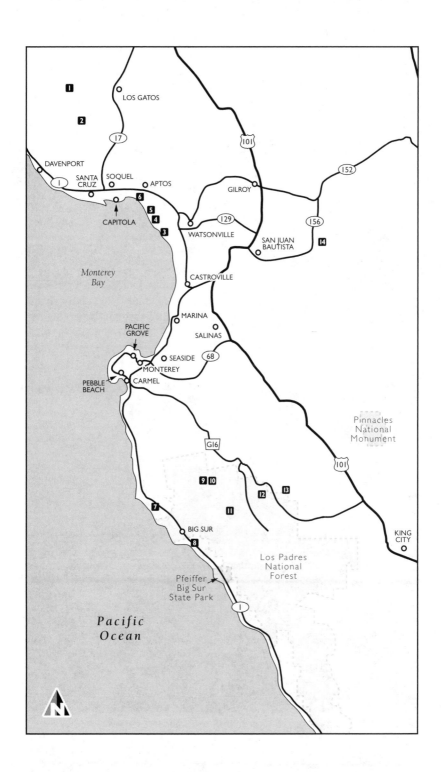

Santa Cruz and the Monterey Area

① Big Basin Redwoods State Park 🌲🌲🌲🌲🌲

Big Basin was the very first state park established in California in 1902, just in time to prevent its mighty virgin redwoods from becoming timber to help rebuild San Francisco following the great earthquake of 1906. As magnificent as some of those Victorian homes in San Francisco are today, they are no match for this place. The basin is 20,000 acres of wild redwood forestland crisscrossed with streams, creeks, and rivers containing dozens of waterfalls. Big Basin is a place for hikers, equestrians, birders, and nature lovers in general. The hike

sites	*155*
🏕	*48 tent-only* *No hookups, RVs to 27 feet*
open	*All year*
reservations	*Up to 8 weeks in advance; California State Parks, 800/444-7275*
contact	*Big Basin Redwoods State Park, 831/338-8860*

Big Basin Redwoods State Park offers panoramic views of the Monterey Bay Area.

along Wadell Creek to the ocean is a spectacular experience. The campsites are scattered over a wide area, so while 155 sites may sound like a lot, keep in mind that these are arranged in small groups. Sites have plenty of space between them and offer a wonderful illusion of privacy. When you first arrive, you may feel that the forest is a bit overdeveloped with park facilities and roads, but Big Basin is spacious with more than 80 miles of hiking trails connecting to adjacent public lands. You can literally get lost for days here; just park, set up camp, and put a little distance between yourself and the car—it will all come together. As is always the case with redwood forests, be prepared for a little dampness, even during the summer, as that coastal fog rolls in and leaves the trees wet every morning.

Facilities: Each site has a picnic table and a fire pit. There are flush toilets, showers, and running water, but some sites are a distance from the restroom facilities. The park headquarters area has basic services, including a grocery area, but watch out for the prices there. Santa Cruz, which is 20 miles away, is your best bet for stocking up on supplies. There is also an RV disposal site.

Getting there: From Santa Cruz, drive east on Highway 9 through Henry Cowell Redwoods State Park and beyond. At the Highway 236 intersection, turn left and continue another 10 miles to the park boundary. Campgrounds are scattered around the forest. Start at the park headquarters to check in and get specific directions to your site.

❷ Henry Cowell Redwoods State Park 🌲🌲🌲🌲🌲

Crane your neck and squint; the treetops are up there. Somewhere. Normally when you think of coast redwoods, the tallest trees on Earth, the northern reaches of California—Humboldt and Del Norte Counties, in particular—come to mind.

sites	112
🏕️ 🚐	No hookups, RVs to 35 feet
open	March to November
reservations	Up to 8 weeks in advance; California State Parks, 800/444-7275
contact	Henry Cowell Redwoods State Park, 831/335-4598

Fact is, however, that the band of redwoods that once dominated the California coast stretched all the way from the Oregon border more than 500 miles south to the Santa Cruz Mountains. There are still some awesomely beautiful redwood stands in this area, including some in Henry Cowell Redwoods State Park. Cowell provides every part of the redwood experience: The wild-running San Lorenzo River bisects the park and is open for steelhead fishing, there are self-guided nature trails for ecology lessons with the kids, and trailheads are located right near the campground for longer day hikes to peaks overlooking the surrounding mountains with views of the Pacific. While the campground is large, it can be as serene and

The Big Sur coast is rugged and wild—just the way we found it.

beautiful as any redwood forest recreation spot. There's something about these old, magnificent trees that brings out the best in people—even when you're in crowded quarters. Privacy is never far off; just take a little walk into the trees and you will find the solitude you're looking for. If at all possible, avoid sites right next to trailheads or too close to day-use picnic areas.

Facilities: Each site has a picnic table and a fire pit. Running water, flush toilets, and showers are available nearby. The park has a large day-use area, including picnic facilities and spots for flyfishing. Santa Cruz is your best bet for supplies.

Getting there: From Highway 1 in Santa Cruz, take the Highway 9 turnoff east and head 3 miles to the park entrance, which is clearly marked.

❸ Sunset State Beach 🌲🌲🌲

This spot on the Monterey Bay coast certainly lives up to its name on those clear evenings when you can watch the sun, burning an amber orange, dip into the ocean. The campground, however, is not one of the best. The sites are on a bluff with no view of the beach or ocean, set in a group of pines. The sites are also poorly laid out, too close together, and crowded in. Because the bluff blocks the ocean out, however, there is protection from the sea breezes. On a particularly negative note, the beach is surrounded on three sides by farmland. If the wind picks up in the wrong direction, the smell of fertilizer will waft into the campground.

sites	90
🏕️ 🚐	Electrical hookups, RVs to 31 feet
open	All year
reservations	Up to 8 weeks in advance; California State Parks, 800/444-7275
contact	Sunset State Beach, 831/763-7062

Facilities: Each site has a picnic table and a fire pit. Running water, flush toilets, and showers are available nearby. The nearest services are in Watsonville.

Getting there: In Watsonville, take the Riverside Drive exit from Highway 1 and head west a short distance to Beach Road. Turn left on Beach Road and continue a short distance to San Andreas Road. Turn right and continue on to the beach entrance.

❹ Manresa Beach State Park 🌲🌲🌲

The campsites, a short walk from the parking area, are among trees on a bluff overlooking the beach. Like most of the public beaches in this area, summers get a large number of day visitors—but don't despair. Somehow, the salt winds through the trees and gorgeous views of the Pacific Ocean help you forget all of that. Ask for a site nearest the beach, as some are set so far back in the trees you would never know you were a stone's throw from the ocean. Surf fishing, tidepooling, and clamming all are popular here.

sites	64
🏕️	
open	All year
reservations	Up to 8 weeks in advance; California State Parks, 800/444-7275
contact	Manresa Beach State Park, 831/724-3750

Facilities: Each site has a picnic table and a fire pit. Running water, flush toilets, and showers are available nearby.

Getting there: From Capitola, drive south on Highway 1 a short distance out of town and exit at San Andreas Road. Turn west on Sand Dollar Drive and continue west a short distance to the park entrance.

Views like this one along the Coast Highway will make you want to gawk and drive at the same time. But pull over instead.

⑤ Seacliff State Beach 🌲🌲🌲🌲

There is an abandoned World War I–era supply ship constructed from concrete that has been parked at the Seacliff State Beach pier since the 1930s. Today, the 400-foot ship is used mostly by anglers looking for a good spot to cast a line into the surf. The campsites are situated on a bluff overlooking the 85-acre beach, which is a popular sun and surf spot during the summer. Because the campground at Seacliff is significantly smaller than those at other state beaches in the area, it is honestly your best bet for camping on the Santa Cruz/Monterey shore. The campground and beach are reasonably quiet and well managed, and the sites are spacious and secluded from the day-use areas.

sites	26
🏕️ 🚐	No hookups, RVs to 40 feet
open	All year
reservations	Up to 8 weeks in advance; California State Parks, 800/444-7275
contact	Seacliff State Beach, 831/688-3222

Facilities: Each site has a picnic table and a fire pit. Flush toilets, running water, and showers are available nearby. There is a small ecology center at the beach. Surf fishing is popular from the pier area.

Getting there: In Capitola, just south of Santa Cruz on Highway 1, take the Seacliff Beach exit from the highway and head west to the park entrance.

⑥ New Brighton State Beach ▲▲▲

What a contrast this place is from the Santa Cruz Beach and Boardwalk just a few miles to the north. No amusement park rides or seafood restaurants overlooking the water here—just a front-row view of Monterey Bay, about 70 acres of beach and tidal marsh, and some prime real estate on a bluff overlooking it all for a campground. The campground is nothing fancy and at times is overrun with locals and their children, but the view and the ambi-

sites	*112*
🏕️ 🚐	*Electrical hookups, RVs to 31 feet*
open	*All year*
reservations	*Up to 8 weeks in advance; California State Parks, 800/444-7275*
contact	*New Brighton State Beach, 831/464-2850*

The Laguna Seca Recreation Area, east of Monterey, comes complete with a feral cat.

The frothing, churning surf creates whitecaps along the Big Sur coast.

ence make it all worth it. Remember, this beach is used heavily by day visitors, but the campground is segregated well enough from picnic areas and the beach itself that amazingly you don't lose too much of the flavor. Guided nature walks are offered during the summer.

Facilities: Each site has a picnic table and a fire pit. Flush toilets and running water are available nearby, as are showers.

Getting there: From Highway 1 in Capitola, take the Capitola/New Brighton Beach exit west and drive a short distance to the entrance to the beach.

Other Santa Cruz and Monterey Area Campgrounds

Public campgrounds in Monterey are next to nonexistent; in fact the state beaches on the Santa Cruz shore are pretty much the only game in town.

The Marina Dunes RV Park has 65 sites with full hookups, along with all the comforts you would expect: showers, flush toilets—even cable television. Marina Dunes State Park, which has no camping, is next door. Call 831/384-6914.

If you get really desperate, you can always go to the Laguna Seca Recreation Area campground, which has 170 sites set on rolling oak-covered hills. This campground is abysmal, however, and it's right next door to a race track and a shooting range. Call 831/422-6138.

Big Sur

❼ Andrew Molera State Park ▲▲▲▲

This is where the land and the sea meet big time. More than 4,700 acres of beach, bluffs, meadows and marshes make up this expansive preserve right at the point where the Big Sur River dives into the Pacific Ocean from the rocky bluffs above.

sites	Variable number
open	All year
reservations	None
contact	Andrew Molera State Park, 831/667-2315 or 831/649-2836

To camp here is a wondrous experience. You can watch gray whales migrate past offshore and sea otters frolicking on the rocks, and enjoy wildflowers, butterflies, and salt breezes through the trees. The preserve seems like the end of the Earth; the sky seems huge. Because the river forms a large lagoon where it meets the sea, this is a great place to watch for shorebirds. In winter, steelhead spawn in the streams. The campground, however, is not a campground at all, but just a meadow where you'll be allowed to pitch a tent. Don't expect anything fancy—it's like backpacking without the big hike.

Facilities: These primitive sites situated in a large meadow have no improvements. Pit toilets and running water are available nearby. Rangers decide how many campers to allow based on demand and park conditions.

Getting there: Drive south on Highway 1 from Carmel for 24 miles to the clearly marked park entrance, which is on the right side of the road. The camp area is a third of a mile from the entrance and you must hike in.

❽ Pfeiffer Big Sur State Park ▲▲▲▲

Everything you've heard is true: Groves of redwood, oak, sycamore, maple, and alder hug high rocky bluffs that drop into the churning Pacific. Rivers and creeks cut deep canyons, then give way to waterfalls cascading directly into the ocean.

sites	218
	No hookups, RVs to 32 feet
open	All year
reservations	Up to 8 weeks in advance; California State Parks, 800/444-7275
contact	Pfeiffer Big Sur State Park, 831/667-2315

Sea otters sun themselves on off-shore rocks and porpoises swim alongside kayakers in the churning surf. Follow hiking trails to overlooks where you can take in dramatic views of the entire coast and surrounding forested canyons, bask in the filtered sunlight on the tree-lined banks of the Big Sur River. There is a magical interplay

Pfeiffer Big Sur State Park is pleasant—but hard to get into.

between the land and the ocean at Big Sur—and you can feel the energy it creates. Campsites are dispersed around about 800 acres of forest. Some sites are near the river and are choice. The setting and scenery are about as close to perfect as you're going to find in this part of the coast. The park does not get a perfect score from us, however, for one reason and one reason only: It's too darn crowded. During the peak recreation season months, cars are lined up as far as the eye can see, and campers packed in like sardines. It's just enough carbon monoxide to spoil the fun just a little. Needless to say, it's a good idea to make a reservation before trying to camp here.

Facilities: Each site has a picnic table and a fire pit. Running water, flush toilets, and showers are available nearby. There are numerous services in the park, including a general store, laundry facilities, an RV disposal station, and an inn with a restaurant.

Getting there: Big Sur is 25 miles south of Carmel on Highway 1. The clearly marked park entrance is on the east side of the highway. Stay to the left when you enter the park; the driveway to the right is for the Big Sur Inn only.

Other Big Sur Area Campgrounds

Most camp areas along the Big Sur coast are privately owned, and when the few public spots are snapped up the private camps are pretty much your only option if you want to pitch a tent in the area. They include Fernwood Park, which has 16 tent sites and 49 RV sites, 831/667-2422; Big Sur Campground, which has 40 sites for RVs (full hookups and the works, 831/667-2322); and Riverside Campground, which has 46 sites for tents or RVs, 831/667-2414. There are another 70 sites at Ventana Campground, 831/667-2688.

Ventana Wilderness

⑨ Bottchers Gap 🌲🌲🌲🌲

This small campground is pretty, quiet, and secluded—and right on the edge of the Big Sur coast in the Mill Creek Canyon at 2,100 feet. Think mixed redwood forest, no RVs, and a place to part ways with the shoulder-to-shoulder madness of places that get a little too popular during nice weather weekends. The great thing about camping here is that it is an escape from the escape. Still, as lovely as this section of forest is and as nice as it is to have a creek flowing by, you may wish you were just a little closer to the ocean. It's a big trade-off.

sites	9
open	All year
reservations	None
contact	Monterey Ranger District, 831/385-5434

Facilities: Each site has a picnic table and a fire grill. Vault toilets are available nearby. There is no running water, so be sure to pack in enough to last for your entire stay.

Getting there: Drive south on Highway 1 for 10 miles from Carmel. At Palo Colorado Road, turn right and continue 9 miles to the campground entrance.

⑩ White Oaks Campground 🌲🌲🌲🌲

Head for the hills. Heed that advice from the fancy schmancy resort town of Carmel and you just may end up here—out in the middle of nowhere, and loving it. White Oaks is situated at 4,000 feet near the banks of Anastasia Creek and in the shadows of the Chews Ridge Lookout and the Mira Observatory, both worth hiking to for a visit. There are—and this is not a typo—1,500 miles of trails in the surrounding wilderness and forest, and several good trailheads leave from near White Oaks, making it a good place from which to stage a backpacking trip. Because the sites are hike-in only, you also don't have to worry about having to imagine what the forest looks like without a big hunk of metal parked in the way.

sites	8
open	All year
reservations	None
contact	Monterey Ranger District, 831/385-5434

Facilities: Each site has a picnic table and a fire grill. Vault toilets and running water are available nearby.

Getting there: From Carmel, drive south on Highway 1 to Carmel Valley Road to just outside of town. Turn left and continue 25 miles to Tassajara Road. Turn right and continue another 9 miles to the campground entrance. There is one fork in the road that may be confusing; stay to the left.

⑪ China Camp 🌲🌲🌲🌲

The Tassajara corridor into Ventana Wilderness is a place to get connected again. Things move more slowly here; it's like Mother Nature's own version of Club Med without the plastic drink beads or activity directors. Set at 4,300 feet, this particular camp is closer to both Chews Ridge and the Mira Observatory than White Oaks, which is similarly appointed. The campground is small, quiet, pleasant—the kind of place where you lose track of what day of the week it is. Watch out for condors, bald eagles, and perigrine falcons where the forest gives way the rocky peaks above the tree line; there are nearly 500 different species of fish, birds, and mammals in this area—including the mountain lion and wild boars (watch out for those). The Pine Ridge Trail route to the South Ventana Cone begins from here; it's a great hike but is best done as an overnighter.

sites	8
open	All year
reservations	None
contact	Monterey Ranger District, 831/385-5434

Facilities: Each site has a picnic table and a fire grill. Vault toilets are available nearby. There is no running water so be sure to pack in enough to last for your entire stay.

Getting there: Drive south on Highway 1 from Carmel a short distance to Carmel Valley Road. Turn left and head out 25 miles to the Tassajara Road intersection. Turn right and continue another 11 miles to the campground entrance. There is one point at which the road forks; when in doubt veer left.

⑫ Arroyo Seco Campground 🌲🌲🌲

I bet you thought the California Gold Rush took place in the Sierra Nevada. It did. But another Gold Rush took place right here in the Ventana region. It all started when a fellow named David Douglas stumbled upon flakes of gold around the roots of a fir tree—some 15 years before the Great Gold Rush was due to kick off. Nobody got rich off Douglas' discovery, but he did end up with a tree named after him. This is how the Douglas-fir got its name. The American River and John Marshall ended up in the history books, not David Douglas and Arroyo Seco Creek.

sites	*50*
	No hookups, RVs to 24 feet
open	*All year*
reservations	*Up to 240 days in advance; U.S. Forest Service Reservations, 800/280-2267*
contact	*Monterey Ranger District, 831/385-5434*

Oh well, this is still a decent place to camp, set as it is at 900 feet in the creek drainage. The river is a nice swimming spot once the spring runoff calms down and there are a couple of small lakes to enjoy. The campground is a bit larger and more crowded than many others in the forest, however, so if you're looking for something a little closer to Mother Nature keep searching.

Facilities: Each site has a picnic table and a fire grill. Running water and vault toilets are available nearby. The campground is less than a mile from the town of Arroyo Seco, where general services are available.

Getting there: Drive south on US 101 from Salinas to the town of Greenfield. Take the Elm Avenue exit and head west to Arroyo Seco Road. Turn left and continue 1 mile to the campground entrance.

⓭ Escondido Campground 🌲🌲🌲🌲

Hikers wanting to disappear for days into the Ventana Wilderness via the Lost Valley Trail and numerous others would be well served using this pleasant and out-of-the way campground as a staging point. Easy trail connections to no fewer than eight designated backpacking camps are had from here. Escondido is set at 900 feet near the confluence of Lost Valley and Arroyo Seco Creeks. This is a lush and vibrant area during the spring, but be careful of stream crossings, as currents can be stronger than you realize.

sites	*9*
open	*All year*
reservations	*None*
contact	*Monterey Ranger District, 831/385-5434*

Facilities: Each site has a picnic table and a fire grill. Vault toilets are available nearby. There is no running water, so be certain to pack enough in to last your entire stay.

Getting there: Drive south on US 101 from Salinas to the town of Greenfield. Take the Greenfield/Arroyo Seco Road exit and drive west 20 miles to Indians Road. Turn left and continue another 10 miles to the campground.

⑭ Fremont Peak State Park 🌲🌲🌲🌲

So far away from the cities and with panoramic views of the landscape of Central California, Fremont Peak is a favorite spot for amateur astronomers who want to do a bit of stargazing without unnatural light pollution. There is an observatory on the mountain, which tops out at 3,169 feet. The surrounding terrain is a mixture of oak woodlands, groves of pine, and open meadows teeming with wildflowers during the spring. During the summer there are astronomical interpretive programs for park visitors. Again, what makes a camp-out here a winner is that the park is so secluded. There are miles and miles of rolling hills, forested patches, and meadows. The hike to the peak pays off with a great view not only of Monterey Bay but of the San Lucia Mountains to the south and the Salinas Valley to the north.

sites 25

No hookups, RVs to 26 feet

open All year

reservations Up to 8 weeks in advance; California State Parks, 800/444-7275

contact Fremont Peak State Park, 831/623-4255

Facilities: Each site has a picnic table and a fire pit. Running water and vault toilets are available nearby. The park is literally out in the middle of nowhere, so don't forget anything.

Getting there: From Highway 156 in San Juan Bautista, drive south on San Juan Canyon Road for 10 miles to the park entrance. The access road is 11 miles long, and while it's paved it is a bit windy. Observe the RV limit.

Other Ventana Wilderness Area Campgrounds

Literally dozens of small established backpacker camps are scattered throughout the Ventana Wilderness high country. Explore them. Other developed campgrounds include the Santa Lucia Memorial Park, which has 12 sites for tents or RVs set at 2,000 feet near numerous trailheads. There are several campgrounds on the Pacific Ocean shore as well, but they are well south of Big Sur in the very northern tip of Southern California (but Southern California nonetheless). One is Kirk Creek Campground, with 33 sites for tents or RVs; another is Plaskett Creek, which is nearby and similarly equipped but with 44 sites. For information about any and all of these campgrounds, call the Monterey Ranger District, 831/385-5434.

Northern Mountains

Don't even try it. The last person who attempted to scale 14,162-foot Mount Shasta in an RV didn't make it. Indeed, the abandoned husk of a 36-foot Winnebago is crumpled at trailside about half way up, a sad reminder that some vacations go awry and end with a long explanation to the insurance company.

This is not to say that car campers and RV riggers should stay completely away from the southern Cascade region. There are plenty of other camper-friendly places, and the great mountain is rarely out of sight (unless it's enveloped in storm clouds). You can enjoy Mount Shasta without necessarily getting anywhere near it! Choose from the Klamath National Forest's Marble Mountain Wilderness, the naked granite spires of Castle Crags State Park, the shores of Lake Shasta or Trinity Lake, the hidden corners of the Trinity Alps, and the banks of the meandering Trinity River. You will wish you had more than one trailer hitch and a larger roof rack because this is boating, rafting, kayaking, canoeing, and flyfishing country—and more.

One of the most important things to remember when exploring this part of the state is that the weather is unpredictable, especially in some areas of the high desert to the east of Mount Shasta. Late summer and early fall can be warm, even downright hot. But freaky storms can have you sunning yourself at the edge of a lazy mountain lake one minute and running for cover the next. Take plenty of layers, and be prepared for rain.

You will also want to pack the geology textbooks. Lassen Volcanic National Park and other lava flow areas will have the kids asking questions that you won't be able to answer (honestly, anyway) unless you brush up on your rock facts before leaving home. Volcanic rock isn't the only thing to inspire, though: Watch for lightning storms that send flashes across the mountainous night skyline, waterfalls cascading ice-cold snowmelt over the granite boulders of the McCloud River, marshes on the shores of Goose Lake in the high desert filled with a variety of waterfowl moving along the Pacific Flyway, and trees growing out of split boulders.

This is a land of curiosities. Just be sure to park the RV in a designated space only!

Northern Mountains

1. Matthews Creek Campground
2. Idlewild Campground
3. Lovers Camp
4. Indian Scotty Campground
5. Mount Ashland Campground
6. Bridge Flat Campground
7. Tree of Heaven Campground
8. Girder Creek Campground
9. Sarah Totten Campground
10. Gray Falls Campground
11. Hayden Flat Campground
12. Minersville Campground
13. Stoney Point Campground
14. East Weaver Campground
15. Hayward Campground
16. Preacher Meadow
17. Mary Smith Campground
18. Trinity River Campground
19. Jackass Springs Camp
20. Big Flat Campground
21. Toad Lake Campground
22. Lake Siskiyou Campground
23. Castle Crags Campground
24. McBride Campground
25. Panther Campground
26. Fowler Campground
27. Sims Flat Campground
28. Medicine Lake Campground
29. Hogue Campground
30. Lava Campground
31. Indian Well Campground
32. Big Sage Campground
33. Cave Lake Campground
34. Plum Valley Camp
35. Stowe Reservoir Campground
36. Emerson Campground
37. Patterson Campground
38. Lakeshore East Campground
39. Nelson Point Campground
40. Hirz Bay Campground
41. Pine Point Campground
42. Moore Creek Reservoir
43. Ellery Creek Campground
44. Madrone Campground
45. McCloud Bridge Campground
46. Hawkins Landing Campground
47. AtAh-Di-Na Campground
48. McArthur Falls Campground
49. Big Pine Campground
50. Northshore Campground
51. Hat Creek Campground
52. Silver Bowl Camp
53. High Bridge Campground
54. Domingo Springs Campground
55. Elam Campground
56. Alder Campground
57. Juniper Lake Campground
58. Cool Springs Campground

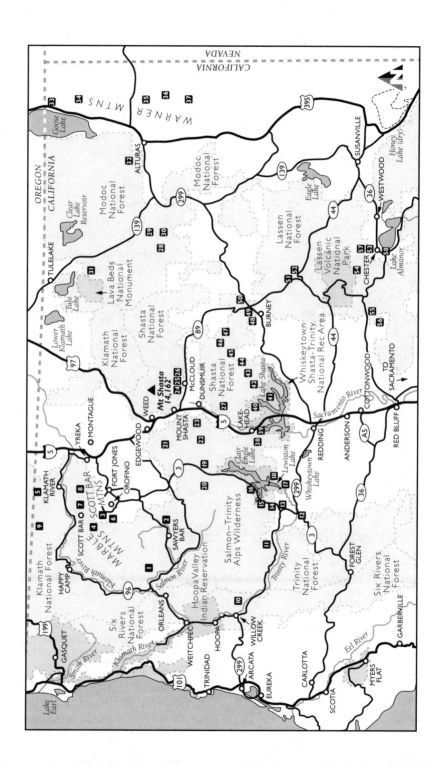

Klamath Region

① Matthews Creek Campground 🌲🌲🌲🌲🌲

If you ever needed proof that everything runs downhill, just come to this small, secluded campground in the Salmon River canyon during the spring runoff. Dozens of small creeks—including Matthews, Black Bear, Methodits, and Indian—become raging torrents during the spring, bringing ice-cold snowmelt from the Marble Mountains. This is more than just a place to watch rushing water, however. In the spring and early summer, rafting and kayaking runs between here and Cody Bar are exquisite. Later in the summer, when the water slows down and the swimming holes start looking a little more friendly, tubing and wading along the same river runs will keep you from being overcome by the heat. In the autumn and winter, salmon and steelhead appear—leave the waterplay gear at home and bring the tackle box instead. The surrounding terrain is lush forested canyon lands loaded with interesting birds and other wildlife. Note that hunters frequent this camp during the autumn and winter. The elevation is 1,760 feet.

sites	8
🏕️🚐	No hookups, RVs to 24 feet
open	May through October
reservations	None
contact	Salmon River Ranger District, 530/468-5351

Facilities: Each site has a picnic table and a fire grill. Running water and vault toilets are available nearby.

Getting there: From Cecilville, drive west on Cecilville Road for 16 miles through Cody Bar and to the campground entrance, which is on the south side of the road. Note that the road is a bit treacherous—the RV limit is for real.

② Idlewild Campground 🌲🌲🌲🌲🌲

sites	12
🏕️🚐	No hookups, RVs to 24 feet
open	May through October
reservations	Up to 240 days in advance on some sites; U.S. Forest Service Reservations, 800/280-2267
contact	Salmon River Ranger District, 530/468-5351

Looking for the grand tour? This is it. This small, quiet campground on the banks of the Salmon River is a favorite staging point for backpacking trips into the Marble Mountains. Suggested itinerary: a few overnight hikes to the northwest to the English Peak Lookout (7,322 feet)—a spot with one of the most stunning views of the southern Cascade region found anywhere. This portion of the forest is studded with beautiful, ice-cold alpine lakes and springs—some of the purest

The Salmon River cuts through the Klamath National Forest. It is a popular but treacherous destination for rafters and other thrill-seekers.

This meadow near Lovers Camp in the Marble Mountain Wilderness can hold snow well into the summer.

water you are going to find anywhere. It's not advisable, of course, but we subsisted on spring water for a week in these parts a few summers ago and were never tempted even once to filter it. The riparian terrain gives way to vast rocky plateau, wide meadows, and rocky peaks. There is every kind of wonder here: rare wildflowers, rattlesnakes, poison oak, and pack mules. Know that the terrain here is rugged and the trails challenging. Mule is the best way to travel. Trails have numerous stream crossings and are horrendously steep, dusty, rocky, and treacherous in places. If you stay at the developed campground the entire time, that's no sloucher either. The campground is set below the severe weather line, at 2,600 feet. The mid- to late summer months are perfect for wading and swimming at low current. Fall and winter ushers in the flyfishing season. Sawyers Bar is nearby for spring and early summer kayaking and rafting. The road getting out this way is a bit winding—so beware if you're an RVer. While you're here, enjoy the big sky, the sound of the wind through the trees, the chatter of songbirds, and the patter of the river dragging gravel downstream.

Facilities: Each site has a picnic table and a fire ring. Running water and vault toilets are available nearby.

Getting there: From Sawyers Bar, take Sawyers Bar Road east and drive for 11 miles before turning north on Mule Bridge Road. Continue another 3 miles to the campground on the left.

❸ Lovers Camp 🌲🌲🌲🌲🌲

Lovers Camp is a front-row seat to the best that the Klamath Forest has to offer. The camp is situated on a 4,300-foot crest facing the Black Marble Mountain and Marble Mountain 3,000 feet overhead. There are trail connections to the higher peaks and easy access to dozens of pristine, high-mountain lakes perfect for an ice-cold dip during the heat of summer. This is big sky country, a place to push your internal reset button. The Marble Mountains Wilderness contains more than 240,000 acres of pine forest, rocky plateau, high mountain meadows and lakes, and stunningly beautiful white rock peaks looking out over the entire northern state. Panoramic views of the Shasta and Lassen regions and glimpses of the redwood coast are had from here on clear days. The Marbles area also wild country—bears, rattlesnakes, poison oak, and just about everything else you want to try to avoid while in the outdoors exist here in abundance. It is most advisable, because of the vastness of the wilderness here, to spend at least part of your time exploring by horseback (or mule since they seem a bit more sure-footed). Deep Lake and Lower Sky Lake are good day trips if you're looking to explore and go for a swim during the summer.

sites	*8*
open	*May through October*
reservations	*Up to 240 days in advance on some sites; U.S. Forest Service Reservations, 800/280-2267*
contact	*Scott River Ranger District, 530/468-5351*

Facilities: Each site has a picnic table and a fire ring. Vault toilets are available nearby. There is no running water, so be sure either to pack enough to last for your entire stay or come prepared to treat creek water. The camp is equipped with corrals for stock.

Getting there: From Fort Jones, drive west on Scott River Road for 14 miles to Forest Road 44N45. Turn right and continue 8 winding miles to the campground at the end of the road.

As far as the eye can see, the forested canyons of the Marble Mountain Wilderness Area are blanketed by the snows of late spring.

④ Indian Scotty Campground 🌲🌲🌲

This is a popular and pleasant spot on the Scott River for autumn flyfishing trips and summer swimming. Just keep in mind that the campground is well-known and RV friendly. While it's in a nice forested area on the banks of a good stretch of river, it does not have that quiet and secluded feel some of some of the smaller, more remote camps. There is a group camp adjacent, which often means even more noise and less privacy. At 3,500 feet, this is often just below the snow line.

sites	35
	No hookups, RVs to 30 feet
open	May through October
reservations	Up to 240 days in advance on some sites; U.S. Forest Service Reservations, 800/280-2267
contact	Scott River Ranger District, 530/468-5351

Facilities: Each site has a picnic table and a fire ring. Vault toilets and running water are available nearby. A public phone is also available.

Getting there: From Fort Jones, drive west on Scott River Road for 14 miles to the campground entrance.

⑤ Mount Ashland Campground 🌲🌲🌲🌲🌲

Talk about being out in the middle of nowhere. Set at 6,600 feet near the Mount Ashland/Siskiyou Botanical Area, this small, secluded campground is actually about as far south in Oregon as you can get and still be able to say you're, technically, still in California. That's because Klamath National Forest and the Siskiyou Mountains are contiguous with Oregon's Rogue River National Forest, and in these parts there are some places where the state line is right down the middle of the trail you're walking on. No matter. The creeks run just as wild, the forests are just as lush and alive, and the panorama is all about California: Shasta, Lassen, and lesser peaks that dominate the northern mountains skyline. This is a quiet, little-known spot where you will find no RVs. The campground can be used as a staging point for hikes along the Pacific Crest Trail segments straddling the state line. In the winter, the campground is closed but this is a happening snow sports area; there are cross-county ski trails and a snow park nearby.

sites	7
open	May through October
reservations	None
contact	Oak Knoll Ranger District, 530/465-2241

Facilities: Each site has a picnic table and a fire ring. Vault toilets are available nearby. There is no running water, so either bring plenty or come prepared to treat creek water.

Getting there: From Yreka, take Highway 96 west and drive for 12 miles to Forest Road 48N01. Turn right and go another 13 miles to the campground entrance, which is on the left side of the road.

⑥ Bridge Flat Campground 🌲🌲🌲

The Scott River is built for kayaking. And rafting, canoeing, fishing, and swimming. Get a spot at Bridge Flat and you can do all of these things (depending on the time of year) or none of them—it's all up to you and which direction the mountain breezes are blowing. Set at 2,000 feet, Bridge Flat is below the severe weather line. The small, quiet campground is one of the last in a series along Scott River Road. River access from here is easy. Rafting and kayaking are best early in the season; in later summer the currents normally subside enough for wading and canoeing. Fishing season comes along in autumn. If the river doesn't interest you, trail connections to the Marble Mountains are nearby.

sites	7
🏕️🚐	No hookups, RVs to 30 feet.
open	May through October
reservations	Up to 240 days in advance on some sites; U.S. Forest Service Reservations, 800/280-2267
contact	Scott River Ranger District, 530/468-5351

Facilities: Each site has a picnic table and a fire ring. Vault toilets are available nearby. There is no running water, so be sure either to pack enough to last your entire stay or come prepared to treat creek water.

Getting there: From Fort Jones, drive west on Scott River Road for 17 miles to the campground entrance.

⑦ Tree of Heaven Campground 🌲🌲🌲

This stretch of the Klamath River is popular among rafters and kayakers during the spring and early summer, but when the river starts to calm down a bit in mid- to late summer it becomes more of a swimming hole. The riparian habitat around the riverside is perfect bird-watching territory; more than 200 species of bird have been documented here. When fishing season begins in the autumn, the campground is used mostly by flyfishers working the Klamath. Later in the season, hunters tend to find this campground conve-

sites	20
🏕️🚐	10 tent-only No hookups, RVs to 34 feet
open	May through October
reservations	Up to 240 days in advance on some sites; U.S. Forest Service Reservations, 800/280-2267
contact	Oak Knoll Ranger District, 530/465-2241

niently located. Note that there is a group camp adjacent. The site is set at 2,200 feet, so it is below the severe weatherline for much of the year.

Facilities: Each site has a picnic table and a fire ring. Running water and vault toilets are available nearby. There is a public telephone at the campground.

Getting there: From Redding drive north on I-5 for 80 miles to the Highway 96 junction near Yreka. Head 7 miles west on Highway 96 to the campground, which is on the south side of the road.

⑧ Grider Creek Campground 🌲🌲🌲🌲

Grider Creek is a tributary of the Klamath River. This spot upstream from the busy Highway 96 corridor provides seclusion and peace in a part of the forest that is often loaded with activity, particularly rafting and kayaking during the spring and summer. The creek flow is best in the spring and early summer. Swimming is good here, as is fly-fishing during the autumn and winter months. Hikers like to use the campground as a staging point for treks along the Pacific Crest Trail, which passes nearby. This part of the forest is a great bird-watching and wildlife viewing area. Bald eagles, songbirds, and numerous varieties of waterfowl are found here, as are deer, bobcats, and the occasional black bear. At 1,400 feet, there is less concern here about severe weather than in other parts of the Klamath region.

sites	10
🏕️🚐	No hookups, RVs to 16 feet
open	All year
reservations	Up to 240 days in advance on some sites; U.S. Forest Service Reservations, 800/280-2267
contact	Oak Knoll Ranger District, 530/465-2241

Facilities: Each site has a picnic table and a fire ring. Running water and vault toilets are available nearby.

Getting there: From Scott Flat, drive north on Scott River Road for 10 miles to Highway 96. Turn west and continue 7 miles to Walker Creek Road. Turn left at the Seiad Valley Work Center complex and continue 3 miles to the campground.

⑨ Sarah Totten Campground 🌲🌲🌲

Sarah Totten is one of just a few campgrounds located on the banks of the Klamath River a few miles upstream from Scott Bar, one of the more popular put-ins for rafting, kayaking, and canoeing in these parts. During the summer, it's all about river access. The river is fickle and unpredictable, however, depending on the rate of snowmelt so be sure to check on conditions before making specific plans. In the spring and early summer, canoeing can be a little rough here. During the autumn run, leave the bathing suit at home and bring the tackle box instead. The river access makes this a good spot for salmon and steelhead flyfishing. Because of its popularity year round, you're unlikely to drop in on an empty space here ever, so be sure to make a reservation. The tent-only sites nearest the river are the best choice. For hikers, the trail access to Tom Martin Peak (7,021 feet) is nearby. The campground is set at 1,400 feet.

sites	20
	5 tent-only
	No hookups, RVs to 22 feet
open	All year
reservations	Up to 240 days in advance on some sites; U.S. Forest Service Reservations, 800/280-2267
contact	Oak Knoll Ranger District, 530/465-2241

Facilities: Each site has a picnic table and a fire ring. Running water and vault toilets are available nearby. A public telephone is located at the camp.

Getting there: From Scott Bar, drive north on Scott River Road for 10 miles to Highway 96. Turn west and continue on Highway 96 for 1 mile to the campground on the right.

Other Klamath Area Campgrounds

There are dozens more developed campgrounds in the Klamath National Forest area, most of them similar in character and amenities to those fully profiled above.

In the Scott River Ranger District, phone 530/468-5351, the O'Neil Creek Campground (18 sites, no hookups, RVs to 21 feet) is set along the banks of a tributary to the Klamath River. Kangaroo Lake Campground (18 sites, no hookups, RVs to 16 feet) is set at 6,500 feet near a pretty alpine lake stocked with steelhead trout. Hidden Horse Campground (6 sites for tents only), in a remote spot near Scott Mountain, is a perfect staging point for backpacking trips into the wilderness area. Trail Creek Camp (12 sites for tents only) is similar to Hidden Horse, except that it's located in the southern reaches of the forest—with Pacific Crest Trail access nearby.

In the Salmon River Ranger District, phone 530/468-5351, East Fork Campground (9 sites, no hookups, RVs to 16 feet) is located near the confluence of the Salmon River's east and main forks. Other campgrounds in this part of the forest include Mule Bridge Campground (3 sites, no hookups, RVs to 24 feet), set at 2,800 feet; and Red Bank Campground (4 sites for tents only) set at 1,760 feet in the river drainage and near good fishing spots and rafting put-ins.

Trinity Region

⑩ Gray Falls Campground 🌲🌲🌲

Of the three good-sized riverside campgrounds near Trinity Village and Salyer, Gray Falls is at the best spot. Maybe it's because the river is a bit more swimmer friendly here in the mid- to late summer; that has everything to do not only with the way the main river chose to find its path here (it zigs and zags a bit), but also with the fact that two large creeks meet the river very nearby, those being Gray and Cow Creeks. Swimming, tubing, and light waterplay are best here once the spring runoff has slowed a little and the water warms, which at 1,000 feet happens early enough in the summer.

sites	36
🏕️🚐	No hookups, RVs to 32 feet
open	All year
reservations	Up to 240 days in advance on some sites; US Forest Service Reservations, 800/280-2267
contact	Weaverville Ranger District, 530/623-2121

Flyfishing is also good near the creeks in the late fall and winter. Keep in mind that because the highway is nearby, there is going to be noise. If you want something a little more peaceful, consider taking a drive up Forest Road 7N26 to the Happy Camp Mountain area and Denny.

Facilities: Each site has a picnic table and a fire ring. Running water and vault toilets are available nearby.

Getting there: From Arcata, drive east on Highway 299 for 22 miles, past Salyer, to the campground entrance, which is on the north side of the road.

⑪ Hayden Flat Campground 🌲🌲🌲🌲

Rafters, kayakers, and those just wanting to take a cold dip during the heat of the summer flock to campgrounds like this one on the banks of the Trinity River. A word to the wise, however: If you're not into water sports, the Trinity River campgrounds along the Highway 299 corridor are probably not the place for you. First off, the campsites are noisy because they are not set back far enough from the highway. Second, only a few of the sites at Hayden are even near the water—

sites	22
🏕️🚐	No hookups, RVs to 24 feet
open	All year
reservations	Up to 240 days in advance on some sites; U.S. Forest Service Reservations, 800/280-2267
contact	Trinity River, Big Bar Ranger District, 530/623-6106

and the odds are against you actually getting to sleep at riverside. On a positive note, this campground and the others lining Highway 299 are reasonably well taken care of and well managed; at 1,200 feet, they are also below the severe weather line. The Brushy Mountain area of the Trinity Alps Wilderness, 5,000 feet up, is accessible via Forest Service roads from just east of this particular campground.

Facilities: Each site has a picnic table and a fire ring. Running water and piped toilets are available nearby. Put-ins for rafters and kayakers are found here.

Getting there: From Weaverville, drive west on Highway 299 for 11 miles through the Del Loma Cave area to the campground entrance, which is on the right side of the road.

⑫ Minersville Campground 🌲🌲🌲🌲

This is one of the nicer RV spots on the lake's shore because it is secluded from a nearby group camp, relatively small, and at the end of a small peninsula near the Cedar Stock Resort. Ridgeville Island is just offshore and Bowerman Island beyond; both have boat-in campgrounds so if that is more your speed, just launch from here and float the gear a short distance out and you'll have all the seclusion you'll need from most lake day visitors and RVs. This section of the lake is at ground zero for water-ski runs and fishing, so be ready for a lot of activity on the water. Bird-watchers should retreat to the east side of the lake, as things are much more productive over there for wildlife of all types.

sites	21
🏕️🚐	No hookups, RVs to 21 feet
open	All year
reservations	Up to 240 days in advance on some sites; U.S. Forest Service Reservations, 800/280-2267
contact	Trinity River, Big Bar Ranger District, 530/623-6106

Facilities: Each site has a picnic table and a fire ring. There is running water after the winter thaw only. Vault toilets are available nearby. There is a public boat ramp a short distance from the campground. The elevation is 2,500 feet.

Getting there: From Trinity Center, go south 9 miles to the campground entrance, which is on the left side of the road. You will see the Mule Creek crossing just before the campground.

⑬ Stoney Point Campground 🌲🌲

Judging from its size and the fact that RVs are not allowed, you would expect this nice campground on the Trinity Lake west shore would be top-of-the-line accommodation. And indeed, the views are pretty and the lake access superb. Fact is however, that this is a particularly busy part of the lake—and the campground has a large group camp adjacent. Between the speedboats and shrieking swimmers on the water, you aren't going to get much shut-eye or rest around here during the height of the summer festivities. It is a the kind of campground where you just know an 8-year-old with a bouncing ball is going to decide that the perfect place to play is right outside your tent at 7 a.m. During the winter fishing season, however, things are a little calmer—you just won't feel like going swimming.

sites	24
open	All year
reservations	Up to 240 days in advance on some sites; U.S. Forest Service Reservations, 800/280-2267
contact	Trinity River, Big Bar Ranger District, 530/623-6106

Facilities: Each site has a picnic table and a fire ring. Running water and vault toilets are available nearby. There is a store in Trinity Center to the north.

Getting there: From Trinity Center drive south on Highway 3 for 8 miles to the campground entrance, which is near the Stewart Fork Bridge on the lake.

14 East Weaver Campground 🌲🌲🌲🌲

A great hike into the Trinity Alps Wilderness departs from here to the 6,998-foot lookout point just west of Monument Peak. This view offers an amazing panorama of the Trinity region—a row of majestic snowcapped peaks with lakes sprawled out beneath them like cobalt blue carpeting. This pretty, secluded campground in a shady canyon on the banks of East Weaver Creek north of the Weaverville township is a good alternative to some of the more crowded and busy campgrounds at Trinity Lake; it's perfect for those of us who enjoy a little hiking and exploring in the uplands as well as good old-fashioned summer waterplay. The elevation is 3,000 feet.

sites	19
	No hookups, RVs to 19 feet
open	All year
reservations	Up to 240 days in advance on some sites; U.S. Forest Service Reservations, 800/280-2267
contact	Trinity River, Big Bar Ranger District, 530/623-6106

Facilities: Each site has a picnic table and a fire ring. There is running water after the winter thaw. Vault toilets are available nearby.

Getting there: From Weaverville, head north and go 3 miles on Highway 3 to the intersection with East Weaver Creek Road. Turn left and continue up the road 4 miles to the campground entrance.

⑮ Hayward Campground 🌲🌲🌲🌲

The beach at Hayward Flat doesn't get near the number of visitors as areas of the lake directly adjacent to the main highway, but the campground is so big that the beach still gets plenty crowded. It's noisy, too. Still, because the campground is on its own little peninsula the area around it can be quite peaceful at times, even when the summer rush is in full swing. Digger Creek just west of the campground can be a good trout and salmon fishing spot during the autumn and winter runs. There is an old-fashioned rope swing at the southernmost end of the peninsula, but be sure not to use it unless the water level is up in the lake—dropping 10 feet into 6 inches of water is no fun, no matter how soft the landing. There are an awful lot of ducks in this part of the lake, so bring lots of bread crumbs. The elevation is 2,400 feet.

sites	100
🏕️🚐	No hookups, RVs to 42 feet
open	All year
reservations	Up to 240 days in advance on some sites; U.S. Forest Service Reservations, 800/280-2267
contact	Trinity River, Big Bar Ranger District, 530/623-6106

Facilities: Each site has a picnic table and a fire ring. Running water and vault toilets are available nearby, as is a public boat ramp. There is a general store in Trinity Center.

Getting there: From Trinity Center, drive south on Highway 3 for 6 miles to the campground access road, which is on the left.

⑯ Preacher Meadow Campground 🌲🌲

This campground is big and noisy, but it's close enough to Trinity Lake that if the shoreline campgrounds are overflowing on a nice summer weekend you might be able to at least get a spot just a few miles away. The highway noise from here is the biggest bother, but the other trouble with this spot is that it seems more like a parking lot than a place to sleep under the stars. Just a few too many cars, big RVs, and people coming and going because they're interested in something nearby—not in the campground itself.

sites	47
🏕️🚐	No hookups, RVs to 36 feet
open	All year
reservations	Up to 240 days in advance on some sites; U.S. Forest Service Reservations, 800/280-2267
contact	Trinity River, Big Bar Ranger District, 530/623-6106

Facilities: Each site is equipped with a picnic table and a fire ring. Running water and vault toilets are available nearby. There is a general store in Trinity Center to the north.

Getting there: From Trinity Center, drive south on Highway 3 for 2 miles to the campground, which is on the right side of the road.

🅱 Mary Smith Campground 🌲🌲🌲🌲🌲

Lewiston Lake is one of those coffee commercial settings: Picture yourself throwing open the sash of your ramshackle farmhouse at 6 a.m. and looking out over the glassy surface of a small lake with steam rising from it in the morning chill. Then there's nothing to do but sip strong coffee and watch the rising sun melt the frozen dew on each blade of grass in the adjacent meadow. It's the speed of the place that makes it special—so slow you're almost moving in reverse. Because it is just downstream from Trinity Dam, the lake level can fluctuate at certain times of the year, but there is always plenty of water here. Fishing for bass, pushing off

sites	17
open	All year
reservations	Up to 240 days in advance on some sites; U.S. Forest Service Reservations, 800/280-2267
contact	Trinity River, Big Bar Ranger District, 530/623-6106

Preacher Meadow Campground within Trinity National Forest is a great place to park the rig for a few nights.

on a inner tube, lazing campside with a good book and a bowl of campfire stew—this place won't make you want to do much important. Bird-watchers will enjoy this camp because of the marshy areas surrounding the lake. The elevation is 2,500 feet. Mary Smith was the sister of Broderick Wallace-Smith, one of the area's first European settlers. The campsite and nearby Neff Peak are named for Mary Smith, whose pet name was "The Neff."

Facilities: Each site has a picnic table and a fire ring. Running water and vault toilets are available nearby. Lewiston township has a general store.

Getting there: From Weaverville, go north on Highway 3 for 4 miles to Trinity Dam Road. It is an 8-mile ride to the campground, which is beyond the dam and the Lewiston township.

⑱ Trinity River Campground ▲▲▲

Sometimes it's the little quiet spot in the corner that will get you through a busy summer weekend in the outdoors. Trinity River Campground is next to Highway 3 and on the Trinity River just upstream from Trinity Lake. There are no other campgrounds nearby. The elevation is 2,500 feet. This makes it an accessible yet secluded place to unfurl the bed roll while still being close enough to where the boat was launched to enjoy the lake during the day. Fishing is good in this part of the Trinity except when upstream hatcheries have large releases. On those days, just lean the rod and reel up against a tree and go swim in the lake instead.

sites	*11*
	No hookups, RVs to 32 feet
open	*All year*
reservations	*Up to 240 days in advance on some sites; U.S. Forest Service Reservations, 800/280-2267*
contact	*Weaverville Ranger District, 530/623-2121*

Facilities: Each site has a picnic table and a fire ring. Running water and vault toilets are available nearby. There is a general store in Weaverville. Boat ramps are 7 miles south on Trinity Lake.

Getting there: From Trinity Center, drive north on Highway 3 for 10 miles to the campground entrance, which is on the left side of the highway.

⑲ Jackass Springs Camp ▲▲▲▲

During the summer, the 145 miles of shoreline and 16,000-acre surface area of Trinity Lake become the Disneyland of waterplay in the Trinity/Shasta region. It's a long, slender lake with many hidden crevices along the shoreline. Fishing for bass, rainbow trout, kokanee salmon, and catfish is good throughout the outdoor season. More than a dozen campgrounds line the shoreline, some with boating access. Of all the campgrounds, however, the definitive spot is not on the west side of the lake where campground row is located, but rather on the east side—at Jackass Springs—where you can camp in virtual isolation from everybody else if you're lucky enough to get a spot and are willing to do a little driving around to get to it. Jackass Springs is near a small cove and a pair of islands below the 4,511-foot Jackass Peak. The surrounding wetlands and marshes are a favorite shorebird area because of the quiet and comfort of this more secluded side of the lake.

sites	20
	No hookups, RVs to 28 feet
open	All year
reservations	Up to 240 days in advance on some sites; U.S. Forest Service Reservations, 800/280-2267
contact	Trinity River, Big Bar Ranger District, 530/623-6106

Because this is the quiet side of the lake, however, keep in mind that there are no public boat ramps around here, nor are there good ski or boating runs for more extreme sports. If skiing is on your agenda, you'll have to settle for something on the other side of the lake, preferably closer to the south end.

Facilities: Each site has a picnic table and a fire ring. Vault toilets are available all year, but running water is available only after the winter freeze.

Getting there: From Weaverville, drive north on Highway 3 for 24 miles to the intersection with Eastside Road near Enrich Gulch. Turn right and head southeast 14 miles to the County Road 119 turnoff. Turn right and proceed a short distance to the campground.

⑳ Big Flat Campground 🌲🌲🌲🌲🌲

Another small, secluded, quiet campground far enough off out of the way to dissuade most RV riggers, this spot is so far south in the Klamath forest that trail connections to the Trinity Alps, Salmon Mountains, and Shasta National Forest

sites	6
	No hookups, RVs to 24 feet
open	May through October
reservations	None
contact	Salmon River Ranger District, 530/468-5351

are not far off. Of course, at nearly 6,000 feet, the campground and adjacent hiking areas are inaccessible during much of the winter and spring—and some years well into the summer, but good things are worth waiting for. This campground is in an extremely rugged and remote area subject to sudden climate changes. Trails are often in less than pristine condition. Think twice before bringing children and/or inexperienced outdoorspeople to these parts.

Facilities: Each site has a picnic table and a fire ring. Running water and vault toilets are available nearby.

Getting there: From Trinity Center, head north on Highway 3 a short distance to Coffee Creek Road. Turn west and continue 20 miles to the campground entrance, which is beyond Rocky Gulch.

Other Trinity Area Campgrounds

The canyons, peaks, riversides, and lakeshores of the Trinity region contain scores more campgrounds within the broad range of those described above. In the Mad River Ranger District, phone 707/574-6233, Baily Cove Campground (27 sites for tents or RVs, no hookups, RVs to 21 feet) is on the shores of Ruth Lake just beyond the forest border in the Six Rivers area.

In the Weaverville Ranger District, phone 530/623-2121, Scott Mountain Campground (10 sites for tents only) in a primitive section of the Klamath forest

Lewiston Lake, seen here from near the Ackerman Campground, is surrounded by snowcaps much of the spring.

to the north but within the Scott Mountains, which is primarily in the Trinity Alps Wilderness.

In the Big Bar Ranger District, phone 530/623-6106, Burnt Ranch Campground (19 sites for tents or RVs, no hookups, RVs to 27 feet) overlooks the Trinity River near the Burnt Ranch area of the Highway 299 corridor. Eagle Creek Campground (19 sites for tents or RVs, no hookups, RVs to 31 feet) is also on the river just north of Trinity Lake at Eagle Creek. Horse Flat Campground (18 sites, no hookups, RVs to 16 feet) is near Burnt Ranch, also on the river. Alpine View Campground (65 sites, no hookups, RVs to 35 feet) is another spot on the river near the small town of Covington Mill. Another option nearby is the smaller Clark Springs Campground (26 sites for tents only). Finally, Tannery Gulch Campground (91 sites, no hookups, RVs to 41 feet) is one of the larger riverside campgrounds, just near the Stuart Fork Bridge in the Ridgeville area.

Ackerman Campground (72 sites, no hookups, RVs to 44 feet) is near Lewiston Lake just beneath the Trinity Dam. The Mary Smith Campground (page 135) is a ways downstream and a quieter alternative.

Mount Shasta

㉑ Toad Lake Campground 🌲🌲🌲🌲

You won't find this small, secluded, nearly impossible-to-reach campground on the official Forest Service map—because it's one of those best-kept secrets. But if you're up for a bumpy ride on some really poorly maintained and unpaved forest roads (in a four-wheel drive!), this lazy, hidden, out-of-the way fishing lake north of the Gumboot trailhead for the Pacific Crest Trail is going to work out just fine for you. There is actually a pair of lakes here; the smaller Porcupine Lake is about a quarter of a mile to the south, along the Pacific Crest route. Of all of the lakes in this section of the Trinity River drainage, Toad has the best-developed camping area. The others, however, are suitable for dispersed camping, and if you explore the area on foot you may just find you have a nice alpine lake all to yourself! You will find trout in most of these lakes for lazy afternoons fishing, but don't count on a big haul. The elevation is 3,300 feet.

sites	10
🏕️	
open	May through October
reservations	None
contact	Mount Shasta Ranger District, 530/926-4511

Facilities: Each site is equipped with a picnic table and a fire ring. Vault toilets are available nearby. There is no running water, so be certain to pack enough in to last your entire stay.

Getting there: From Mount Shasta, drive half a mile south on I-5 to West Lake Road. Head west a short distance to Forest Road 26 and turn right. A short distance later, turn right again at Forest Road 40N26. In 2 miles, you will cross the Sacramento River's south fork. After the bridge, turn right onto the campground access road (unpaved). Continue 12 miles to the campground. Note that the road is often in poor shape.

㉒ Lake Siskiyou Campground 🌲

If you're really hard up for a campsite near the lakeshore and struck out getting in at Lake Shasta or Trinity, this very large sprawling camp area near Lake Siskiyou will at least provide you with a place to pitch a tent, park the RV, and swim or fish. But as you can imagine, 400 campsites is just a few too many—and the result is just what you would expect: lots of noise and a few too many concrete slabs where the forest should be. You will survive the experience if it becomes necessary, but we say skip this one if you can avoid it. The elevation, incidentally, is 1,000 feet.

Facilities: Each site has a picnic table and a fire grill. Running water, flush toilets, and showers are available nearby.

sites	400
	225 tent-only
	100 full hookups, 50 electrical hookups, 25 no hookups, RVs to 40 feet
open	All year
reservations	Up to 240 days in advance; U.S. Forest Service Reservations, 530/926-2618
contact	Mount Shasta Ranger District, 530/926-4511

Getting there: From Mount Shasta village, go south on I-5 for half a mile to West Lake Road. Go west a short distance to S. Old Stage Road and turn right. At the lakeshore, take W.A. Barr Road to the right and go another 2.5 miles to the campground entrance, which is on the north side of the road beyond the dam site.

23 Castle Crags Campground 🌲🌲🌲🌲🌲

The main attraction here is the 6,000-foot crags, polished granite formations carved out by a slow-moving glacier millions of years ago that point to the mountain sky like a row of long, bony fingers protruding from the ground. There is an awful lot more to do here, however. The Sacramento River is nearby for swimming during the summer and fishing later in the season. There are nearly 30 miles of hiking trails, including a short hike to a 3,000-foot lookout that provides spectacular views of Mount Shasta. In addition, there are easy trail connections to the Shasta region segment of the Pacific Crest Trail, the Castle Crags Wilderness Area part of Shasta-Trinity National Forest, and points beyond. The hike to the 4,966-foot Castle Dome is a workout, but what a view! Castle Lake, Echo Lake, and dozens of small alpine lakes scattered around the Gumboot area just west of the park also are great spots to unlace the hiking shoes and take in some quiet time. The campsites are distributed through a

sites	82
	6 tent-only
	No hookups, RVs to 29 feet
open	All year
reservations	Up to 8 weeks in advance; California State Parks, 800/444-7275
contact	Castle Crags State Park, 530/235-2684

pretty pine forested area, and while there are a lot of them, they are spread out well enough that the campground does not seem packed in too tight. The six hike-in sites are your best bet. This park gets a large number of day visitors. The elevation is 2,500 feet.

Facilities: Each site has a picnic table and a fire ring. Running water, flush toilets, and showers are available nearby.

Getting there: From Dunsmuir, head south on I-5 and drive for 3 miles to the Castle Crags State Park exit. Follow the signs west to the park entrance.

㉔ McBride Springs Campground 🌲🌲🌲

If you're looking for a place comfortably near sea level to lay back and look up at the 14,162-foot summit of Mount Shasta (while trying to muster up the courage to actually climb up there some day), this may just be the perfect spot. The climb to the Shasta summit is a grueling two days of trudging through the snow and ice and eating MREs (meals ready to eat); this campground you can almost drive to. You decide which is more your style. As small as the campground is and as well situated in the Shasta mountain's foothills, don't be fooled by appearances: It is one of the most popular camp-grounds in the north state and is constantly overrun with climbing parties planning their trip into high country. The area around the campground also attracts a fair number of day visitors. Because of the campground's proximity to the highway and the Mount Shasta village, this area can get downright busy. The elevation is 3,500 feet.

sites	10
open	All year, weather permitting
reservations	None
contact	Mount Shasta Ranger District, 530/926-4511

Facilities: Each site has a picnic table and a fire ring. Running water and vault toilets are available nearby. The nearest services, such as equipment rentals and general purchases, are in the town of Mount Shasta.

Getting there: From Mount Shasta village at I-5, take the East Lake Road turnoff to Everitt Memorial Highway. Turn left and follow the highway for 5 miles to the campground on the north side of the road.

㉕ Panther Meadow Campground 🌲🌲🌲🌲

Because it is out of the thoroughfare, this small and secluded base camp at the foot of Mount Shasta provides a bit more privacy and serenity than you will find at McBride Springs (above). Again, this camp is in a foothills setting with spectacular views of the 14,162-foot Shasta summit overhead. It is a fabulous place to watch the sky—few peaks are so high that you can actually see storm clouds colliding with the Earth, but it happens here. The summit is often hidden in a blur of extreme weather. The camp is used primarily by climbing parties preparing to embark upon the two-day summit climb, but it is always possible to nab a spot here even if you're not quite ready to go all the way. Backpackers coming down the mountain are always ready and willing to talk about their conquest, making this a great place to gain inspiration.

sites	10
open	All year, weather permitting
reservations	None
contact	Mount Shasta Ranger District, 530/926-4511

Facilities: Each site has a picnic table and a fire ring. Running water and vault toilets are available nearby. The nearest services are in the village of Mount Shasta, west of the campground.

Getting there: From the Mount Shasta village at I-5, take the East Lake Road exit to the Everitt Memorial Highway turnoff. Turn east and follow the road 7 miles (it turns into County Road A10) to the very end. Park at the Bunny Flat parking area and walk a short distance away to the campground.

㉖ Fowler Campground 🌲🌲🌲🌲

It isn't always necessary to get your splash guards muddy to reach a really pleasant place to camp. At Fowler, all you've got to do is try to forget the fact that there is a state highway just a few hundred yards away from your tent and instead enjoy being on the banks of a lovely river, nestled in a cluster of pines among rocky canyon lands. There are two waterfalls on the McCloud very near the campground, and

sites	42
	No hookups, RVs to 29 feet
open	All year
reservations	Up to 240 days in advance; U.S. Forest Service Reservations, 800/280-2267
contact	McCloud Ranger District, 530/964-2184

plenty of pooled and coved spots on the river for summer dips (the water is a bit icy before midsummer rolls around). The waterfalls also, however, attract a fair share of day visitors to this section of the river, so don't be fooled by the relatively small size of the campground, as there will be plenty of people milling about. Bird-watchers will find an interesting array of songbirds, owls, woodpeckers, and waterfowl in this area. Hike past the upper falls to the more rocky terrain and high peaks, and birds of prey are often visible overhead. There also is decent trout and salmon fishing in the river beginning with the fall runs.

Facilities: Each site has a picnic table and a fire ring. Running water and vault toilets are available nearby. There is a general store in McCloud.

Getting there: From McCloud, drive east on Highway 89 for 6 miles. The campground entrance is on the right side of the road.

㉗ Sims Flat Campground 🌲

Feel like pitching a tent for the night without having to scout around forever looking for a campground? This is about as easy as they come. Because it is literally a stone's throw from I-5, you won't have the "out there" feeling you would if you were to cruise around the forest roads looking for a more private spot (hard to do with the sound of truck engines reverberating through the forest), but the sites are near the banks of the Sacramento River and the campground is small enough that you won't feel crowded in.

sites	*18*
	No hookups, RVs to 18 feet
open	*All year*
reservations	*None*
contact	*Mount Shasta Ranger District, 530/926-4511*

Trout and salmon fishing isn't bad here beginning with the autumn run, but it is naturally much better in sections of the river south of Lake Shasta. There is easy trail access to Tombstone Mountain (5,613 feet) and Yellowjacket Mountain (5,016 feet), so don't lose sight of the fact that Sims Flat may make a good staging area for a day-long hike. The elevation at the campground is 1,000 feet.

Facilities: Each site has a picnic table and a fire ring. Running water and flush toilets are available nearby.

Getting there: From Lakehead, go north on I-5 for 12 miles to the Sims Road turnoff; the campground is 1 mile south on Sims.

Other Mount Shasta Area Campgrounds

The looming Shasta summit will follow you everywhere you go in this region; there is simply no escape from it. There are numerous campgrounds in addition to those described above. Also consider Cattle Campground (22 sites for tents or RVs, no hookups, RVs to 29 feet), an overflow camp for the more popular Fowler Campground (see above) but still a very nice spot. Contact the McCloud Ranger District, 530/964-2184 or inquire through Forest Service Reservations, 800/280-2267.

Another secluded forested setting is found at Harris Springs Campground (17 sites for tents or RVs, no hookups, RVs to 35 feet) near the town of Bartle east of McCloud. Call the campground directly at 530/964-2184.

Modoc Region

28 Medicine Lake Campground ▲▲▲▲

Take an ancient crater and drop a whole lot of pure, fresh, ice-cold water into it and what do you end up with? Medicine Lake would be one example. The evolving landscape in the Medicine Lake region tells us a story: Everything is interconnected; we are all the result of cause-and-effect events that unfold in nature. There is a vast area of lava flows a short walk from the northern shore of the lake. The Glass Mountain area and Lava Beds National Monument both are nearby, and are doable as day trips from Medicine Lake camp. Because camping is so limited at the national monument, many visitors end up staying at the lake instead. The campsites are near the lakeshore in a pretty forested area. During the summers, swimming and boating are popular here, as is fishing for stocked brown trout. Don't count on waterplay during the off-season, though; at 6,700 feet you're going to find the lake frozen and the forest blanketed in snow.

sites	22
🏕️ 🚐	No hookups, RVs to 22 feet
open	July through October
reservations	None
contact	Doublehead Ranger District, 530/667-2246

Facilities: Each site has a picnic table and a fire grill. Vault toilets and running water are available nearby, as is a public boat ramp. Minimal supplies are available at the lake's marina. Boat rentals are available.

Getting there: From Tule Lake, go south on Highway 139 through the town of Perez. At County Road 197, turn west and continue 7 miles to the campground and lake.

29 Hogue Campground ▲▲▲▲

The north banks of Medicine Lake are dotted with dozens of campsites, most of them overflow camping for the more popular Lava Beds National Monument nearby. Don't pass this area over, however, if you're not looking for a place to camp. It's a nice high-desert summer watersports area and an interesting sight at that: The lake is really an ancient crater that filled up with melting snow from surrounding peaks.

sites	24

 No hookups, RVs to 22 feet

open	July through October
reservations	None
contact	Doublehead Ranger District, 530/667-2246

Facilities: Each site has a picnic table and a fire grill. Running water and vault toilets are available nearby, as are a public boat ramp and a full service marina with boat rentals. Limited services are available at the marina.

Getting there: From Tule Lake, go south on Highway 139 through the town of Perez. At County Road 197, turn west and continue 7 miles to the campground and lake.

③⓪ Lava Campground 🌲🌲🌲

This very secluded campground just above the tree line in the Sugar Pine Ridge area of the forest, at 4,400 feet, is a great place to pitch a tent if you want to be equal distance between awesome lava flow areas and a place to play in the water.

sites	12

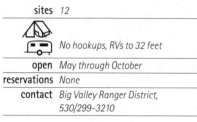 No hookups, RVs to 32 feet

open	May through October
reservations	None
contact	Big Valley Ranger District, 530/299-3210

The Whitehorse Flat Reservoir is in one direction and the Burnt Lava Flow Geologic Area is in the other. There is also a fun waterhole just a short distance south for swimming during the summer. Note, however, that once hunting season starts in the fall you're likely to find this part of the forest crawling with guys and guns. If that's not your thing, skip it. The campground is nicely arranged with private sites and excellent views. Because it accommodates bigger RVs, you run the danger of being near larger rigs.

Facilities: Each site has a picnic table and a fire grill. Vault toilets are available nearby. There is no running water, so be sure to pack in enough to last your entire trip or come prepared to treat creek water.

Getting there: From Adin, drive north on Highway 139 past Harris Springs, and then turn west on Forest Road 41N10. Continue for 12 miles and turn left on Forest Road 42N03. At Forest Road 42N23, turn right. The campground is a short distance straight ahead.

③ Indian Well Campground 🌲🌲🌲🌲

If you can't get a campground reservation at the moon and are really bummed about it, this may very well be the spot for you. Lava Beds National Monument is a geologist's answer to Disneyland. Ancient lava flows, lava caves, cinder cones, and lava tubes dominate the almost surreal landscape here—and you are pretty much free to explore cave openings and the like without restriction (just be careful). During winter months, it all looks like a blanket of jagged ice chunks, as the lava flows are buried in snow. The campground, we must note, is often full of schoolchildren studying geology and California history so don't be disappointed if you don't have perfect peace and quiet during your stay. The scenery makes it all worth it, so focus on that instead.

sites	40
🏕️🚐	No hookups, RVs to 16 feet
open	All year
reservations	None
contact	Lava Beds National Monument, 530/667-2282

Facilities: Each site has a picnic table and a fire ring. Running water and flush toilets are available nearby, but during the severe winter months they are unavailable.

Getting there: From Tule Lake, head south on Highway 139 through the town of Perez. At County Road 197, turn right and proceed 2 miles to Lava Bed National Monument Road/Hill Road. The entrance to the monument and the campground is at the end of the road.

③ Big Sage Reservoir 🌲🌲🌲🌲

Big Sage Reservoir is out in the middle of nowhere and pretty much secluded from just about everything, but there is a tiny campground on its southern shore for those who want an out-of-the-way place to launch the boat and cast a line for a few brown trout or catfish. At 5,100 feet, you're not going to find too many hot summer nights at the lake's edge unless you're camping out in the late summer. Drop in here when everything is just right, however, and the luck of timing will pay off big time with a rare private experience in a lovely waterplay setting. Note that the campground is quite small, so if you find it filled up don't be surprised. There is no campground host and no fee.

sites	6
🏕️🚐	No hookups, RVs to 22 feet
open	May through October
reservations	None
contact	Devil's Garden Ranger District, 530/233-5811

Facilities: Each site has a picnic table and a fire grill. Vault toilets are available nearby. There is a public boat ramp adjacent. There is no running water here, so be sure to bring enough to last your entire stay or come prepared to treat creek water.

Getting there: From Alturas, drive west on Highway 299 for about 3 miles to Airport Road/County Road 72. Turn right and continue another 4.5 miles to County Road 180. Turn right again and look for the campground a short distance ahead.

33 Cave Lake Camp 🌲🌲🌲🌲🌲

You know the feeling: Wanting to get away from it all so badly that you end up in the farthest reaches—so far, in fact, that you're within a stone's throw of falling off the edge of the California map. That's pretty much what we're dealing with here. At Cave Lake, the Oregon border is over one shoulder and the Nevada border is over the other. This is indeed out of the way, and it feels like it. This is a quiet and secluded campground, remarkably easy to reach when you consider the desolate feeling of the place. This is the high desert, so expect weather extremes even during the summer. Set at 6,600 feet, the Cave Lake area sees cool nights and rain storms even during the summer. If you're looking for a time to actually swim or do other water play, August is your best bet. Because Goose Lake is nearby, bird-watchers will find Cave Lake a suitable waterfowl watching place; geese, ducks, warblers, and numerous others pass through this area in droves during the annual migrations. The lake is also good for rainbow trout during the summer.

sites	7
	No hookups, RVs to 16 feet
open	July through October
reservations	None
contact	Warner Mountain Ranger District, 530/279-6116

Facilities: Each site has a picnic table and a fire ring. Running water and vault toilets are available nearby. Pack in all gear, as this is a remote site with no services nearby.

Getting there: Drive north on US 395 from Alturas for 32 miles, toward the Oregon border. Half a mile from the border, turn east on County Road 2. Follow the signs to the campground, which is on the left side of the road.

The Warner Mountains Wilderness Area boundary is dotted with numerous campgrounds at the beginning of the Cascade range.

34 Plum Valley Camp 🌲🌲🌲🌲

This small, little-known campground is near the banks of the south fork of Davis Creek, is a decent spot for weekend flyfishing trips if you don't mind brown trout.

sites	7
	No hookups, RVs to 16 feet
open	June through October
reservations	None
contact	Warner Mountain Ranger District, 530/279-6116

The spot, set at the 5,600-foot elevation, is equal distance between Upper Alkali Lake and Goose Lake and so makes a good stopover for those who want to see both. Remember that extreme weather occurs here year round. Rain during the summer is not uncommon—so come prepared.

Facilities: Each site has a picnic table and a fire grill. Vault toilets are available nearby. There is no running water, so be sure to pack enough in to last your entire stay or come prepared to treat creek water. There is a store in Davis Creek, which is about 4 miles to the west.

Getting there: From Alturas, drive north on US 395 for 22 miles to the Davis Creek township. Turn east of County Road 11 and continue 2.5 miles to the fork in the road. Take the right fork and continue 1 mile to the campground, which is on your left.

35 Stowe Reservoir Campground ▲▲▲

Cedar Mountain, Bear Mountain, Payne Peak, the Cedar Ski Hill, and the town of Cedarville all are very near this quiet and pleasant campground near a small reservoir once used by cattle ranchers to water their herds. While the lake sits at 6,300 feet, surrounding peaks range on up over 8,000 feet; often, there are snowcaps well into the summer and the water running through the creeks is exquisitely cold. Pine forest and rocky plateau are the predominant terrain around here. Expect to encounter bobcats, raccoons, weasels, and plenty of deer in these parts.

sites	14
	No hookups, RVs to 22 feet
open	May through October
reservations	None
contact	Warner Mountain Ranger District, 530/279-6116

Facilities: Each site has a picnic table and a fire grill. Vault toilets and running water are available nearby. Cedarville, a few miles to the east, has basic services and essentials.

Getting there: Drive north on US 395 for 6 miles to Highway 299. Turn east and continue to the campground entrance about 12 miles out on the right side of the road. If you reach the town of Cedarville, you have gone too far.

36 Emerson Campground ▲▲▲▲

Backpackers planning to take the Emerson Trail through the South Warner Mountains like to use this small, quiet, pleasant campground on the edge of the wilderness area as a jumping-off point or as a place to gather themselves after a few days in the backcountry. This is prime real estate: Both Eagle Peak (9,892 feet) and Dusenbury Peak (9,097 feet) are accessible from this trailhead, which also connects to trail systems leading to virtually every part of the wilderness area. The small town of Eagleville is just 5 miles away, as is Middle Alkali Lake. The campground is set at 6,000 feet and often is not thawed out in time even for midsummer camping unless it's in snow gear.

sites	4
	No hookups, RVs to 16 feet
open	July through October
reservations	None
contact	Warner Mountain Ranger District, 530/279-6116

Facilities: Each site has a picnic table and a fire grill. Vault toilets are available nearby. There is no running water, so be certain to pack in enough to last your entire trip or come prepared to treat creek water.

Getting there: From Alturas, go south on US 395 for 25 miles to the smaller township of Madeline. Turn east on County Road 510/Patterson Sawmill Road.

Proceed another 22 miles to the intersection with Highway 81. Turn left on Emerson Road and continue a short distance to the campground, which is just outside the wilderness area boundaries.

㊲ Patterson Campground 🌲🌲🌲

This is one of five small developed campgrounds situated right on the border of the South Warner Mountain Wilderness area. All are perfect starting points for backpacking trips to the higher peaks. Patterson is at both the East Creek Trail and Summit Trail entrances to the wilderness; both trails connect to the entire network covering hundreds of miles of backcountry. Because of its small size and relatively easy access from the south end of the wilderness area, this is the campground out of the five that is most likely to be filled to capacity during backpacking season. The surrounding terrain is a mixed conifer forest with wide meadows and meandering creeks; there are good views of Emerson Peak and Bald Mountain.

sites	5
	No hookups, RVs to 16 feet
open	July through October
reservations	None
contact	Warner Mountain Ranger District, 530/279-6116

Facilities: Each campsite has a picnic table and a fire grill. Vault toilets and running water are available nearby.

Getting there: From Alturas, go south on US 395 for 25 miles to the smaller township of Madeline. Turn east on County Road 510/Patterson Sawmill Road and proceed 12 miles to the campground entrance, which is on the right side of the road.

Other Modoc Region Campgrounds

There are more than a dozen other campgrounds within the Modoc National Forest boundaries, and they cover all types of settings and terrain. The full profiles listed above represent a cross-section of what is available.

In the Big Valley Ranger District area, 530/299-3210, Ash Creek Campground (7 sites for tents or RVs to 22 feet), is set at 4,800 feet on the banks of a nice creek. Trash must be packed out here and there is no running water. Lower Rush Creek Campground is at 4,400 feet (10 sites for tents or RVs to 22 feet). Upper Rush Creek Campground is similar, but 800 feet further up. Willow Creek Campground (8 sites, for tents or RVs to 22 feet) is another.

In the Doublehead Ranger District, 530/667-2246, the Hemlock Campground (19 sites for tents or RVs to 22 feet) is on the banks of Medicine Lake. Headquarters Campground (9 sites) is also at the lake. Elsewhere, the Payne Springs Campground (6 sites for tents or RVs to 20 feet) is set at 6,500 feet.

The Warner Mountain Ranger District area, 530/279-6116, has five other campgrounds, including Pepperdine, Mill Creek Falls, and Soup Springs, all near trailheads on the border of the forest wilderness area. These are among the nicest campsites in the forest, and are best suited for backpackers heading into the wilderness areas. Note that Mill Creek is the largest, with 19 sites.

In the Devil's Garden Ranger District area, 530/233-5811, you'll find Cottonwood Campground, set at the 4,700-foot elevation west of the Devil's Garden township (10 sites for tents or RVs to 22 feet). Howard's Gulch Campground (11 sites for tents or RVs to 22 feet) is located nearer Duncan's Reservoir.

Another small campground on the banks of Lake Britton, with 7 sites, is able to accommodate RVs to 21 feet. Call Pacific Gas & Electric Company, 916/923-7142, for information.

Lake Shasta

38 Lakeshore East Campground ⚑

Location is everything, and in this case that isn't necessarily good. Because the campground is located so close to a full-service marina and other amenities in Lakehead, people with the most complicated RV rigs, the biggest and loudest boats, the most obnoxious monster trucks, and the yappiest dogs flock to this large sprawling campground on the Sacramento River arm of the lake. If you get stuck here, you'll no doubt survive, but any trouble you have to go through to avoid it will make your trip many times more bearable. Don't say you weren't warned. The elevation is 1,000 feet.

sites	38
	No hookups, RVs to 37 feet
open	All year
reservations	Up to 240 days in advance on some sites; U.S. Forest Service Reservations, 800/280-2267
contact	Lake Shasta Ranger District, 530/275-1587, or the Lake Shasta Information Center, 530/257-1589

Facilities: Each site has a picnic table and a fire ring. Running water and flush toilets are available nearby. There is a public boat ramp just north of the campground at Antlers.

Getting there: From Lakehead, head south on I-5 to the Antlers Road exit and go west a short distance to the intersection with Lakeshore Drive. Turn south and continue another 3 miles to the campground entrance, which is on the left.

39 Nelson Point Campground 🌲🌲🌲🌲

Things are little more private and secluded at Nelson Point because the campground is set on the banks of the Salt Creek Inlet to Shasta Lake and not on the main lake itself. Because the inlet is a dead end for ski boats and house boats, you don't see very many of them on this part of the water. Catfish and brown trout colonies are well established here; bring the aluminum fishing boat. The campground is oddly private despite its close proximity to I-5, but the ease with which it is

sites	10
	No hookups, RVs to 18 feet
open	All year
reservations	Up to 240 days in advance on some sites; U.S. Forest Service Reservations, 800/280-2267
contact	Lake Shasta Ranger District, 530/275-1587, or the Lake Shasta Information Center, 530/257-1589

reached can attract crowds. A marina and public boat launch facilities are nearby. The elevation is 1,000 feet.

Facilities: Each site has a picnic table and a fire ring. Vault toilets are available nearby. There is no running water, so be sure to bring plenty to last your entire stay. The nearest boat ramp is to the north at Lakehead.

㊵ Hirz Bay Campground 🌲🌲🌲🌲

This is a quiet and peaceful spot on the McCloud River arm of Lake Shasta, but the campground fills up easily and is quite large. There are also, count them, two group camps next door. While the trout and catfish action is good on this part of the lake, be prepared to share space if you land here. Shasta has 340 miles of shoreline and a surface area covering almost 30,000 acres. Fishing, swimming, water-skiing, and summer cookouts are in store when you drop in here for a weekend. A good excursion is the hike to the Hirz Mountain lookout, which stands at 3,540 feet and provides a good panoramic view of the entire lake. The elevation at the campground is 1,000 feet.

sites	50
	No hookups, RVs to 31 feet
open	All year
reservations	Up to 240 days in advance on some sites; U.S. Forest Service Reservations, 800/280-2267
contact	Lake Shasta Ranger District, 530/275-1587; Lake Shasta Information Center, 530/257-1589

Facilities: Each site has a picnic table and a fire grill. Running water and flush toilets are available nearby. There is a public boat ramp just west of the campground.

Getting there: From Lakehead, drive south on I-5 for 7 miles before turning east on Gilman Road at the lake. Follow Gilman 10 miles to Hirz Bay Road. Turn south and continue 1 mile to the campground.

Getting there: From Lakehead, head south on I-5 and drive 3 miles to the Salt Creek Road exit. Go left and continue 1 mile north to the campground entrance, which is on the west side of the road.

㊶ Pine Point Campground 🌲🌲🌲

The vantage point is a little different from this small, pretty campground set on a small bluff overlooking the lake. Sites are set within a grove of pine trees that gives way to the waterfront. This is a narrow point in the river crossing; it's possible to drift over to the other side and visit Samwell Cave without having to unpark the rig and drive around the north end of the lake or go for a long hike. It is not unusual, however, for temperatures to climb well into the 90s and beyond during the summer here—so keep in mind that the cool breezes off the lake are going to be a little farther off should you decide to camp out in a forest setting away from the shore. The elevation is 1,000 feet.

sites	*16*
🏕️ 🚐	*No hookups, RVs to 23 feet*
open	*All year*
reservations	*Up to 240 days in advance on some sites; U.S. Forest Service Reservations, 800/280-2267*
contact	*Lake Shasta Ranger District, 530/275-1587; Lake Shasta Information Center, 530/257-1589*

Facilities: Each site has a picnic table and a fire grill. Running water and vault toilets are available nearby. The nearest boat ramp is to the south at Hirz Bay.

Getting there: From Lakehead, take I-5 south to the Gilman Road exit and head east 16.5 miles to the campground, which on the right side of the road.

The vistas from the McCloud arm of Lake Shasta, near Ellery Creek Campground, include the forested hills upstream of the lake.

42 Moore Creek Campground 🌲🌲🌲🌲

Things move a little more slowly and are a little calmer on this part of the McCloud arm of Lake Shasta, just north and upstream of the Hirz Bay complex. With Hirz Mountain towering directly overhead, this is a pretty spot both in terms of waterfront scenes and surrounding topography. Ducks and other shore birds come here in droves; the trout and catfish spots are numerous. This is the section of the McCloud arm where the waterway begins to resemble a wide, slow-moving river. Because of this, it almost has the feeling of the tropics, particularly during the high heat of summer; dream hard enough and you will swear you're on the Amazon in the jungles of South American, only without all the scary critters. The elevation is 1,000 feet.

sites	13
🏕️ 🚐	No hookups, RVs to 21 feet
open	All year
reservations	Up to 240 days in advance on some sites; U.S. Forest Service Reservations, 800/280-2267
contact	Lake Shasta Ranger District, 530/275-1587, or the Lake Shasta Information Center, 530/257-1589

Facilities: Each site has a picnic table and a fire grill. Running water and vault toilets are available nearby.

Getting there: Drive I-5 south from Lakehead to the Gilman Road exit and go 10 miles east to Hirz Bay Road. The campground is just beyond Hirz Bay Road.

43 Ellery Creek Campground 🌲🌲🌲🌲

Just north of Hirz Mountain on the northern stretch of Lake Shasta's McCloud arm, the mouth of Ellery Creek forms a nice little drop basin where brown trout like to hide out when larger fish are feeding. This makes the Ellery Creek Campground and surrounding waterfront a great place to cast a line from the shore. The scenery here is quite striking: pretty pine forest giving way to outcroppings of limestone. The creek flows high well into the summer with snowmelt from the higher peaks. Boating activity begins to drop off this far north on the McCloud because it is out of reach of decent ski runs and the nearest public ramp is several miles to the south. The camp has no neighbors, so enjoy the peace.

sites	20
🏕️ 🚐	No hookups, RVs to 31 feet
open	All year
reservations	Up to 240 days in advance on some sites; U.S. Forest Service Reservations, 800/280-2267
contact	Lake Shasta Ranger District, 530/275-1587; Lake Shasta Information Center, 530/257-1589

Facilities: Each site has a picnic table and a fire grill. Running water and vault toilets are available nearby. The nearest boat ramp is at the Hirz Bay Campground to the south.

Getting there: From Lakehead, take I-5 south to the Gilman Road exit and continue 15 miles along the north shore of the lake to the campground, which is on the right side of the road.

44 Madrone Campground 🌲🌲🌲🌲

It's a long, windy, treacherous drive on yucky Forest Service roads to get from this small, secluded campground on Hoffmeister Creek to all the action on Lake Shasta—but that can be a good thing. Here you will find the peace and quiet you were looking for: Let everyone else sit at the edge of the lake listening to the shrieks of amateur waterskiers and the drone of motorboats or the "hee haw" of trout fishers reeling in the catch of the day. Nonetheless, flyfishing in the late autumn and winter can be quite good both here and on nearby Beartrap Creek; so don't forget the tackle box. The elevation is 2,700 feet.

sites	*13*
	No hookups, RVs to 18 feet
open	*All year*
reservations	*Up to 240 days in advance on some sites; U.S. Forest Service Reservations, 800/280-2267*
contact	*Lake Shasta Ranger District, 530/275-1587; Lake Shasta Information Center, 530/257-1589*

Facilities: Each site has a picnic table and a fire ring. Vault toilets are available nearby. There is no running water, so be certain to bring enough to last your entire stay.

Getting there: From Redding, head east on Highway 299 for 25 miles to Fenders Ferry Road. Turn left and continue another 20 miles to the campground.

45 McCloud Bridge Campground 🌲🌲🌲🌲🌲

If you're one of those people who likes to be all the way at the top of the mountain, or the end of the road, this is the perfect camp spot for you at Lake Shasta. McCloud Bridge is literally as far north as you can get on the lake without having to do dispersed camping out in the forest. Access to the McCloud River is excellent here, as is the fishing for both catfish and brown trout. There are also good trail connections for day hikes into the surrounding forest, including to the Green Mountain summit (4,059 feet) and Nawtawaket Mountain (4,551 feet), both of which provide spectacular panoramas of the lake, Mount Shasta to the north, and the meandering Sacramento River snaking its way south through the valley.

sites	20
	No hookups, RVs to 31 feet
open	All year
reservations	Up to 240 days in advance on some sites; U.S. Forest Service Reservations, 800/280-2267
contact	Lake Shasta Ranger District, 530/275-1587; Lake Shasta Information Center, 530/257-1589

Bird-watchers should note that these parts are the best place to spot birds of prey such as bald eagles and peregrine falcons. There is no boat ramp, but you can launch a small fishing boat from the shoreline anywhere.

Facilities: Each site has a picnic table and a fire grill. Running water and vault toilets are available nearby. There is a general store nearby in O'Brien.

Getting there: From Lakehead, take I-5 south to the Gilman Road exit and head east 20 miles to the campground entrance on the north shore of the lake to the right.

46 Hawkins Landing 🌲🌲🌲🌲

Iron Canyon Reservoir is one of a series of pretty lakes in the Pit River drainage where you can melt into a lounge chair at the water's edge and slowly absorb a new attitude. Getting to Hawkins Landing requires a bit of back-road driving, but the

sites	11
	No hookups, RVs to 31 feet
open	All year
reservations	None
contact	Pacific Gas & Electric Company, 916/923-7142

minute you arrive you'll know for certain that the trekking off the main drag is worth the effort. There are trail connections from here to Little Bagley Mountain, with a 3,867-foot summit from which you will get a unique view of Shasta from the east. Bagley Mountain is on to the south, with a 4,387-foot summit and slightly wider panorama. There is, however, no need to be so ambitious in a setting like this. It's perfectly okay to cast a line into the reservoir and stay put. You may even get a bit of brown trout—if you can get yourself motivated enough to reel it in.

Facilities: Each site has a picnic table and a fire ring. Running water and vault toilets are available nearby. There is a general store in Big Bend, a short distance to the east.

Getting there: From Redding, drive east on Highway 299 for 35 miles to Hillcrest. Turn left on Big Bend Road and proceed another 20 miles north to the campground.

47 AtAh-Di-Na Campground 🌲🌲🌲

Visitors to Lake McCloud love this small secluded campground on the banks of the McCloud River just a few miles downstream from the actual lakeshore. That's because it is possible to have the quiet and solitude of a campsite in a nice forested canyon setting with the more rambunctious scene on the lake out of sight. Lake McCloud is a popular boating, fishing, swimming, and picnic area frequented mostly by day visitors (there are no campgrounds on the lake itself). There are trail connections to the 4,697-foot Bald Mountain overlook from the campground, and nice walking areas along the riverbanks. If you go to the lake, note that the east side around Star Creek is the most peaceful. For boating and waterplay, stick to the west side.

sites	18
🏕️🚐	No hookups, RVs to 31 feet
open	All year
reservations	None
contact	McCloud Ranger District, 530/964-2184

Facilities: Each site has a picnic table and a fire ring. Running water and flush toilets are available nearby.

Getting there: From Lakehead drive north on I-5 for 47 miles to Highway 89. Head east on Highway 89 and drive 12 miles to McCloud. Turn south on Squaw Valley Road/Forest Road 11 and continue 10 miles to the lake and campground.

48 McArthur Falls Campground 🌲🌲🌲🌲

You might be a bit surprised to find such a green and lush forested area in this part of the Southern Cascade range, but not everything is lava rock and open plateau up here. At McArthur-Burney Falls, the sugar pine and Douglas-fir forests are kept misty and wet by spray from a 130-foot waterfall on Burney Creek. Lake Britton is nearby and there are nice views of the surrounding peaks. The water is super cold, however, so don't bring your bathing suit unless you're a polar bear. Some campsites are a bit more private and luxurious than others, and because of the size of this campground you may find yourself feeling a bit of a squeeze. This is one of the few spots in the region where you're going to find such luxuries as flush toilets and showers.

sites	130
🏕️🚐	No hookups, RVs to 36 feet
open	All year
reservations	Up to 8 weeks in advance; California State Parks, 800/444-7275
contact	McArthur-Burney Falls Memorial State Park, 530/335-2777

Facilities: Each site has a picnic table and a fire grill. Running water, flush toilets, and showers are available nearby, as is a sanitary dump station for RVs.

Getting there: From Burney, go east on Highway 299 for 6 miles to the intersection with Highway 89 and turn left. The campground is straight ahead on the left.

49 Big Pine Campground 🌲🌲🌲🌲

Potato Butte (over 5,000 feet) and the smaller peaks surrounding it provide a picturesque backdrop for this small, quiet campground in the Hat Creek drainage. Fishing is lousy at the spot, but of the half dozen or so campgrounds within shouting distance of the main entrance to Lassen Volcanic National Park this is by far the nicest. It is more quiet and a bit more secluded from the main highway. RVs also tend to be less common here because access is a bit more difficult due to lack of pavement.

sites	19
🏕️🚐	No hookups, RVs to 22 feet
open	May through October
reservations	None
contact	Eagle Lake Ranger District, 530/336-5521

Facilities: Each site has a picnic table and a fire ring. Running water and vault toilets are available nearby. The access road is unpaved and parking is limited. There are wintertime snowmobile areas close by.

Getting there: From Redding, drive north on I-5 for 6 miles to Highway 299, then turn northeast to the Highway 89 connector. Continue 14 miles to the campground entrance, which is on the left.

50 Northshore Campground 🌲🌲🌲

This is one of the nicer small lakeside campgrounds owned and operated by Pacific Gas &Electric. Burney Lake spills into Burney Creek, which drops 130 feet to the adjacent state park. The area is a pretty sugar pine and Douglas-fir forest in the midst of the lava flow terrain that dominates the high plains in this part of the Southern Cascade range. There is decent fishing for brown trout during the summer. Large groups of RVs tend to camp here.

sites	30
🏕️🚐	No hookups, RVs to 31 feet
open	May through October
reservations	None
contact	Pacific Gas & Electric Company Recreation Office, 916/923-7142

Facilities: Each site has a picnic table and a fire grill. Vault toilets and running water are available nearby.

Getting there: From Redding, go east on Highway 299 for 6 miles to Highway 89. Turn left and continue to the campground entrance, which is just before Four Corners.

Other Lake Shasta Area Campgrounds

Clear Creek Campground (9 sites for tents or RVS, no hookups, RVs to 21 feet), phone 530/623-2121, is northwest of Lake Shasta in a pretty canyon on the banks of a free-running creek.

Holiday Harbor (26 sites for tents or RVs, electrical hookups, RVs to 40 feet), phone 530/238-2383, offers a few more amenities than most others around the lake—including showers—but it's basically a parking lot for camp rigs.

Salt Creek Campground (60 sites for tents or RVs, electrical hookups, RVs to 40 feet) is another RV parking area they call a campground. Call 530/238-8500 if you'd like to see for yourself.

Gregory Creek Campground (19 sites, no hookups, RVs to 23 feet) is on the Sacramento just downstream from Lake Shasta, in the spray of the spillway. Call 530/238-2824.

Antlers Campground (60 sites for tents or RVs, no hookups, RVs to 31 feet) is one of the largest campgrounds on the Sacramento River and also south of the lake. Call 530/275-1512.

Lassen Region

51 Hat Creek Campground 🌲🌲🌲

Hat Creek is a good place to fish for planted rainbow trout when the timing is right. Logan Lake is a short distance down the hill, and a good spot for a dip— during the hot late summer months only! This is one of the half dozen campgrounds used by day visitors to Lassen Volcanic National Park who want to avoid the rushing crowds in the mornings and nights.

sites	73
	No hookups, RVs to 22 feet
open	May through October
reservations	Up to 240 days in advance on some sites; U.S. Forest Service Reservations, 800/280-2267
contact	Hat Creek Ranger District, 530/336-5521

Facilities: Each site has a picnic table and a fire ring. Flush and vault toilets are available nearby, as is running water.

Getting there: From Redding, drive north on I-5 for 6 miles to Highway 299. Go northeast to the junction with Highway 89 then south 22 miles to the campground entrance.

52 Silver Bowl Camp 🌲🌲🌲🌲🌲

Location means everything. The forested plateau making up the Caribou Peak Wilderness area of Lassen National Forest is littered with living evidence that the greenery regenerates over time following a volcanic period. Lava flows, cinder cones, craters, and strewn rock are garnished with patches of pine, fir, and hemlock. Silver Lake is right on the southeastern boundary of the wilderness and is near the Caribou Lake trailhead, a great staging ground for days-long backpacking trips into the wilderness. There are literally hundreds of smaller lakes along the trail route. The highest point in the wilderness is the 8,370-foot summit of Red Cinder. Silver Lake has a quiet and peaceful feel to it, and at the height of the late summer backpacking season it feels like a real hiker's camp. Earlier in the season, it is occupied mostly by RV rigs and boaters. Summer fishing is best for catfish and brown trout.

sites	18
	No hookups, RVs to 30 feet
open	May through October
reservations	None
contact	Almanor Ranger District, 530/258-2141

Facilities: Each site has a picnic table and a fire ring. Running water and vault toilets are available. Nearby are a marina with boat rentals and a public boat ramp.

Getting there: From Redding, drive north on I-5 for 6 miles to Highway 299. Turn right and continue to the Highway 89 intersection. Turn right again and follow Highway 89 through the Lake Almanor area and Highway 44. At Highway 44, turn left and make an immediate right on Silver Lake Road. It is another 9 miles to the campground on the lakeshore.

⑤ High Bridge Campground 🌲🌲🌲🌲🌲

When trying to figure out if a campground is going to be a winner, one thing you can often count on is this: the worse the road getting to it, the less likely it is that you're going to find grandma and grandpa parked there in the Winnebago. This is

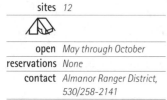

sites	12
open	May through October
reservations	None
contact	Almanor Ranger District, 530/258-2141

the case with High Bridge Campground, a small and cozy necklace of a dozen primitive campsites set at 5,200 feet near the upper portion of the Feather River. The surrounding pine and fire forestlands are brimming with wildlife; look for deer, bobcats, raccoons, and even the occasional wayward migrating waterfowl. Despite the fact that you are on the section of river upstream from Lake Almanor, fishing for rainbows and brown trout can be quite good. You can also use this camp as a staging point for day trips north to Lassen Volcanic National Park, or for longer backpacking trips along the Pacific Crest Trail segment connecting the lakes region with the southern Cascades.

Facilities: Each site has a picnic table and a fire ring. Vault toilets and running water are available nearby. There are decent views of a number of impressive peaks around the Lassen region from here. These include North Stover Mountain and Ice Cave Mountain to the west and north.

Getting there: Take Highway 36 out of Susanville east to Chester. Turn north on Feather River Road and go about 5.5 miles to the campground entrance, which is on the west side of the road. As noted, it is not a good idea to make this trip in an RV or while pulling a trailer, as the road is unpaved and only intermittently maintained.

⑤ Domingo Springs Campground 🌲🌲🌲🌲

Getting to this small, little-used campground south of Lassen Volcanic National Park is a little more work than is the case with others, but those who would like a

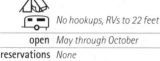

sites	18
	No hookups, RVs to 22 feet
open	May through October
reservations	None
contact	Almanor Ranger District, 530/258-2141

more primitive and secluded experience will enjoy this campground at 5,200 feet near the upper portion of the Feather River. Trail connections north to the volcanic park area and south through the forest peaks west of Lake Almanor also are available easily from here, making this spot a good staging point for longer backpacking adventures along the Pacific Crest Trail. The surrounding terrain is rocky plateau with intermittent pine and hemlock. It's a great viewing spot for birds of prey who frequent the surrounding peaks.

Facilities: Each site has a picnic table and a fire ring. Running water and vault toilets are available nearby.

Getting there: Drive east on Highway 36 from Susanville to the town of Chester, then get on Warner Valley Road heading north for an additional 6.5 miles. At Forest Road 311, turn left and continue another 2.5 miles to the campground.

55 Elam Campground 🌲🌲🌲🌲🌲

There is a series of small campgrounds along Highway 32 between Butte Mountain and Mill Creak Plateau, all on or near the banks of Deer Creek. The creek and its smaller tributaries are the main attraction in this area, a rocky and grassy

sites	15
🏕️ 🚐	No hookups, RVs to 22 feet
open	May through October
reservations	None
contact	Almanor Ranger District, 530/258-2141

meadow plateau set at 4,600 feet with lush pine and fir forests closest to the water. Slate Creek, Elam Creek, Alder Creek, and Swamp Creek flow into the Deer Creek basin at this location—take your pick of good flyfishing spots during the summer. Keep note, however, that the game refuge area is just west of Highway 32, and during the autumn hunters use this part of the forest, camps included. Because of the relatively easy access to Elam and other camps from the highway, this place is popular with RVers. If you're looking for something more remote and out of the way, find a better hidden corner.

Facilities: Each site has a picnic table and a fire ring. Running water and vault toilets are available nearby.

Getting there: From Susanville, drive east on Highway 36 for 40 miles to the intersection with Highway 32. Go south for 3 miles on Highway 32 to the campground, which is on the west side of the road.

56 Alder Campground 🌲🌲🌲🌲🌲

Let's keep this spot our little secret. Of the half dozen small campgrounds in the Deer Creek drainage, Alder is by far the place to be if you're a tent camper. The reasons are simple: It's small, it's quiet, it's hidden, and RVs can't get in. During the spring, Round Valley Creek and Deer Creek are running at full volume with ice-cold snowmelt; this creates a wonderful, lush energy in the forested plateau. Fishing is particularly good here during the summer for browns and rainbows, as is the case all along the Highway 32 corridor. Humboldt Peak and Colby Mountain are both nearby and are suitable places to break in the hiking shoes. Mill Creek Plateau to the north is also a great spot to see the high mountain wildflower blooms during the spring. The campground is a dark, quiet, big-sky kind of place where you can relax with the sound of rushing water and the wind through the trees—and wish you never had to leave. Note, however, that this part of the forest is not a convenient staging point for Lassen Volcanic National Park. Stop here to check out for a while and stay in one place—not during one of those trips where you're trying to get a turbo tour of everything.

sites	5

open	April through November
reservations	None
contact	Almanor Ranger District, 530/258-2141

Facilities: Each site has a picnic table and a fire ring. Running water and vault toilets are available nearby.

Getting there: From Susanville, drive east on Highway 36 for 40 miles to the intersection with Highway 32. Go south for 9 miles on Highway 32 to the campground.

57 Juniper Lake Campground 🌲🌲🌲🌲🌲

Thousands of years of volcanic activity created the rocky plateau known as the Lassen region and nowhere is the entrancing regeneration of the landscape more accessible than at Lassen Volcanic National Park. There are seven campgrounds within the park boundaries and numerous others in the national forest outside the park. Of the seven, however, the small, quiet lakeside setting at Juniper Lake is far superior to the others for a variety of reasons. First, the campground is remote—far from the busy main entrances of the national park that attract the most day visitors. Of course, because there is no RV access here, tent campers rule. Trail connections to the Pacific Crest Trail that cut through the northern boundaries of the park are easily accessed from Juniper, as are trails to two nearby peaks, Fairfield and Crater Butte. Sweeping views of the volcanic preserve are had from the peaks, or from Inspiration Point, a shorter hike accessed from the northeast corner of the lake.

sites	20

open	May through October
reservations	None
contact	Lassen Volcanic National Park, 530/595-3262

Facilities: Each site has a picnic table and a fire ring. Pit toilets are available nearby. There is no running water so be sure to either pack in enough to last your entire stay or come prepared to treat creek water.

Getting there: From Susanville, take Highway 36 east to Chester. Drive north about 1 mile on Warner Valley Road to the Chester/Juniper Lake Road intersection. Turn right and continue another 10 miles to the campground and lake.

58 Cool Springs Campground 🌲🌲🌲

What makes this small, quiet campground on the eastern banks of Butt Valley Reservoir a smart choice is its seclusion from the busy water sports areas on adjacent Lake

sites	32
🏕️ 🚐	No hookups, RVs to 36 feet
open	May through October
reservations	None
contact	Pacific Gas & Electric Company, 916/923-7142

Almanor. The lake is a fraction the size of Almanor but has just one other campground on its banks, a fair distance away. It also attracts far fewer day visitors than its sister lake. Butt Creek and the north fork of the Feather River are nearby for those who want to try a little flyfishing with the lake action. Water levels are usually best in the spring and early summer months.

Facilities: Each site has a picnic table and a fire ring. Running water and vault toilets are available nearby.

Getting there: From Susanville, drive west on Highway 36 through the town of Chester, passing Lake Almanor. Turn south on Highway 89 and proceed 5 miles to the Prattville/Butt Reservoir Road turnoff to the left. The campground is straight ahead.

Other Lassen Area Campgrounds

In the Eagle Lake Ranger District, 530/257-4188, Butte Creek Campground (12 sites for tents or RVs, no hookups, RVs to 22 feet) is a pretty and quiet spot on the banks of the creek for which it is named. No running water is available and the setting is quite primitive. Crater Lake Campground (21 sites for tents only), another pleasant and quiet spot on Crater Mountain, is set in nosebleed country at 6,800 feet. Want to get away from it all? This could be the place. Bogard Campground (20 sites for tents or RVs, no hookups, RVs to 31 feet) is located on the banks of Pine Creek and is popular for trout action.

One large campground in Lassen Volcanic National Park, 530/595-3262, is Summit Lake Campground (100 sites for tents or RVs, no hookups, RVs to 32 feet), a bit crowded during the summer but in a pleasant waterfront setting and a great way to see the park. Manzanita Lake Camp (184 sites for tents or RVs, no hookups, RVs to 36 feet) is the most popular campground in the park because of its proximity to visitor centers and services, but it's plenty crowded and noisy—especially during the summer. Reservations are not accepted at any of the national park campgrounds here.

Another good spot in the Almanor Ranger District, 530/258-2141, is along the Highway 32 corridor in the Deer Creek drainage at Potato Patch Campground (20 sites for tents or RVs, no hookups, RVs to 22 feet), a great spot for swimming in the mid- to late summer and a good trout location that is easy to reach.

Central State

Remember the V8 motor?

Back in the good old days—before they took the lead out of gasoline and started pushing little hotbox Hondas for their fuel efficiency—even our mothers and grandmothers tooled around with the mighty power of a V8 motor under the hood. The most innocent wood-paneled station wagon packed enough power back then to blow the doors off anything on the road today. Well, if you miss those days when everybody drove gas guzzlers that could pull a houseboat up a hill without breaking 2000 RPMs, it's time for a trip to the Delta, the Sacramento Valley, or the San Joaquin Valley.

The middle of the state is a blue-collar recreational playground, the kind of place where the 1970s never ended. The cars and trucks are big and American, the beer is Budweiser and Coors, and the ski boats crackle like thunder while the choking smell of exhaust and gasoline trail behind them. This is aluminum fishing boat country too, and the kind of place where camper rigs contain all the trappings of your typical suburban tract home. The World War II generation plays here and retires here—and their children and grandchildren come along to keep them company.

All of this aside, however, the "middle of the state" is simply a great place to launch a boat and make for the waters. The network of rivers and sloughs between Sacramento and Stockton in particular are a water sports paradise. Nowhere will you find more public campgrounds at the water's edge, complete with public boat ramps, full-service marinas, and swimming beaches. While the fishing can be less than stupendous in this area because of water conditions during the summer, it is indeed a great place for windsurfers, water-skiers, and anyone who enjoys being next to the water.

If you enjoy water sports, fishing, lazing around the water's edge with a beer in your hand, and being able to wear white socks with dress shoes and shorts to dinner, the Central State region may indeed be worth checking out. Most camp facilities are at riverside, on sloughs, or at reservoirs. Boating access is easy everywhere. Be prepared, though, for an overabundance of asphalt and a lack of tree shade at most places, as getting a boat on the water is the top priority here—not communing with nature.

Central State

1. Whiskeytown Lake
2. McCumber Reservoir Campground
3. Woodson Bridge State Recreation Area Campground
4. Lake Red Bluff Campground
5. Colusa/Sacramento River State Recreation Area
6. Englebright Lake Boat-in
7. Sandy Beach County Park
8. Westgate Landing County Park
9. Brannan Island State Recreation Area
10. Dos Reis Park
11. Caswell Memorial State Park
12. George Hatfield State Park
13. San Luis Reservoir State Recreation Area

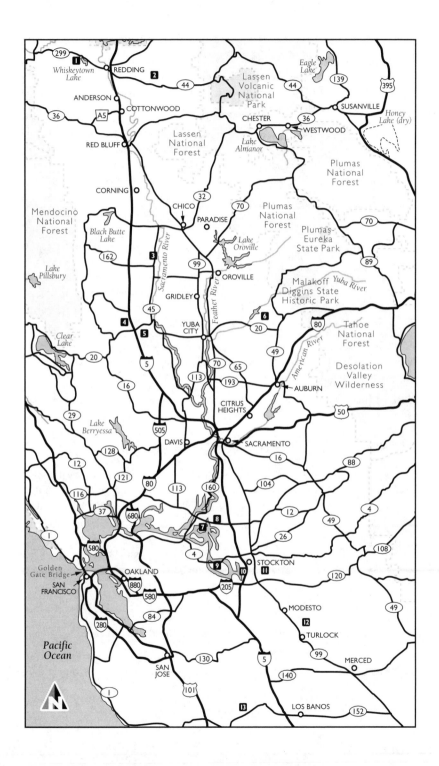

Sacramento Valley

❶ Whiskeytown Lake 🌲🌲🌲

Bigger isn't always better—especially when you're talking about campgrounds. For this reason, visitors to Whiskeytown Lake should camp at the Brandy Creek Campground on the lake's south shore rather than Oak Bottom Campground on the north shore. Brandy Creek has 45 of the 195 sites found at the lake. The lake is a popular water sports and fishing spot year round, but hikers looking for a staging point into the Shasta and Trinity wilderness areas may also find it inviting. The campground caters mostly to the RV set though; so if you're expecting a quiet wilderness experience, pass this one by. The elevation is 1,500 feet.

sites	195
🏕️🚐	No hookups, RVs to 30 feet
open	All year
reservations	Up to 240 days in advance; Forest Service Reservations, 800/280-2267
contact	Whiskeytown Unit, Shasta-Trinity National Forest, 530/241-6584

Facilities: Each site has a picnic table and a fire pit. Running water, flush toilets, and showers are provided. Public boat ramps, a full-service marina, and boat rentals are on hand.

Getting there: From Redding, drive west on Highway 299 for 10 miles to the lake.

❷ McCumber Reservoir Campground 🌲🌲🌲

Fishing for rainbow trout is the main draw at this small, pretty lake near Lassen National Forest. You will need a float tube or rowboat to get out on the water, since motors are not allowed. The sites are well cared for and the campground laid out nicely. The surrounding terrain is mixed forest with high peaks visible. In summer, this is one of those lazy, quiet spots perfect for unwinding. Although the campground is not well known, it fills up easily on weekends during the summer because of its size. Get there early. The elevation is 2,500 feet.

sites	20
🏕️🚐	No hookups, RVs to 22 feet
open	All year
reservations	None
contact	Pacific Gas & Electric Company, 916/923-7142

Facilities: Each site has a picnic table and a fire grill. Vault toilets and running water are available. There is a boat ramp nearby.

Getting there: From Redding, drive east on Highway 44 for 12 miles, then go left on Lake McCumber Road. The lake is 5 miles out.

③ Woodson Bridge State Recreation Area Campground 🌲🌲🌲🌲

These thick oak woodlands hugging the banks of a wide section of the Sacramento River are a terrific place to seek shady refuge from the valley heat during the summer. Woodson Bridge covers 250 acres on both sides of the river; the two sections of the park are connected by a bridge. Fishing for salmon, steelhead, striped bass, catfish, and blue gill is best in the late summer and autumn. Summer is also waterplay time; coved areas on the shore are perfect for wading but there is plenty of room for skiers as well. Bird-watchers looking for any variety of migratory species known to travel along the Pacific Flyway also won't be disappointed here during the winter or spring flight. The campsites are situated in a pleasant forested area, and are spacious.

sites	41
🏕️ 🚐	No hookups, RVs to 30 feet
open	All year
reservations	Up to 8 weeks in advance; California State Parks, 800/444-7275
contact	Woodson Bridge State Recreation Area, 530/839-2112

Facilities: Each site has a picnic table and a fire grill. Running water, showers, and flush toilets are available. A public boat ramp and a marina are nearby.

Getting there: From Corning at I-5, drive south on South Avenue for 10 miles to the recreation area on the river.

④ Lake Red Bluff Campground 🌲🌲🌲🌲

Bird-watchers, waterskiers, and those interested in studying the unique river ecosystem of the Sacramento Valley will enjoy this quiet spot on the banks of the Lake Red Bluff. The lake has 15 miles of shoreline behind the Red Bluff diversion dam on the Sacramento River. There are day-use facilities for picnickers and swimmers, but the campground has plenty of quiet time since there is no through traffic. The best wildlife viewing is during the spring and autumn.

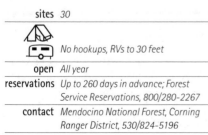

sites	30
🏕️ 🚐	No hookups, RVs to 30 feet
open	All year
reservations	Up to 260 days in advance; Forest Service Reservations, 800/280-2267
contact	Mendocino National Forest, Corning Ranger District, 530/824-5196

There is an observation platform where spawning salmon can be seen climbing man-made fish ladders to get past the dam.

Facilities: Each site has a picnic table and a fire pit. Running water, flush toilets, and showers are available. There is a public boat ramp nearby for river access. You can also use the lake campground as a staging area for hikes in the nearby 30,000-acre Ishi Wilderness.

Getting there: Drive I-5 to Red Bluff and exit the freeway at Sale Lane. Head south 2 miles on Sale Lane to the park campground entrance on the left.

⑤ Colusa/Sacramento River State Recreation Area 🌲🌲🌲🌲

There are 67 acres of willow trees, meadows, and marshes on the banks of the Sacramento River here—and rumor has it that John Muir himself camped at this very spot during one of his famous boating excursions through the valley. The key to enjoying this place, however, is to arrive at the correct time of year for your favorite activities. Bird-watchers enjoy viewing a wide variety of waterfowl migrating along the Pacific Flyway in winter and seeing roosting birds in spring. In summer, this is ski country—don't go anywhere near this place unless you're into fast-moving fiberglass and loud motors. In fall, the steelhead and salmon fishing can be superb here, and things begin to calm down. The campground is small and quiet.

sites	15
🏕️🚐	No hookups, RVs to 30 feet
open	All year
reservations	Up to 8 weeks in advance; California State Parks, 800/444-7275
contact	Colusa/Sacramento River State Recreation Area, 530/458-4927

Facilities: Each site has a picnic table and a fire grill. Running water, flush toilets, and showers are nearby. A public boat ramp and a bait and tackle shop are on site.

Getting there: From Sacramento, go 32 miles north on I-5 to the Highway 20 intersection. Drive east on Highway 20 for 10 miles to Colusa. Turn right on 10th Street and continue a short distance to the recreation area.

⑥ Englebright Lake Boat-in 🌲🌲🌲🌲

During the Gold Rush years, Englebright Dam was built on the Yuba River to help capture tailings from upstream mining operations. The result was this unusual 9-mile-long lake in the foothills near Marysville. Today the lake is used mostly for water storage and recreation. All sites are for boat-in access only but those without boats can easily rent them at the lake's marina. Englebright is primarily a water

sites	*100*

open	*All year*
reservations	*None*
contact	*Englebright Lake, 530/962-1600*

sports destination; on the lower 5 miles of the lake speedboats and water-skiers are present throughout the summer. The surface area is 815 acres when the water level is at normal. The lake is stocked with rainbow trout, black bass, catfish, sunfish, and Kokanee salmon and is a suitable place to teach young children how to cast out. The elevation is 2,100 feet. This area gets very hot during the summer.

Facilities: Each site has a picnic table and a fire grill. Pit toilets are available nearby. Boat rentals are available near the park entrance. All sites are reachable only by boat.

Getting there: From Marysville drive east on Highway 20 for 20 miles. Turn left on Marysville Road and continue another 10 miles to the lake.

The Delta

⑦ Sandy Beach County Park ▲▲▲

The small, little-known camping area on the Sacramento River near the Rio Vista Bridge is a slight improvement over Brannan Island (see below), but still if your focus is not getting on the water in some kind of boat you may find the experience

sites	40
	No hookups, no RV limit
open	All year
reservations	Sandy Beach County Park, 707/374-2097
contact	Sandy Beach County Park, 707/374-2097

a bit disappointing. The facility is simply a lot of asphalt with lawn and trees, and not very well maintained. During our inspection, we also noticed a few old, abandoned RVs that looked like they belonged in a junkyard. As a consolation, the beach can be quite nice—especially on hot days.

Sandy Beach Campground near Rio Vista has easy river access.

Facilities: Each site has a picnic table and a fire ring. Running water, flush toilets, and showers are available nearby. There is a public boat ramp.

Getting there: From I-80 at Fairfield, drive east on Highway 12 for 15 miles to Rio Vista. Use the Main Street exit and continue two blocks to Second Street. At Beach Street, turn east and continue to the end, where the park entrance is located.

⑧ Westgate Landing County Park 🌲🌲🌲

Water access camping spots on the Delta can seem crowded and noisy, but this one is small enough and far enough off the beaten path that you won't have to worry too much about being overrun. The sites are well cared for and water access is easy. Water skiing, fishing, and boating are the main activities out this way since most of the surrounding land is in private hands and used for farming. The Delta is flat, hot, and sprawling during the summer, its sloughs labyrinthine. Once you're on the water, however, this region of the state takes on the lazy feel of a bayou in the South. Small resort settlements with green lawns line the riverbanks and shores; retirees sprawled out on lawn chairs wave and smile as you go by. Along the sloughs and highways you will also see another throwback to times past: old-fashioned drawbridges, which in other parts of the state are rapidly being replaced by elevated highway over-crossings.

sites	14
🏕️ 🚐	No hookups, RVs to any length
open	All year
reservations	None
contact	San Joaquin County Parks, 209/953-8800

Facilities: Each site has a picnic table and a fire pit. Flush toilets, running water, and showers are available nearby. There are guest slips and a public boat ramp.

Getting there: From I-80 in Fairfield, drive east on Highway 12 for 24 miles through and beyond Rio Vista to Terminous. Turn left on Glasscock Road and continue north 2 miles to the park entrance, which is at the end of the road.

⑨ Brannan Island State Recreation Area 🌲🌲

If you have a boat and want a decent place to camp out for the weekend while having fun on the Delta, this is a reasonable spot to set up camp. The campground, however, is little more than a vast expanse of asphalt with scattered lawn here and there. It very much has the feel of a parking lot, and can get pretty noisy. Again, unless your focus is boating, pass this one by because it's not at all peaceful.

sites	*100*
🏕️🚐	*No hookups, RVs to 36 feet*
open	*All year*
reservations	*Up to 8 weeks in advance; California State Parks, 800/444-7275*
contact	*Brannan Island State Recreation Area, 916/777-6671*

Facilities: Each site has a picnic table and a fire grill. Running water, flush toilets, and showers are available nearby. There is a public boat ramp.

Getting there: From I-80 in Fairfield, drive east on Highway 12 for 15 miles to Rio Vista. Turn right on Highway 160 and continue west for 3.5 miles to the park entrance on the left side of the road.

Brannan Island State Recreation Area is most popular with boaters.

⑩ Dos Reis Park 🌲🌲🌲

While it is on the east edge of the Delta away from the most popular fishing and boating areas, this small little-known county park on the banks of the San Joaquin River is a much quieter and less crowded spot—especially when compared to Brannan Island (see above) and others. Numerous private islands are found in the area, some long abandoned and without the "no trespassing" signs that make a little squatter's picnic out of the question for those unwilling to take chances. Note, though, that during the heat of summer many of these islands catch fire, leaving the park and anything upwind in a smoky haze. During fire season, you will be tempted to just keep heading north for more lush surroundings.

sites	25
🏕️🚐	No hookups, RVs to any length
open	All year
reservations	None
contact	San Joaquin County Parks, 209/953-8800

Facilities: Each site has a picnic table and a fire grill. Flush toilets, running water, and showers are available. There is a public boat ramp on the river.

Getting there: From Stockton, drive south on I-5 for 3 miles to the Lathrop Road exit. Go north a short distance to Dos Reis Road. Turn left and proceed to the end of the road and the park entrance.

San Joaquin Valley

⑪ Caswell Memorial State Park 🌲🌲🌲🌲

Two centuries ago, before Europeans began settling California's Central Valley and diking off huge swaths of land, you would have found vast areas of riparian habitat—sprawling oak forests and free-flowing rivers spilling over their banks during the spring snowmelt and creating a vast floodway. While most of the area looks nothing like it did before, Caswell Memorial State Park is virtually unchanged. The area is 250 acres of oak woodlands and floodplain at the confluence of the Stanislaus and San Joaquin Rivers. Good fishing spots

sites	65
🏕️ 🚐	No hookups, RVs to 24 feet
open	All year
reservations	Up to 8 weeks in advance; California State Parks, 800/444-7275
contact	Caswell Memorial State Park, 209/599-3810

Along the shore of the San Joaquin River you'll find hundreds of hidden spots for quiet reflection.

and swimming holes are found along its beaches, and a fantastic nature trail through the oaks is a favorite among bird-watchers. Many rare species are found here, including the endangered San Joaquin kit fox and more that 200 different birds. There are interpretive tours during the summer. The campground is rather large and uninviting, but its surroundings make up for that.

Facilities: Each site has a picnic table and a fire pit. Running water, flush toilets, and showers are available. There is a public boat ramp but no marina or fishing equipment.

Getting there: From Stockton, go 15 miles south on I-5 to Austin Road. Head east 5 miles to the campground entrance.

12 George Hatfield State Park 🌲🚶

This small, quiet campground is actually on an island surrounded by a split in the Merced River, right near where it meets the San Joaquin. Native American artifacts are found among the sprawling riparian terrain. Watch out during heavy weather events, as this area can easily flood. Bird-watching here is exceptional, as are fishing and swimming. The campground, however, is out in the middle of nowhere. If you're stopping for a night or two while on your way to the Yosemite region, this area is good for a change of pace—but it stops being interesting pretty quickly. Note that a large group camp near the main campground is often overrun.

sites	20
🏕️🚐	No hookups, RVs to 32 feet
open	All year
reservations	Up to 8 weeks in advance; California State Parks, 800/444-7275
contact	George Hatfield State Park, 209/826-1196

Facilities: Each site has a picnic table and a fire grill. Running water, flush toilets, and showers are available nearby. There is a public boat ramp and small marina/store.

Getting there: From Modesto, go south on I-5 for 14 miles to Stur Road. Go east 4 miles to where Stur becomes Hills Ferry Road. Continue another 6.5 miles to the campground/park entrance.

13 San Luis Reservoir State Recreation Area

This campground is little more than a sprawling parking lot for enormous RVs. If you're a car camper, backpacker, or anyone looking for some semblance of quiet and being in the outdoors, there is really no reason at all for you to stop here.

sites	500
	50 sites with electrical hookups; 350 RVs to 28 feet, 80 RVs to 32 feet, 50 RVs to any length
open	All year
reservations	Up to 8 weeks in advance, California State Parks, 800/444-7275
contact	San Luis Reservoir State Recreation Area, 209/826-1196

Facilities: Each site has a picnic table and a fire grill. Running water, flush toilets, and showers are available nearby. There are public boat ramps, a full-service marina, and store at the lake.

Getting there: From Los Banos, drive west on Highway 152 for 12 miles to the lake site.

Northern Sierra

For some of us it's the cold, clean mountain water cascading through countless high mountain canyons, the tall pines swaying when Delta breezes kick up in the afternoon, the morning sunlight being shattered into a kaleidoscope by tree branches, or the smell of wood fires teasing us with the scent of outdoor living. All this, and much more, draws us again and again to the Northern Sierra.

Here the outdoor adventurer is faced with waterfalls and granite walls, scars in the landscape caused by nineteenth-century gold miners, and wild rivers spilling into the world's largest man-made lakes. And then there's the crown jewel, Lake Tahoe, whose cobalt hue and legendary clarity make it an entrancing place. Tahoe means "big water" in the language of Washoe Indians, who inhabited this area before Europeans arrived in 1844. But the Tahoe and Northern Sierra region encompasses much more than the popular ski resorts and water sports areas around the lake. Indeed there are thousands of acres of high mountain forest-lands stretching from Plumas to the southern edge of the Cascade range.

What you choose to do with all of that room is entirely up to you. Between Plumas and El Dorado National Forests in the Sierra foothills and the high country forestlands of the immediate Tahoe region, there are five major rivers, hundreds of small lakes, an abundance of campgrounds, and enough space to hold you when you feel the need to load up the camping gear and disappear. One thing we can say for certain is that there is always a hidden corner of the Northern Sierra waiting to be discovered.

Dive from the rocks at D. L. Bliss State Park on the Tahoe lakeshore, lounge lazily at the nearly deserted Ice House Reservoir or its neighbor, Wrights Lake, in El Dorado National Forest. Take a wrong turn off Carson Pass and drop in at Silver Lake; cast a line and take a snooze. The campgrounds in this region run the gamut from busy and brimming with Baywatch beach action to being so remote you'll forget what it feels like to hit the snooze alarm five times in the morning or be woken up by the noise of a garbage truck on your street.

Rip this chapter out of the book and stuff it in one of those extra pockets in your pack. We'll hold your calls.

Northern Sierra

1. Loafer Creek Campground
2. Haskins Valley Campground
3. Whitehorse Campground
4. Sundew Campground
5. Little Beaver Campground
6. Milsap Bar Campground
7. Plumas-Eureka State Park Campground
8. Boulder Creek
9. Lone Rock Campground
10. Crocker Campground
11. Grizzly Campground
12. Nevada County Fairgrounds
13. South Yuba Campground
14. Malakoff Diggins State Historic Park Campground
15. Lake Spaulding Campground
16. Canyon Creek Camp
17. Cold Creek Campground
18. Lower Little Truckee Camp
19. Davies Creek Campground
20. Logger Campground
21. Lakeside Campground
22. Lodgepole Camp
23. Donner Memorial State Park
24. North Fork Campground
25. French Meadows Campground
26. Sugar Pine Point State Park
27. Tahoe State Recreation Area Campground
28. D. L. Bliss State Park Campground
29. Emerald Bay State Park
30. Fallen Leaf Campground
31. Auburn State Recreation Area
32. Peninsula Campground
33. Folsom Lake
34. Sly Park Campgrounds
35. Lake Almanor Campground
36. Sand Flat Campground
37. Ice House Campground
38. Wrights Lake Campground
39. Loon Lake Camp
40. Sunset Campground
41. Hope Valley Campground
42. Kit Carson Campground
43. Caples Lake
44. Kirkwood Lake
45. Silver Lake

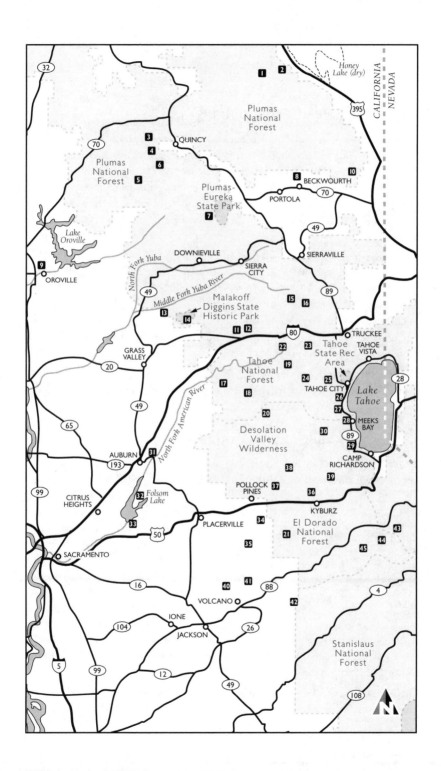

Plumas Region

❶ Loafer Creek Campground 🌲

Yet another big asphalt slab on the banks of a reservoir—packed to capacity. The dam on the Feather River, at 770 feet, is the largest earth-filled dam in the world. The lake, a popular bass fishing destination covers 28,000 acres. While it is a fun boating and swimming spot for day use, camping here can be a bit frustrating, as there are far too many people and way too much noise. Those who really want to get in the water should just use the lake as day visitors and find somewhere smaller and nicer to set up camp.

sites	140
🏕️🚐	No hookups, RVs to 42 feet
open	All year
reservations	Up to 8 weeks in advance; California State Parks, 800/444-7275
contact	Lake Oroville State Recreation Area, 530/538-2200

Facilities: Each site has a picnic table and a fire ring. Running water, flush toilets, and showers are available. Nearby are a public boat ramp, a full-service marina with boat rentals, and a general store.

Getting there: From Oroville, go 1.5 miles north on Highway 162 to Loafer Creek Road. Turn west and proceed a short distance to the park/campground entrance.

❷ Haskins Valley Campground 🌲🌲🌲

Thar she blows! Years backs someone started a bizarre "Lock Ness monster" rumor about this small, out-of-the way reservoir owned by Pacific Gas & Electric. As finny as the story was (and obviously a hoax), the end result wasn't so great: Now everybody knows about the place. Summer weekends and holidays are a lost cause here unless you head out early enough to nab a site. Swimming, fishing, hiking, and bird-watching will keep you plenty occupied there—but don't count on seeing any sea monsters. That old story was probably made up by the same guy who invented Bigfoot (another local monster we have yet to see in the flesh). The elevation is 5,700 feet.

sites	70
🏕️🚐	No hookups, RVs to 32 feet
open	All year
reservations	None
contact	Pacific Gas & Electric Company, 916/923-7142

Facilities: Each site has a picnic table and a fire ring. Running water and vault toilets are available. A public boat ramp and a general store are nearby.

Getting there: From Quincy, go 17 miles west on Bucks Lake Road to Bucks Lake. The campground is on the right-hand side of the road.

❸ Whitehorse Campground 🌲🌲🌲

Backpackers looking to explore the woods in the Bucks Lake Wilderness Area, at Plumas National Forest, enjoy staging from this small, quiet campground in the forest just a few miles from the shores of the lake itself. There is far less noise and human activity here than at the other campgrounds on the lakeshore, and because of its relatively small size it can be quite peaceful, particularly at night when traffic passing through on the access road to the lake calms down a bit. It is a good idea to make reservations between Memorial Day and Labor Day, as summer weekends and holidays tend to fill up, especially if the lakeside sites are taken. On off-peak weekends, however, this is a great spot, as you can have the best of both worlds—the high country and the lake waters. The elevation is 5,200 feet.

sites	*21*
🏕️🚐	*No hookups, RVs to 32 feet*
open	*May through October*
reservations	*Up to 240 days in advance; Forest Service Reservations, 800/280-2267*
contact	*Mount Hough Ranger District, 530/283-0555*

Facilities: Each site has a picnic table and a fire ring. Running water and piped toilets are available nearby. A public boat ramp and a general store are nearby.

Getting there: From Quincy, drive 15 miles west on Bucks Lake Road toward the shore of Bucks Lake. The campground is 2 miles before the lakeshore on the right-hand side of the road.

❹ Sundew Campground 🌲🌲🌲

Bucks Lake Dam is another one of those engineering marvels, and this small, quiet campground on a secluded section of the lakeshore is a great vantage point from which to enjoy not only the dam but both the upper and lower lakes. Fishing, swimming, hiking, boating, and bird-watching are quite good here. There are some unusual nesting colonies of shorebirds at either end of the dam structure. A small cove just west of the campground is a great bluegill spot. Bucks

sites	*18*
🏕️🚐	*No hookups, RVs to 36 feet*
open	*May through October*
reservations	*Up to 240 days in advance; Forest Service Reservations, 800/280-2267*
contact	*Mount Hough Ranger District, 530/283-0555*

Mountain, Bald Eagle Mountain, and Buck Creek, which are excellent spots for hiking and flyfishing, are all nearby. The elevation is 5,200 feet.

Facilities: Each site has a picnic table and a fire ring. Running water and vault toilets are available. A public boat ramp and a general store are nearby.

Getting there: From Quincy, take Bucks Lake Road and head 10 miles west toward Buck Lake, but instead of continuing directly to the lakeshore turn right on Bucks Lake Dam Road and go another 4 miles to the campground.

⑤ Little Beaver Campground 🌲🌲

Day hikers looking for a nice spot to stage a trek up the 6,200-foot Bald Mountain will enjoy this sprawling lakeside campground (or one of four others nearby), as it is a nice place to stash gear and rest at the end of the day. We may be starting to sound like a broken record, however, when we issue this warning: This place is a lot of asphalt, vehicles, and noise. Fishing for rainbow trout is good during the summer, but you will need a boat to get to the nicest fishing holes. Despite its size, the campground has a tendency to fill to capacity during the summer and on holidays. The elevation is 5,100 feet.

sites	122
🏕️🚐	No hookups, RVs to 36 feet
open	May through October
reservations	Up to 240 days in advance; Forest Service Reservations, 800/280-2267
contact	Mount Hough Ranger District, 530/283-0555

Facilities: Each site has a picnic table and a fire ring. Running water and flush toilets are available. A public boat ramp and a general store are nearby.

Getting there: From Quincy, go east on Highway 162 about 8.5 miles to Quincy/La Porte Road. Turn right and continue a short distance to the campground entrance on the right.

⑥ Milsap Bar Campground 🌲🌲🌲

If you're looking for a convenient spot to put in for a hot rafting trip down the middle fork of the Feather River, this large, well-equipped campground is the perfect spot, as there are several good Class II and Class III runs downstream. Stay here only if the rafting is the focus of your desire, however, as getting a serene camping experience at this spot is quite difficult because of the campground's size and resultant crowds. Fishing on the river for steelhead and salmon is quite good in winter, but the campground doesn't stay open for the best part of the fishing season. The elevation is 1,600 feet.

sites	223

	No hookups, RVs to 36 feet
open	May through October
reservations	Up to 240 days in advance; Forest Service Reservations, 800/280-2267
contact	Mount Hough Ranger District, 530/283-0555

Facilities: Each site has a picnic table and a fire ring.

Getting there: From Quincy, go south on Bald Rock Road for half a mile to Milsap Bar Road. Turn left and go another 7.5 miles to the campground, which is on your right.

7 Plumas-Eureka State Park Campground

More than three years after the famous discovery at Sutter's Mill east of Sacramento that touched other California Gold Rush, a second gold strike at this location in May 1959 touched off a second scramble for gold on Eureka Peak, the crown jewel of this sprawling state preserve in the Sierra Nevada foothills. Today, this spot offers a variety of activities for outdoorspeople. There are two lakes and a creek for fishing. Bluegill and rainbow trout action is best during the summer. Bird-watchers also flock to the surrounding forests to catch a glimpse of rare woodpeckers and humming birds in the surrounding pines. Parents love to bring their children to this location to learn about Gold Rush history, as there is a museum and numerous displays explaining the mining operations that existed here through the mid- to late nineteenth century. The campground is very pleasant and well equipped. Because there are showers and flush toilet, the sites get snapped up pretty quickly on weekends and holidays. Be sure to make reservations during the peak season between Memorial Day and Labor Day. The elevation is 5,400 feet.

sites	64
	No hookups, RVs to 31 feet
open	May 1 to October 15
reservations	California State Parks, 800/444-7275
contact	Plumas-Eureka State Park, 530/ 836-2380

Facilities: Each site has a picnic table and a fire ring. Running water, flush toilets, and showers are available. There is an RV sanitary dump station. The nearest store is in Quincy.

Getting there: From Quincy, drive east on Highway 70/89 for 18 miles to the intersection with Highway 89. Head south on 89 to County Road A half a mile away. The campground and park entrances are on your right, along the county road, clearly marked from the highway.

⑧ Boulder Creek 🌲🌲🌲

This is one of two reasonably large, family-oriented campgrounds at Antelope Lake, another popular boating and fishing spot in this section of the Sierra Nevada. The campground caters mostly to large family groups with lots of equipment—especially RVs. Don't come here looking for silence and solace or you will be sorely disappointed. The 7,700-foot Clarks Peak nearby is a popular day hike. The elevation is 5,000 feet.

sites	73
🏕️🚐	No hookups, RVs to 32 feet
open	May through October
reservations	Up to 240 days in advance; Forest Service Reservations, 800/280-2267
contact	Mount Hough Ranger District, 530/283-0555

Facilities: Each site has a picnic table and a fire pit. Running water, flush toilets, and showers are available nearby. At the lake you will find a public boat ramp and a marina.

Getting there: From Susanville, go south on South Wheatherlow Road a short distance to Richmond Road. Turn right and continue for 4 miles. At Gold Run Road, turn left. After half a mile, turn left on Skyline Mountainway. After a short distance, turn right on Diamond Mountain Road and go for 4 miles, through Bear Valley, to Fruit Growers Road. The campground is a short distance ahead on the banks of the lake.

⑨ Lone Rock Campground 🌲🌲

Why they call it Antelope Lake is anyone's guess, because we've never seen an antelope within a 100-mile radius of this place. Lone Rock is, however, on the shores of a lake so-named. If you're looking for a place to launch the aluminum fishing boat and knock back a couple of Coors Lights, you'll be in heaven here. The campground tends to be noisy, and doesn't promote rest and relaxation. Just so we don't undersell it, though, you might find a quiet spot somewhere along the lakeshore if you put a boat on the water and putter far enough from ground zero. The elevation is 5,000 feet.

sites	84
🏕️🚐	No hookups, RVs to 32 feet
open	May through October
reservations	Up to 240 days in advance; Forest Service Reservations, (800) 280-2267
contact	Mount Hough Ranger District, (530) 283-0555

Facilities: Each site has a picnic table and a fire pit. Running water, flush toilets, and showers are nearby. You will find a public boat ramp and a marina at the lake.

Getting there: From Susanville, go south on South Wheatherlow Road a short distance to Richmond Road. Turn right and continue for 4 miles. At Gold Run Road, turn left. After half a mile, turn left on Skyline right on Mountainway. After a short distance, turn right on Diamond Mountain Road and go 4 miles, through Bear Valley, to Fruit Growers Road. The campground is a short distance ahead on the banks of the lake.

⑩ Crocker Campground 🌲🌲🌲🌲

This is one of four nice, relatively small, and quiet campgrounds in the Lake Davis area of Plumas National Forest—and a particularly good choice since it is tucked away in a quiet pine grove far from all the activity on the lake surface. Here, you can have your quiet nights by the fire and lazy days at creekside while the lake is just a short distance down the road. There are fewer day visitors to contend with and no noise from ski-boat motors. While there is RV access here, the campground is usually packed in with cars and tents only. Fishing is quite good not only on the lake, but also on nearby Grizzly Creek. The elevation is 5,800 feet.

sites	10
	No hookups, RVs to 34 feet
open	May through November
reservations	Up to 240 days in advance; Forest Service Reservations, 800/280-2267
contact	Beckwourth Ranger District, 530/836-2575

Facilities: Each site has a picnic table and fire ring. Vault toilets are available. There is no running water. Four public boat ramps are nearby.

Getting there: From Beckwourth, drive west on Highway 70 for half a mile to Grizzly Road. Turn north and proceed 7 miles to Crocker Mount Road. The campground is near the end of the road, within shouting distance of Lake Davis.

⑪ Grizzly Campground 🌲🌲🌲🌲

sites	53
	No hookups, RVs to 34 feet
open	May through October
reservations	Up to 240 days in advance; Forest Service Reservations, 800/280-2267
contact	Beckwourth Ranger District, 530/836-2575

What you give up in quiet and solitude at Crocker Campground (above) you make up for in fun and excitement at this much larger and more frequently used campground right on the shores of Lake Davis in Plumas National Forest. Water-skiers, swimmers, anglers, and people just looking to unwind in a nice alpine lake setting flock to this spot during the summer. Lakeshore marshes attract an eclectic variety of waterfowl. Day visitors tend to congregate en masse on this side of the lake since highway access is the easiest, so don't be surprised if strangers walk through your campsite during the day. The elevation is 5,900 feet.

Facilities: Each site has a picnic table and a fire ring. Running water and flush toilets are available nearby. Also nearby are a sanitary dump station, a boat launch, and a general store.

Getting there: From Beckwourth head half a mile east on Highway 70 to Grizzly Road and turn left. Continue 4 miles to Lake Davis and the campground entrance, which is clearly marked.

Other Plumas Area Campgrounds

There are more than a dozen campgrounds in the Plumas region in addition to the cross-section described above.

In the Quincy area, within the Mount Hough Ranger District, 530/283-0545, the others include North Fork Campground (20 sites for tents or RVs, no hookups, RVs to 24 feet) on the banks of the North Fork River in an area with good steelhead and salmon runs. Also in this area is Black Rock Campground (22 sites for tents or RVs, no hookups, RVs to 36 feet) at Little Grass Valley Reservoir. Also at Little Grass Valley Reservoir is Running Deer Campground (44 sites for tents or RVs, no hookups, RVs to 21 feet).

In the Susanville area, contact the Mount Hough Ranger District, 530/283-0555. Choices include the very large and very RV-friendly Almanor Campground (100 sites for tents or RVs, no hookups, RVs to 36 feet) in a popular boating area on the region's largest lake. More silence and solitude is had, however, at Last Chance Creek Campground nearby (14 sites for tents only), where the creek enters Lake Almanor.

In the Beckwourth area, contact the Beckwourth Ranger District, 530/836-2575, and consider Frenchman Campground (41 sites for tents or RVs, no hookups, RVs to 36 feet) on the shores of Frenchman Lake, a much quieter spot than Almanor.

At Lake Oroville, contact Lake Oroville State Recreation Area, 530/538-2200. Here Bidwell Canyon Campground (70 sites mainly for RVs, full hookups, RVs to 42 feet) is a rare find, since it is both a public campground and one with full amenities for RV campers. Just accept that it's basically a big flat asphalt area where very large rigs park. It is not recommended for tents.

Northern Gold Rush Country

12 Nevada County Fairgrounds 🌲

Unfortunately, the Nevada County Fairgrounds are a little more than a parking lot for RVs. If your idea of the great outdoors is something different, don't bother stopping here. It's just a place to stop the RV rig for a night or two before moving on to something a little more rustic.

sites	134
🚐	Full hookups, RVs to 42 feet
open	All year
reservations	Nevada County Fairgrounds, 530/273-6217
contact	Nevada County Fairgrounds, 530/273-6217

Facilities: Each site has a picnic table and a fire grill. There are flush toilets, showers, running water, and an RV disposal site provided.

Getting there: From Nevada City, go south on Golden Center Highway for 14 miles to Grass Valley. At Empire Street, exit and continue to the Highway 20 intersection. Follow Highway 20 a short distance to Mill Street. Turn right and proceed to the fairgrounds entrance.

13 South Yuba Campground 🌲🌲🌲🌲

Just downstream of the fabulous Malakoff Diggins State Historic Park (page 194) is a well-hidden, small, quiet campground near the banks of the south fork of the Yuba River. Fishing and swimming in the river and its tributaries or just melting into a favorite lounge chair or hammock with a good book are about all you'll want to do here. Farther downstream you may even want to do a little tubing or canoeing if water levels are high enough. Raccoons are aggressive in this area; be sure to lock food up, particularly at night.

sites	17
⛺ 🚐	No hookups, RVs to 30 feet
open	May to October
reservations	None
contact	U.S. Bureau of Land Management, 530/985-4474

Facilities: Each site has a picnic table and a fire grill. Piped water and pit toilets are available. The nearest services are in Nevada City.

Getting there: From Nevada City, go north half a mile on Coyote Road and turn right on North Bloomfield/Graniteville Road. Go 8 miles to the town of North Bloomfield. From there, turn right on Relief Hill Road and continue a short distance to the campground.

⑭ Malakoff Diggins State Historic Park Campground ▲▲▲▲

During the mad rush for gold that is the cornerstone of California history, huge hydraulic canons were used to wash away entire hillsides, and gold ore was extracted from the ensuing mud-flows. The result was not only vast wealth for those who got in early enough to stake a claim, but also blunt cliffs hundreds of feet high where once there had been rolling foothills of pine and fir. Here, the naked cliffs are a stark reminder of the magnitude of the Gold Rush's

sites	*32*
	No hookups, RVs to 25 feet
open	*May to October*
reservations	*Up to 8 weeks in advance; California State Parks, 800/444-7275*
contact	*Malakoff Diggins State Historic Park, 530/265-2740*

The Yuba River, just downstream of Malakoff Diggins State Park, carried tailings from hydraulic mining during the Gold Rush. The hillsides adjacent to the Malakoff camp-grounds still bear the historic scars.

effect on the foothills environment. The cliffs, still eroding, are a strangely beautiful scar in the hillsides, magnificent in their unusual grandeur. This is bear, mountain lion, coyote, and bobcat county, so come prepared to deal with wildlife and take proper precautions with food. There is a small lake near the campground, but fish aren't biting most of the time. The elevation is 3,400 feet.

Facilities: Each site has a picnic table and a fire grill. Running water and flush toilets are available. The nearest store is in North Bloomfield, and the nearest services are in Nevada City.

Getting there: From Nevada City, drive north half a mile on Coyote Road to North Bloomfield/Graniteville Road. Turn right and continue for 12 miles to the park entrance, which is on the right side of the road.

Truckee and Bowman Lake Region

⑮ Lake Spaulding Campground 🌲🌲🌲🌲

Just how deep can blue get? At Lake Spaulding you're going to find out soon enough. This pleasant emerald of a reservoir in the foothills east of Nevada City is a great place to unwind at the water's edge. So lazy is the feeling here that you'll hope you don't get a bite—because that will only mean you'll end up having to reel it in, and that may seem like work. The campground is small and well situated on the banks of the lake with a great view of surrounding forested hills and peaks.

sites	27
🏕️🚐	No hookups, RVs to 21 feet
open	May through October
reservations	None
contact	Pacific Gas & Electric Company, 916/923-7142

This is a good staging point for gold country expeditions, as some of the most impressive hydraulic mining sites are in the vicinity. History hikes are all the rage.

Facilities: Each site has a picnic table and a fire ring. Running water and vault toilets are available. There is a public boat ramp nearby.

Getting there: From Auburn, go east on I-80 for 26 miles to the Highway 20 exit at Yuba. Turn left and proceed 2 miles to Lake Spaulding Road. There, turn right and continue 200 feet to the campground.

⑯ Canyon Creek Camp 🌲🌲🌲

Parents can't go wrong with this spot. Kids love it! A popular gold panning spot near Bowman Lake, Canyon Creek Camp draws hordes of children during the summer, particularly those who are about the age that they are being taught California history in school. When school is in session, there could be a group milling around the creek because of a field trip. If you are lucky enough to get a site here on a weekend, though, you might find some peace and quiet. It is indeed a lovely spot in among the pines and firs in a cold-running creek carrying

sites	21
🏕️	
open	May through October
reservations	Up to 240 days in advance; Forest Service Reservations, 800/280-2267
contact	Nevada City Ranger District, 530/265-4531

snowmelt from surrounding peaks. Lake Faucherie is nearby. The elevation is 6,000 feet.

Facilities: Each site has a picnic table and a fire grill. Running water and vault toilets are available. There is a public boat ramp nearby. The nearest store is in Marsh Mill.

Getting there: From Marsh Mill, go 4 miles east on Meadow Lake Road. At the fork, veer left and continue a short distance to Bowman Lake. When you reach the lake, continue past to the campground, about 2 miles out.

⓱ Cold Creek Campground 🌲🌲🌲

Cold Creek brings icy snowmelt from the 7,085-foot Treasure Mountain and connects to the Truckee River here in a quiet and pleasant forested area very near some popular trails leading through Bear Valley. In winter, this is a popular snow sports area—the brave use the campground for snow camping during ski season but it is officially closed, so if you think you want to try it you weren't encouraged to do so by us. Cold Creek is a favorite steelhead or salmon spot during the autumn and winter runs. The campground is small enough and has a low enough RV length limit that you don't have to worry about it being overrun. Cottonwood Campground is just a short distance north if you find this one full. The elevation is 5,600 feet.

sites	13
🏕️🚐	No hookups, RVs to 21 feet
open	May through October
reservations	Up to 240 days in advance; Forest Service Reservations, 800/280-2267
contact	Truckee Ranger District, 530/587-3558

Facilities: Each site has a picnic table and a fire grill. Running water and vault toilets are available. There is a store in nearby Sierraville.

Getting there: From Truckee, take Highway 89 from the intersection with I-80 and drive north for 12 miles. The campground is on the left side of the road.

⓲ Lower Little Truckee Camp 🌲🌲🌲🌲

Take your pick. This small campground on the banks of a pretty, forested stretch of the Truckee River is within shouting distance of four popular lakes: Stampede, Independence, Boca, and Prosser. Those looking to visit several lakes over the course of a few days will do well to set up camp here. The spot is also a good summer hiking and backpacking staging point for those headed into the Sagahen Hills, Sardine Peak, or Treasure Mountain areas. The campground has great river

sites	15
	No hookups, RVs to 21 feet
open	May through October
reservations	Up to 240 days in advance; Forest Service Reservations, 800/280-2267
contact	Truckee Ranger District, 530/587-3558

access for flyfishers as well. The small RV size keeps monster rigs out, but the highway can be a little too close for comfort if you're looking for total silence and solitude. The elevation is 6,000 feet.

Facilities: Each site has a picnic table and a fire grill. Running water and vault toilets are available. The nearest general store is in Sierraville. There are public boat ramps at all of the aforementioned lakes.

Getting there: From Truckee, go north on Highway 89 for 7 miles. The campground is on the left side of the road.

⑲ Davies Creek Campground 🌲🌲🌲🌲

There is no running water and the toilets are a little more scary here, but if you really insist on camping at Stampede Reservoir you're definitely better off coming

sites	10
	No hookups, RVs to 36 feet
open	May through October
reservations	None
contact	U.S. Bureau of Land Management, 530/582-0120

here than cramming into Logger Campground (page 199) on weekends and holidays. Set in a small coved area on the lake's north shore, this small campground is just the spot to ground the aluminum fishing boat for the weekend. Davies Creek runs through Sardine Valley and cascades into the lake very near the campground. The fish don't bite often, but when they do this makes a great spot for teaching young ones to cast a line.

Facilities: Each site has a picnic table and a fire grill. There is no running water. Pit toilets are available. The nearest public boat ramp is at the south end of the lake.

Getting there: From Truckee, go 4 miles east on I-80 to the Boca/Hirschdale exit. Go left at Stampede Dam Road for 11 miles. At County Road S460 turn left and continue a short distance to the campground.

⑳ Logger Campground 🌲

Especially during the heat of summer, when everyone is looking for a place to take a dip, this expansive slab of pavement on the banks of Stampede Reservoir is

sites	252
🏕️🚐	No hookups, RVs to 38 feet
open	May through October
reservations	None
contact	U.S. Bureau of Land Management, 530/582-0120

a popular spot with RVers. The typical car camper, however, is going to be disappointed with this campground, since anywhere you can park hundreds of RVs all at the same time isn't going to seem much like the great outdoors. Want to waterski, swim, fish, or picnic at the water's edge? Then camp somewhere else and visit Stampede Reservoir during the day instead. The elevation is 6,000 feet.

Facilities: Each site has a picnic table, fire ring, piped water, showers, and flush toilets. There are disposal stations for RVs.

Getting there: From Truckee, go east on I-80 for 4 miles to the Boca/Hirschdale exit. Turn left on Stampede Dam Road and continue for 7 miles. At Dog Valley Road, turn left and continue a short distance to the campground entrance.

㉑ Lakeside Campground 🌲🌲🌲

As spooky as it may sound, this is the spot where the ill-fated Donner Party camped out when they ran into that severe winter in 1846 that wiped out so many. Today, the area is a popular swimming, boating, fishing, and picnicking spot for

sites	30
🏕️🚐	No hookups, RVs to 31 feet
open	May through October
reservations	Up to 240 days in advance; Forest Service Reservations, 800/280-2267
contact	Truckee Ranger District, 530/587-3558

day visitors and campers alike passing through the Truckee/Tahoe region. Lakeside Campground is one of three small, very pleasant camps on the shores of Prosser Reservoir. The surrounding terrain is primarily pine forest, with high mountain springs and creek canyons frequented by an array of interesting wildlife. Birdwatchers in particular enjoy Woodchoppers Spring just north of the campground. Water skiing is popular on the lake, as is fishing for catfish, striped bass, and bluegill. There is a group camp nearby. The elevation is 5,700 feet.

Facilities: Each site has a picnic table and a fire grill. Running water and vault toilets are available. There is a public boat ramp nearby. The nearest store is in Hobart Mills.

Getting there: From Truckee, take Highway 89 from the I-80 junction and drive north for 3 miles. At Hobart Mills, turn right and proceed a short distance to the campground.

22 Lodgepole Camp 🌲🌲🌲🌲🌲

Push your canoe out onto the placid waters of Lake Valley Reservoir on a still, sunny summer morning and glide into a picture-perfect backdrop of forested hills in high surrounding high mountain peaks. This small, pretty lake lies in the

sites	20
🏕️ 🚐	No hookups, RVs to 21 feet
open	May through October
reservations	None
contact	Pacific Gas & Electric Company, 916/923-7142

shadows of Black Mountain, Quartz Mountain, Cisco Butte, and Monumental Ridge; Yuba Gap and Emigrant Gap are nearby. The campground is small and quiet. Only small RVs are allowed, so there is no danger of being overrun by large rigs. This area is most popular during the winter for its cross-country skiing and snowshoeing areas; some brave souls do snow camp here also, but they're not supposed to. This is a great spot for boating, fishing, swimming, bird-watching, or staging a hike into surrounding forest and wilderness areas.

Facilities: Each site has a picnic table and a fire ring. Running water and vault toilets are available. There is a public boat ramp.

Getting there: From Emigrant Camp, go east on I-80 for 2.5 miles. At Lake Valley Road, go south 1 mile to Sky Mountain Road. Turn right and continue 200 feet to the campground entrance.

✗ 23 Donner Memorial State Park 🌲🌲🌲🌲

Often called the jewel of the Sierra Nevada, Donner Lake, set in pine and fir forestlands before the granite peaks of Donner Pass, is a terrific boating, swimming, skiing, bird-watching, picnicking, camping, and hiking spot and a good place to seek refuge from the Tahoe region on busy summer weekends. Trail access to the Granite Chief Wilderness area between the I-80 and US 50 corridors is easily had from Donner Lake. The park has numerous interpretive walks,

sites	*150*
	*No hookups, RVs to 32 feet*
open	*May through September*
reservations	*Up to 8 weeks in advance; California State Parks, 800/444-7275*
contact	*Donner Memorial State Park, 530/582-7892*

an impressive history museum, and a memorial to members of the ill-fated Donner Party. The campground is a bit large and overpaved, but it is well managed and well kept—a great place to park the RV and stick a boat in the water or a stage for longer hikes into the national forest and wilderness. The elevation is 5,850 feet.

Facilities: Each site has a picnic table and a fire grill. Running water, flush toilets, and showers are available nearby. There is a public boat ramp on the lake.

Getting there: From Truckee, go west on I-80 for 6 miles to the Donner park exit. The park and campground are just a short distance south of the highway.

㉔ North Fork Campground 🌲🌲🌲

Kayakers and rafters enjoy this small, little-known spot on the north fork of the American River, with Class II and Class III runs nearby. The camp is a great place

sites	*18*
	*No hookups, RVs to 6 feet*
open	*All year*
reservations	*Up to 240 days in advance; Forest Service Reservations, 800/280-2267*
contact	*Nevada City Ranger District, 530/265-4531*

to stage a rafting trip. The RV restrictions keep this spot, in a pretty forested grove that sometimes gets a little marshy, from becoming overrun. Thus, it stays relatively quiet and peaceful . . . the sort of place where you can nap during the day. Do make your rafting trip before midsummer, however, as this stretch of river can run a little low once snowmelt slows down. Canoes are another option. The elevation is 4,400 feet.

Facilities: Each site has a picnic table and a fire ring. Running water and vault toilets are available.

Getting there: Drive Emigrant Gap Road south from Emigrant Gap at I-80 and continue 6 miles, past the point at which the road changes to Texas Hill Road, to the campground entrance.

Still more downstream, the Yuba River canyon narrows.

✗ ㉕ French Meadows Campground ▲▲▲▲▲

What a spot! This is exactly the kind of place we have in mind when we say, "Get out and press that reset button—you need it." French Meadows is where the reflection of clouds in the water, the number of stars in the sky, the distance a flat rock will skip across the surface of a lake, and any number of other wonders take on a special importance. The sweet smell of the pines on the wind, the beautiful stench of a smoldering campfire, the sound of bullfrogs serenading you—this is the reason you own a sleeping bag and can pretend for a time that you aren't afraid of

sites	*75*
	No hookups, RVs to 36 feet
open	*May through October*
reservations	*Up to 240 days in advance; Forest Service Reservations, 800/280-2267*
contact	*Foresthill Ranger District, 530/367-2224*

bears or snakes. The campground is well situated on the banks of a pretty reservoir with pine and fir forest all around. Despite its size, the campground stays quiet and relatively sparsely populated, probably because the long drive scares RV riggers away. Take advantage of that. Fishing is good for kokanee salmon and steelhead, bluegill, crappie, catfish, and bass. The elevation is 5,300 feet.

Facilities: Each site has a picnic table and a fire ring. Running water and vault toilets are available. There is a public boat ramp just west of the campground.

Getting there: From Westville, go 22 miles east on Forest Hill Road. Just after Sunflower Hill, turn right on French Meadows Reservoir Road and continue about 7 more miles to the campground.

Other Truckee Area Campgrounds

In the Nevada City area, contact Nevada City Ranger District, 530/265-4531, Jackson Creek Camp (15 sites for tents only) is a nice spot on the banks of Jackson Creek. Bowman Lake Campground (9 sites for tents only) is another quiet spot on the shore of Bowman Lake—great for fishing. Woodcamp Campground (10 sites for tents or RVs, no hookups, RVs to 24 feet) is a BLM property, phone 530/582-0120, at Meadow Lake. Fir Top Campground (13 sites for tents or RVs, no hookups, RVs to 24 feet) is at Meadow Lake also, in the boating area. Contact BLM for information on this campground as well. Another BLM campground is Pass Creek Campground (15 sites for tents or RVs, no hookups, RVs to 24 feet), at Jackson Meadow Reservoir, with boating facilities adjacent. Finally, East Meadow Campground (48 sites for tents or RVs, no hookups, RVs to 45 feet) is a larger campground at Jackson Meadow.

In the Truckee area, the main contact is the Truckee Ranger District, 530/587-3558. Upper Little Truckee Camp (25 sites for tents or RVs, no hookups, RVs to 21 feet) is on the banks of the Truckee River, near Lower Little Truckee Camp (profiled above). Boca Rest Camp (29 sites for tents or RVs, no hookups, RVs to 21 feet) is another popular water sports area on Boca Reservoir. Boca Springs Campground (16 sites for tents or RVs, no hookups, RVs to 21 feet) is a BLM campground at Boca, 530/582-0120. Granite Flat Campground (75 sites for tents or RVs, no hookups, RVs to 31 feet, is near Donner Memorial State Park (page 200).

Tahoe Region

26 Sugar Pine Point State Park

The 2 miles of rocky shoreline found at Sugar Pine Point drop straight down into 300-foot-deep water, an ice-blue cold splash for those who want to hurl themselves off the cliffs and then swim ashore to dry off in the summer heat. Fishing from the rocks for salmon and trout is a favorite activity here. The 2,000 acres of pine forest, rocky shore, scrub, and beach were home to the Washoe Indians during summer months; they fished and swam from the same spots summer revelers use today to cool off. Later it was used as a homestead for San Francisco businessman I. W. Hellman. As a state park, it is a prime camping location for those who wish to enjoy Tahoe from the lakeshore. Be warned, however, that this and all other lakeshore camping spots at Tahoe are extremely popular: On hot summer weekends and holidays they are packed not only with campers but also with hordes of day visitors. While the recreation lands around Tahoe contain many hidden corners, you have to seek them out. Don't expect privacy and serenity here. The elevation is 5,900 feet.

sites	180
	No hookups, RVs to 31 feet
open	June 1 to November 15
reservations	Up to 8 weeks in advance; California State Parks, 800/444-7275
contact	Sugar Pine Point State Park, 530/583-3642

Facilities: Each site has a picnic table and a fire grill. Flush toilets and running water are available nearby. The nearest services are in Tahoe City or South Lake Tahoe.

Getting there: From Truckee, head south about 23 miles on Highway 89 to Tahoe City. Near Tahoma, turn right at the campground entrance.

27 Tahoe State Recreation Area Campground

Despite the fact that this pretty, quiet spot in the pine and fir forest groves north of Lake Tahoe is an overflow area for the more popular lakeshore campgrounds in the vicinity, it is actually preferable in some ways to those spots. First of all, there are far fewer day visitors trouncing through this part of the forest. Additionally, because there are fewer sites than at most others, it tends to be less crowded. These trade-offs, however, may not be worth it to

sites	32
	No hookups, RVs to 21 feet
open	All year
reservations	Up to 8 weeks in advance; California State Parks, 800/444-7275
contact	Tahoe State Recreation Area, 530/583-3074

those who insist on having Tahoe's legendary blue waters in view. Also, there is some highway noise here at night. The elevation is 5,900 feet.

Facilities: Each site has a picnic table and a fire ring. Running water, flush toilets, and showers are available. The nearest services are in Tahoe City or South Lake Tahoe.

Getting there: From Truckee, drive south on Highway 89 for about 23 miles to Tahoe City. Turn onto Highway 28 and head north 1 mile to the campground entrance, which is on the left side of the road.

✕ ㉘ D. L. Bliss State Park Campground 🌲🌲🌲🌲🌲

Now you know what it's like to camp on the moon. The rockscape found adjacent to the pine and fir groves, rocky shores, and beaches at D. L. Bliss State Park is definitely a curiosity. One giant granite boulder known as the "balancing rock" rests precariously on just a sliver at its base. The next earthquake will probably knock it down. This is just part of what makes these 1,800 acres of wild land on the lake's western shore special. Because the campground is set in from the highway, this is one of the few spots where you can have the best of both worlds at Tahoe—a wonderful setting right on its shores with a fabulous view of its legendary blue waters, and the kind of peace and quiet that might have existed before highways and casinos came along. The sites are not particularly private, but there are many hidden corners to Bliss. This is, in fact, one of the largest campgrounds in Northern California we are willing to give a perfect rating—simply because the tradeoffs associated with packing people in a little too closely are actually made up for in the way of natural beauty. Swimming, boating, fishing, bird-watching, and hiking are favorite activities here. There also is a bicycle trail system that passes through the park. The elevation is 5,900 feet.

sites	170
🏕️🚐	No hookups, RVs to 21 feet
open	June 1 to November 15
reservations	Up to 8 weeks in advance; California State Parks, 800/444-7275
contact	D. L. Bliss State Park, 530/525-7277

Facilities: Each site has a picnic table and a fire ring. Running water, flush toilets, and showers are provided. There is no boat access to the lake here, but there are beaches. The nearest services are in South Lake Tahoe.

Getting there: From South Lake Tahoe, go north 17 miles on Highway 89 to the park entrance, which is on the right side of the highway.

Near the Zephyr Cove campground and beach facilities, cyclists ride a ring around Lake Tahoe.

㉙ Emerald Bay State Park

Where else can you sink your teeth into scuba and Scandinavian architecture all at once—while camping? Emerald Bay, you see, is the location of Vikingsholm, an

sites	100
🏕️ 🚐	No hookups, RVs to 21 feet
open	All year
reservations	Up to 8 weeks in advance; state parks reservations, 800/444-7275
contact	530/541-3030

unusual medieval-style miniature castle nestled on a small island in the middle of the bay on the north end of Lake Tahoe. How it got there is a long story; suffice it to say sometimes people with money do unusual stuff. There is also an underwater park in the bay that provides some of the best scuba diving you can ask for at Tahoe. Just be prepared to shiver a bit; the water is less than 60 degrees year-round. The campground overlooks one of the lake's most popular boating areas. Sites are large but arranged cookie cutter–style without much privacy. This is also a particularly noisy spot. This is the price you pay for being able to camp out on some of the most prime real estate you're going to find west of the Mississippi. The elevation is 5,900 feet.

Facilities: Each site has a picnic table and a fire ring. Running water, flush toilets, and showers are available. The nearest services are in South Lake Tahoe.

Getting there: From South Lake Tahoe, drive north on Highway 89 for 22 miles to the park entrance, which is on the right side of the road.

㉚ Fallen Leaf Campground

Those wishing to escape the crowds at Lake Tahoe might do well to consider camping out at Fallen Leaf, which while extremely popular in its own right is

sites	225
🏕️ 🚐	75 tent-only No hookups, RVs to 38 feet
open	June 1 to October 15
reservations	Up to 240 days in advance; Forest Service Reservations, 800/280-2267
contact	Tahoe Ranger District, 530/544-0426

secluded enough that it doesn't get anywhere near the amount of day visitor traffic seen elsewhere. The lake is a blue gem tucked in a hidden pine and fir forested canyon, and there are cascades falling over the rocks and into the lake. This is a perfect place for climbing and picnicking. While it's not the main attraction in the Tahoe Basin, Fallen Leaf is by far one of the most stunning alpine lake settings in the Sierra Nevada with such well developed camping facilities and easy access. Swimming and fishing are favorite activities, but remember that the water is cold. The walk-in sites are prime for obvious reasons. The elevation is 6,200 feet.

Facilities: Each site has a picnic table and a fire ring. Running water and flush toilets are available.

Getting there: From South Lake Tahoe, drive north on Highway 89 for 21 miles to the Fallen Leaf access road near Camp Richardson. Turn left and continue another 7 miles to the lake.

 ③ Auburn State Recreation Area ♠♠♠♠

The north and middle forks of the American River traverse this wild and scenic stretch of canyon downstream from the original California gold discovery site in Coloma. Now that the gold miners are long gone, this 35,000 acres of scrub and forest lands is a vast wildlife preserve and creation center. Rafters flock to the campgrounds, as they can stage for runs ranging from Class II to Class IV in difficulty on both forks of the river. Gold panning, dirt bike riding, hiking, swimming, fishing, and boating are also favorite activities here. Lake Clementine is a favorite spot for bottom fishing and boating, although no motorboats are allowed on the water. Campers enjoy a primitive feeling here without actually having to venture too far into the backcountry; this is why so many parents seem to bring young children here for their first camping adventures. The sites are dispersed throughout the recreation area. Some are very well hidden and private. Mountain lions and bears are found in this area, so take precautions. The elevation is 2,400 feet.

sites	75
open	All year
reservations	None
contact	Auburn State Recreation Area, 530/885-4527

Facilities: Each site has a picnic table and a fire grill. Pit toilets are available nearby. There is no running water, so pack your own.

Getting there: From Auburn, go 1 mile south from the I-80 intersection on Highway 49. The campground entrance is on the right side of the road.

③ Peninsula Campground ♠♠♠♠

This difficult-to-reach spot on the eastern shores of Folsom Lake is much nicer than the main campground because the terrain at this end of the reservoir is more like a natural riparian riverside environment. Oak trees and rolling green hills give way to the water's edge. The ensuing marshlands attract a wide variety of waterfowl. Fishing and hiking are favorite activities here. On weekends, the campground tends to fill up with retirees who know this secret back entrance to

sites	*100*

△ *No hookups, RVs to 43 feet*

open	*All year*
reservations	*Up to 8 weeks in advance; California State Parks, 800/444-7275*
contact	*Folsom Lake State Recreation Area, 530/988-0205*

Folsom Lake. During the week, the crowds disappear and things are much more quiet and peaceful. The elevation is 1,500 feet.

Facilities: Each site has a picnic table and a fire ring. Running water, flush toilets, and showers are available. There is a public boat ramp.

Getting there: From Placerville at US 50, take Highway 49 north and drive for 25 miles, through the city of Coloma and beyond, to Rattlesnake Bar Road. Turn left and drive 9 miles to the end of the road. Sections of the road are narrow, so be careful.

㉝ Folsom Lake 🌲🌲

Slap another state flag sticker to the back of the camper and get yourself a Styrofoam cup full of night crawlers—it's time to go fishin'. This sprawling camping spot on the banks of one of the state's most productive reservoirs is used mostly by anglers and boaters during the summer. Swimming, water skiing, and casting out for bass, catfish, and crappie are really all that goes on here. The campground is a good staging point for all of this. The good fishing and easy RV access attract a fair share of retirees and families. Don't come here looking for a serene setting—that requires a backpack, some good shoes, and a long walk. The elevation is 1,500 feet.

sites	*74*

△ *No hookups, RVs to 32 feet*

open	*All year*
reservations	*Up to 8 weeks in advance; California State Parks, 800/444-7275*
contact	*Folsom Lake State Recreation Area, 530/988-0205*

Facilities: Each site has a picnic table and a fire ring. Running water, flush toilets, and showers are available. There is a public boat ramp nearby, as well as a dam visitor center. There is a sanitary disposal station for RVs.

Getting there: From US 50, take the Folsom exit north and continue 8 miles to the lake. Turn right on the lakeshore access road and continue to the campground, which is just beyond the visitor center.

⟶⟶ 34 Sly Park Campgrounds 🌲🌲🌲🌲

This pretty reservoir south of US 50 is a great getaway spot but becomes extremely crowded with locals on hot weekends and holidays—so be prepared to share the splendor with plenty of others. While the campsites are not spread out well or private enough, the lake is pleasant and the surrounding pine and fir forest pristine. Some sites overlook the lake from cliffs high above the north shore. Fishing, boating, swimming, and hiking are favorite activities here. Hazel Creek at the east end of the lake is a great place for a dip on hot summer days.

sites	154
	No hookups, RVs to 32 feet
open	May to October
reservations	530/644-2545
contact	Sly Park Recreation Area, 530/644-2545

Facilities: Each site has a picnic table and a fire ring. Running water and pit toilets are available. A full-service marina, public boat ramp, and general store are available nearby. The elevation is 3,700 feet.

Getting there: From Pollock Pines, drive south for 4 miles on Sly Park Road to the campground entrance and lake, which are located on the left side of the road.

✕ 35 Lake Almanor Campground 🌲🌲

Looking for a big slab of asphalt to pitch your tent or park your RV? This would be the place. This sprawling, noisy, uncomfortably packed campground may be heaven for someone who enjoys camping in Wal-Mart parking lots, but if you're looking for peace, quiet, and relaxation, not even the lovely Lake Almanor is going to make up for how little this place has going for it. There are smaller campgrounds around the lake, so go there instead if you want something peaceful. That said, if you're just looking for a place to launch your boat, this will do.

sites	140
	No hookups, RVs to 32 feet
open	May through October
reservations	Up to 240 days in advance; Forest Service Reservations, 800/280-2267
contact	Lake Almanor Ranger District, 530/258-2141

Facilities: Each site has a picnic table and a fire ring. Running water and vault toilets are available. A sanitary dump station and a public boat ramp are nearby.

Getting there: From Susanville, go east on Highway 36 for 18 miles through Chester. Go north on Highway 89 and continue another 2 miles to the campground, which is on the left.

Time seems to stand still at Sly Park Campgrounds in El Dorado National Forest.

Other Tahoe Region Campgrounds

Just about all of the remaining campgrounds on the lakeshore are privately owned and operated. There are also numerous other private campgrounds in the surrounding national forest lands. Call the Forest Service Reservations, 800/280-2267, for a rundown on where the best facilities are for your needs.

The remaining campgrounds include Yellowjacket Campground (42 sites for tents or RVs, no hookups, RVs to 21 feet) at Union Valley Reservoir. Call El Dorado National Forest, 530/644-6048. Also in El Dorado is Woods Lake Campground (25 sites for tents only) on the banks of Woods Lake near Markleeville.

Crystal Springs Campground (23 sites for tents or RVs, no hookups, RVs to 21 feet) is in Toiyabe National Forest, 702/882-2766, on the banks of the Carson River near Woodfords. Turtle Rock Campground (30 sites for tents or RVs, no hookups, RVs to 28 feet) is near Crystal Springs, also adjacent to the river. Grover Hot Springs State Park (80 sites, 30 for tents only, 13 for RVs only, no hookups, RVs to 28 feet) is also near Markleeville. Situated in a beautiful high mountain meadow, its hot springs are the main attraction. Call California State Parks, 800/444-7275, for more information.

Tahoe Basin

✕ ㊱ Sand Flat Campground ▲▲▲▲

Rafters looking to rocket their way down the south fork of the American River love to make a weekend of it by camping out at this secluded spot on the banks of the river in a pretty stretch of canyon few US 50 travelers get a chance to really enjoy. The sites are not particularly private, so plan on making the camp-out a social event. The layout makes this a perfect spot for large groups of rafters who want to camp out in the same spot. During the winter run, steelhead and salmon wander by here, but not in great numbers most years. Still, this can make quite a suitable camping spot for fishing. Those wishing to venture deeper into the forest should consider the numerous campgrounds on the north side of US 50. The elevation is 2,900 feet.

sites	29
🏕️🚐	No hookups, RVs to 22 feet
open	April 15 to November 15
reservations	Up to 240 days in advance; Forest Service Reservations, 800/280-2267
contact	El Dorado National Forest, 530/644-6048

Facilities: Each site has a picnic table and a fire ring. Running water and vault toilets are available.

Getting there: The campground is just off the south shoulder of US 50, about 20 miles east of Pollock Pines.

✕ ▷ ㊲ Ice House Campground ▲▲▲▲▲

Although you have to drive through a vast area of ugly clearcuts to get to it, Ice House Reservoir and the surrounding mixed pine forests are indeed great places to enjoy nature and unwind. Sun yourself on the boulder-lined north shore, push off for skiing or fishing, rest in one of the many shady coves for an afternoon picnic—you get the picture. . . . This is just another lovely, lazy place to do a little bit of nothing. The high mountains surrounding this part of El Dorado

sites	83
🏕️🚐	No hookups, RVs to 24 feet
open	June 1 to October 15
reservations	Up to 240 days in advance; Forest Service Reservations, 800/280-2267
contact	El Dorado National Forest, 530/644-6048

"Crystal Lake" Sub station : 530-293-3510

Sand Flat Campground within El Dorado National Forest is a great spot for rafters and canoers visiting the American River canyon.

National Forest remain snowcapped well into the late summer, and this provides a stunningly beautiful backdrop for the lake and campground. The campsites aren't quite as large or private as those found at nearby Wright's Lake (page 214) but this is a winner nonetheless. Ice House is simply a great place to relax. While it doesn't officially open until June, the Forest Service allows camping before then, depending on the weather. Be sure to check with the main ranger station if you're looking to pitch a tent in late April or May. The elevation is 5,500 feet.

Facilities: Each site has a picnic table and a fire ring. Running water and vault toilets are available nearby, as are a public boat ramp and an RV sanitary disposal station.

Getting there: From Pollock Pines, drive east on US 50 for 16 miles to the Ice House Road exit. Go north 6 miles to the reservoir and campground, following the Forest Service road signs carefully.

㊳ Wright's Lake Campground

In the still heat of summer, the surface of Wright's Lake looks like a sheet of deep blue glass. Drop a pebble in and the ripples disturb a deafening peace. No place is so quiet and undisturbed, it seems. Imagine yourself camped out on the banks of a high mountain lake so pictur-esque and peaceful that you'd swear you were in a postcard for the Sierra Nevada. The high snowcapped peaks of the Sierra tower over the sprawling pine-forested hills and meadows surrounding the lake. Time stops here. Enjoy. The campground is situated along the banks of the lake and an adjoining creek. Sites are dispersed throughout a grassy area of light brush and sparse trees. The sites are large and private, and despite the campground's relatively easy access from US 50, your fellow campers here tend to be mellow and courteous. Fishing on the lake during the late summer will yield an occasional rainbow trout, catfish, or bluegill. Back-packers enjoy using this campground to stage hikes into the Wright's Botanic Area, or to Blue Mountain or Four Cornered Peak. The elevation is 7,000 feet.

sites	75
	No hookups, RVs to 21 feet
open	June 15 to October 15
reservations	Up to 240 days in advance; Forest Service Reservations, 800/280-2267
contact	El Dorado National Forest, 530/644-6048

Facilities: Each site has a picnic table and a fire ring. Running water and vault toilets are available. There is a public boat ramp but few other amenities.

Getting there: From Pollock Pines, drive east on US 50 for 16 miles. Turn north at Ice House Road and follow the signs up to Wright's Lake, about 15 miles in.

⟶ 39 Loon Lake Camp 🌲🌲🌲🌲

This is taking "off the beaten path" to the extreme. Imagine a crystal-clear, freezing cold alpine lake smack dab in the middle of forest so remote you feel like you might run into the next Ishi around every corner. Because of the extreme weather in this part of the Sierra, count on dealing with snowpack even during the summer. But it is the snow, remember, that feeds this amazingly pristine lake, a favorite among backpackers who want to enter Desolation Wilderness from the west end instead of staging from Tahoe. Tell's Peak, McDonnel Peak, and numerous smaller lakes within Desolation are within a few hours' hike from campground. The elevation is 6,500 feet.

sites	65
🏕️🚐	No hookups, RVs to 24 feet
open	June 15 to September 15
reservations	None
contact	El Dorado National Forest, 530/644-6048

Facilities: Each site has a picnic table and a fire ring. A public boat ramp is nearby. There is no running water. Vault toilets are available.

Getting there: From Pollock Pines, go 16 miles east on US 50 to Ice House Road. Turn left and continue up for 32 miles. At the Schlein Ranger Station, turn right and proceed to the campground, which is clearly marked. The roads are very winding and steep in some places.

⟶ 40 Sunset Campground 🌲🌲🌲🌲

This is the nicest of six campgrounds on the banks of Union Valley Reservoir, a popular water sports and fishing area in the forest lands north of US 50. A little tip: 30 of the sites here, located toward the rear of the campground, are for walk-in campers only. This means no RVs or cars at the sites, and it also means things are a bit more peaceful. The mixed pine forest surrounding the reservoir is home to many varieties of songbirds, so bird-watchers should be sure to bring spotting scopes and cameras. Some waterfowl also are found on the banks of the lake. Wildlife runs the gamut, from raccoons and foxes to bears and

sites	165
🏕️🚐	30 tent-only. No hookups, RVs to 21 feet
open	June 1 to October 15
reservations	Up to 240 days in advance; Forest Service Reservations, 800/280-2267
contact	El Dorado National Forest, 530/644-6048

1-877-444-6777

bobcats. While the campground doesn't officially open until June, sometimes the Forest Service allows people to camp here before that, depending on the weather. Be sure to check with the ranger station if you're in the area during late April and or May. Late summer can get pretty loud and packed here because of the number of campsites. If you're looking for something more quiet and secluded, consider Wrights Lake, described above. The elevation is 4,900 feet.

Facilities: Each site has a picnic table and a fire ring. Running water and vault toilets are available nearby. A public boat ramp and RV sanitary dump station are nearby.

Getting there: From Pollock Pines, drive east on US 50 for 16 miles to the Ice House Road turnoff. Head north 24 miles, following the signs to the campground.

41 Hope Valley Campground 🌲🌲🌲🌲

Those who find a little too much competition at Kit Carson Campground (below) may want to consider casting out instead at this small, quiet campground nestled on the banks of the Carson River a short distance upstream. Brown trout and rainbow are the main fare here. This campground is also used by the occasional rafting party, as there are a number of good Class II runs in the area. The elevation is 6,600 feet.

sites	20
	No hookups, RVs to 21 feet
open	June 1 to October 15
reservations	None
contact	Toiyabe National Forest, 702/882-2766

Facilities: Each site has a picnic table and a fire ring. Running water and vault toilets are available. The nearest services are in Markleeville, 4 miles away.

Getting there: From Makleeville, drive north on Highway 89 for 8 miles to the Highway 88 junction. Turn east on Highway 88 and continue a short distance over the Marsh Creek bridge. At Blue Lakes Road, turn left to the campground entrance.

42 Kit Carson Campground 🌲🌲🌲

Of all the places to camp out along the scenic Carson River corridor, this is one of the nicest, set along the banks of the river in a beautiful grove of mixed pine. Fishing for brown trout and the occasional rainbow and salmon is the main attraction here, so bring tackle if you want to fit in. Those wishing to stage longer hikes into the backcountry may want to choose something a little deeper in—the highest trail segments are in the 8,000-foot range and the elevation here is just 6,600 feet.

sites	15
🏕️🚐	No hookups, RVs to 21 feet
open	June 1 to October 15
reservations	Up to 240 days in advance; Forest Service Reservations, 800/280-2267
contact	Toiyabe National Forest, 702/882-2766

Facilities: Each site has a picnic table and a fire ring. Running water and vault toilets are available.

Getting there: From Markleeville, go 8 miles north on Highway 89 to the Highway 88 junction. Continue another 1.5 miles to the campground, which is on the right side of the road.

43 Caples Lake 🌲🌲🌲

If this nice campground in the scrublands of Carson Pass were at least some distance from Highway 88, we'd have given it a higher rating. But, alas, there is no escape from the midnight whining and grinding of wayward big rigs trying to make their way toward Nevada or descend in high gear toward the Sacramento Valley. It is a constant stream of loud motors and annoying headlights. Fishing, however, is quite good here—so if that's your priority just bring a set of earplugs and have at it. Rainbows, browns, steelhead, crappie, and catfish are found in the lake at varying times of year. The elevation is 7,800 feet.

sites	45
🏕️	30 tent-only
🚐	No hookups, RVs to 21 feet
open	June 1 to October 15
reservations	Up to 240 days in advance; Forest Service Reservations, 800/280-2267
contact	El Dorado National Forest, 530/644-6048

Facilities: Each site has a picnic table and a fire ring. Running water and vault toilets are available. There is a public boat ramp. The nearest services are in Markleeville, 18 miles away.

Getting there: From Markleeville, go 8 miles north to the Highway 88 junction. Drive west on Highway 88 for 10 miles to the lake, which is on the left side of the road.

44 Kirkwood Lake 🌲🌲🌲

When you see this place, you will need someone to pinch you to let you know you're not dreaming—because it is one dreamy spot. The small, quiet campground near Kirkwood Meadows rests on the shores of a small lake surrounded by mixed pines. There are stunning views of several higher peaks from here, including Carson Spur, Martin Point, and Thunder Mountain. The lake's waters run ice cold through the summers, as it is fed by high mountain streams receiving snowmelt for most of the year. Occasionally, however, it actually gets hot enough in these parts for people to want to take a dip. More likely, though, you'll want to bring a fishing boat, a rod and reel, a good book to read, and maybe a hammock. The lazybones bug is contagious here. If you find this campground overflowing, consider stopping at the nearby Silver Lake or Caples Lake, as both have a lot more room. The elevation is 7,600 feet.

sites	12
open	June 16 to October 15
reservations	None
contact	El Dorado National Forest, 530/644-6048

Facilities: Each site has a picnic table and a fire ring. Running water and vault toilets are available. There is a public boat ramp nearby. The nearest services are 20 miles away in Markleeville.

Getting there: From Markleeville drive north on Highway 89 for 8 miles to the Highway 88 exit. Go west another 12 miles to Kirkwood lake, which is on the right.

45 Silver Lake 🌲🌲🌲

If the sequel to *A River Runs Through It* were set here, the title would have to be *A Highway Runs Through It*. Indeed, the campgrounds here are bisected by Highway 88, the busy alternate route into the Tahoe basin via Carson Pass. While sections of the campgrounds are well protected from the highway noise, getting a site a little too close can be a problem. The best sites are on the south side of the highway nearest the lake or an adjacent pond. The 30 walk-in sites are prime. The surrounding mixed pine forest is teeming with

sites	95
	30 tent-only
	No hookups, RVs to 28 feet
open	June 1 to October 15
reservations	Up to 240 days in advance; Forest Service Reservations, 800/280-2267
contact	El Dorado National Forest, 530/644-6048

wildlife, including black bear, bobcats, raccoons, mountain lions, and wild pigs. The numerous high mountain lakes and reservoirs in this part of the Sierra also attract a fair amount of waterfowl. Silver Lake is a favorite fishing spot for bass and catfish. The elevation is 7,200 feet.

Facilities: Each site has a picnic table and a fire ring. Running water and vault toilets are available. Flush toilets are available at the full-service marina on the south side of Highway 88. A public boat ramp is located at the marina.

Getting there: From Markleeville, go 8 miles north on Highway 89 to the Highway 88 junction. Go west on Highway 88 for 12 miles to the campground, which is situated on both sides of the highway. The left (south) side is preferable.

Southern Sierra

It's the water.

Follow the water from the frozen glaciers in Yosemite's high country, down through sheer granite-walled canyons, over mighty falls, through valleys and forests, and into popular fishing and boating lakes of the Sierra foothills and the Central Valley and you will understand: Water not only drives the economy of the Golden State, it is the lifeblood of the state's outdoor recreation areas. This is especially true here in the Southern Sierra where the region's predominant geologic features need water.

What would Yosemite Valley be, after all, without its infamous waterfalls? And Hetch Hetchy Lake? Just another dry meadow in the mountains. Would Mono Lake look like anything more than a rock pile?

The developed campsites inside Yosemite National Park are usually booked many months in advance during the prime outdoor season. But those in the know forego Yosemite Valley campgrounds and instead head to the national forest campgrounds at each of the park's main entrances. Or travel east of Yosemite, along the US 395 corridor. Full of its own natural wonders, this region includes Mono Lake with it's placid waters and moonscape appearance, Mammoth Mountain's towering snowcapped peak, and the splendor of the Ansel Adams Wilderness. You may discover that staying outside the park may actually make a visit to Yosemite a much more enjoyable experience.

During much of the year, the eastern Sierra and Yosemite regions are separated from each other, as Sonora, Ebbetts, and Tioga Passes are closed to traffic. What many outdoors enthusiasts don't realize, however, is that the US 395 corridor can be accessed via the Lake Tahoe basin in Nevada before the roads into Yosemite open in late spring. This is a terrific time to visit Mono Lake and Mammoth Mountain, as the rush of visitors has not started yet.

Yosemite and the public lands that surround it—shaped by water and where John Muir got his inspiration while living as "John of the Mountains"—are the definitive reset button for the soul.

Southern Sierra

1. Upper Pines Campground
2. Lower Pines Campground
3. North Pines Campground
4. Sunnyside Campground
5. Wawona Campground
6. Hodgdon Meadow Campground
7. White Wolf Campground
8. Tuolumne Meadows Campground
9. Crane Flat Campground
10. Tamarack Flat Campground
11. Yosemite Creek Campground
12. Bridalveil Creek Campground
13. Big Bend Campground
14. Saddlebag Lake Campground
15. Tioga Lake Campground
16. Junction Campground
17. Ellery Lake Campground
18. Minaret Falls Campground
19. Sonora Bridge Campground
20. Obsidian Campground
21. Robinson Creek Campground
22. Bootleg Campground
23. Buckeye Campground
24. Lower Twin Lakes Campground
25. Summit Campground
26. Summerdale Campground
27. Jerseydale Campground
28. Tuttletown Campground
29. Woodward Reservoir Campground
30. Moccasin Point Campground
31. Horseshoe Bend Campground
32. Big Sandy Campground
33. Chilkot Campground
34. Forks Campground
35. Lupine-Cedar Campground
36. Upper Highland Lake Campground
37. Union Reservoir Campground
38. Alpine Lake
39. Mill Creek Campground
40. Niagara Creek Campground
41. Pigeon Flat Campground
42. Lumsden Campground
43. Cherry Lake Campground
44. Lost Claim Campground
45. Sweetwater Campground

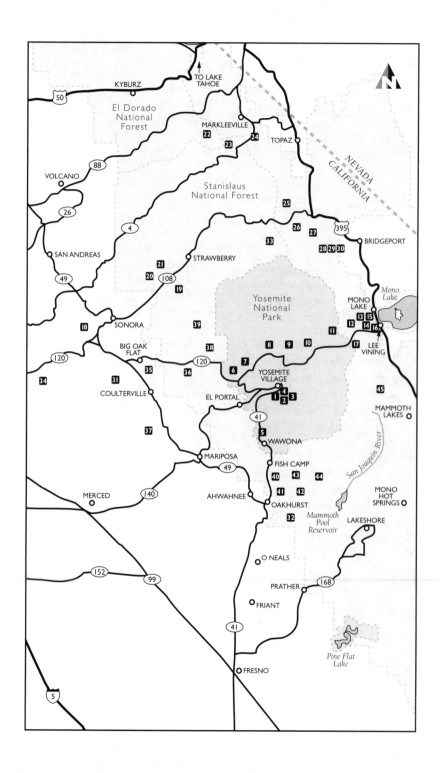

Yosemite Valley

① Upper Pines Campground 🌲🌲🌲🌲🌲

The morning thaw is the most special time when you're camping out in Yosemite Valley. Morning is the time that you can most easily forget the crowds. When the rising sun first crests over the walls of the valley, there is a brilliant white glow as the flat gray granite become engorged in light. Frozen waterfalls begin the thaw, sending sheets of ice crashing hundreds of feet to the valley below.

sites	238
🏕️ 🚐	No hookups, RVs to 38 feet
open	All year
reservations	Up to 5 months in advance beginning the 15th of each month; National Park Service, 800/436-PARK, or http://reservations.nps.gov
contact	Yosemite National Park, 209/372-8502

Upper Pines is perhaps the most difficult campground in the entire state to secure a reservation, as people tend to plan their Yosemite Valley outings here many months or even years in advance. Cradled by the Merced River and adjacent to some of the valley's most interesting nature trails, the campground has an amazingly private and uncrowded feel for its size. That's because the 238 sites are arranged among six reasonably small loops. Those sites in the easternmost corner of the campground are prized, as they are the most private. Views of Glacier Point, Vernal Falls, and Half Dome are very good from this part of the valley. The trailhead to the popular John Muir Trail is just a few yards from the campground. Because Happy Isles Nature Center and other attractions are nearby, there tends to be a fair amount of day-visitor foot traffic in this part of the valley, but because paths are designed to keep day visitors out of the camp area, you hardly notice it. This is a great camping spot for families with children. Note, however, that if you're looking for a more primitive camping experience this is probably going to be disappointing. This is a family camp-out spot or a good place from which to stage day hikes into the high country.

Facilities: Each site has a picnic table and a fire grill. Running water, flush toilets, and showers are available nearby. There is a general store in Yosemite Village.

Getting there: From Yosemite Village, drive east on Southside Drive for 3 miles through the valley to Curry Village. Turn left and cross the bridge to the campground, which is on your right.

❷ Lower Pines Campground 🌲🌲🌲🌲

Go ahead and pinch yourself. This is not a dream, and it's not Fantasy Island. The granite walls and waterfalls are real. That is no Hollywood backdrop you see.

sites	80
🏕️🚐	No hookups, RVs to 40 feet
open	March through October
reservations	Up to 5 months in advance beginning the 15th of each month; National Park Service, 800/436-PARK, http://reservations.nps.gov
contact	Yosemite National Park, 209/372-8512

Yosemite Valley is indeed a place where you catch yourself double checking to make sure the stage props and giant Styrofoam boulders have not been removed yet—it seems that postcard perfect. Lower Pines is a great spot on a small peninsula along the banks of the Merced River. Because of the path the river takes here, you are surrounded by water on two sides. While it is ludicrous to complain about any camping spot in a place like this, it should be noted that this is probably the least desirable of the five campgrounds on the valley floor because of its proximity to Curry Village and the main Yosemite Valley day-use parking areas. Note that some sites in this campground were damaged in 1997 by a flood. Work is underway for repairs. Adjacent Upper River and Lower River camps have been closed since.

Facilities: Each site has a picnic table and a fire grill. Running water and flush toilets are available nearby. There is a general store in Yosemite Village.

Getting there: From Yosemite Village, drive east on Southside Drive through the valley for 3 miles to Curry Village. Turn left before the Merced River bridge to get to the campground.

❸ North Pines Campground 🌲🌲🌲🌲

The spot where Tenaya Creek meets the Merced River is a great place for summertime wading. The small island formed at the confluence is the setting for North Pines Campground, a prime Yosemite Valley camping spot because of its seclusion from other amenities in the park. In addition to easy river access, trail connections to Mirror Lake and Mirror Meadow are nearby. There are also trail connections to Yosemite Village directly from the campground. An important fact: This is the only one of the five main campgrounds in

sites	85
🏕️🚐	No hookups, RVs to 40 feet
open	April through October
reservations	Up to 5 months in advance beginning the 15th of each month; National Park Service, 800/436-PARK, http://reservations.nps.gov
contact	Yosemite National Park, 209/372-8502

Yosemite Valley not located next to a roadway carrying through traffic. The result is a much more natural ambience—to the extent that is possible with 40-foot RVs parked all over the place. Remember that even though you're on a river here, environmental controls on the Merced and its tributaries restrict the amount of recreational fishing allowed. At certain times of year, it is prohibited. Be sure to check with the park service before turning your camp-out into a fishing trip.

Facilities: Each site has a picnic table and a fire grill. Running water and flush toilets are available nearby.

Getting there: From Yosemite Village, go east on Southside Drive east through the valley for 3 miles to Curry Village. Turn left at the end of the road and cross the bridge. The campground is to the left just after the bridge crossing the Merced River.

④ Sunnyside Campground 🌲🌲🌲🌲🌲

The thunderous crash of Yosemite Falls seems jarring at first, like the growling stomach of a large, hungry animal. After a while, however, the roar of the falls becomes a soothing background noise, like soft jazz on a quiet night or the purr of a kitten. Sunnyside Campground is one location in Yosemite Valley where the elegant nature sounds are most pronounced. Because the campsites are walk-in only, there are no RV noises to compete with. The campground is also a great fallback for those of us who haven't planned our trip to Yosemite Valley months in advance, as it's virtually the only way to get a developed campsite during the peak outdoor season—even if the weather is lousy. To secure a site here, however, requires a bit of savvy; the campground is virtually guaranteed to fill up every day. The key is arriving early and being prepared to stake your claim. An important note: Some days the demand is so high for campgrounds that more than one party will be assigned to a site. The limit is six persons per campsite, so if your party is smaller than that you may very well end up sharing.

sites	*35*
open	*All year*
reservations	*None*
contact	*Yosemite National Park, 209/372-8502*

Facilities: Each site has a picnic table and a fire ring. Running water, flush toilets, and showers are available nearby. There is a general store in nearby Yosemite Village.

Getting there: Upon entering Yosemite Valley, follow Southside Drive through Yosemite Village to the Valley Visitor Center. The parking area for the campground is beyond the visitor center, near the base of Yosemite Falls. It is a short hike to the campground itself.

⑤ Wawona Campground 🌲🌲🌲🌲

The Mariposa Grove—where giant Sequoias are nearly 3,000 years old and among the largest (by volume) living organisms on the planet—should not be overlooked by visitors to Yosemite Valley and its environs. There are easy trail connections from the Mariposa/Wawona end of the park to Chilnualna Falls, Crescent Lake, and Buck Camp (for backpackers), all terrific hiking destinations during the summer—after the spring thaw uncovers the high country. Wawona Camp is a great place from which to stage summer hikes in the south end of Yosemite as well as day visits to Mariposa. The camp is large and spread out over a pretty wooded area nestled on the banks of the south fork of the Merced River. Often Wawona is your best chance of landing a campsite within the park boundaries during the peak season when Yosemite Valley is packed in. While there is a drive required to reach the valley, there is far less activity in this part of the park, so the camp-outs tend to be a little more peaceful. Sites nearest the river are prime.

sites	*100*
	No hookups, RVs to 34 feet
open	*All year*
reservations	*Required May through September, up to 5 months in advance beginning the 15th of each month; National Park Service, 800/436-PARK, http://reservations.nps.gov*
contact	*Yosemite National Park, 209/372-8502*

Facilities: Each site has a picnic table and a fire grill. Running water and flush toilets are available nearby. There is a general store in the town of Fish Camp, which is just outside the south entrance to Yosemite National Park.

Getting there: From Yosemite National Park's south entrance on Highway 41, drive north 6 miles on Wawona Road toward Yosemite Valley. The campground entrance is on the left side of the road. Yosemite Valley is another 10 miles north.

⑥ Hodgdon Meadow Campground 🌲🌲🌲🌲

Another good alternative to squeezing into Yosemite Valley with the 4 million other people who visit the park each year is the Hodgdon Meadow site near the Highway 120 entrance to Yosemite. There are excellent trail connections from this part of Yosemite to the Hetch Hetchy Valley area as well as to Aspen Valley on the south fork of the Tuolumne River. Because the campground is operated on a first come, first served basis during the off-season, Hodgdon Meadow can be a prime place for a Yosemite visit in April or October, as both months can be reasonably pleasant depending on the climate cycle at that time of year. During the peak

sites	100

No hookups, RVs to 33 feet

open	All year
reservations	Required May through September, up to 5 months in advance beginning the 15th of each month; National Park Service, 800/436-PARK, http://reservations.nps.gov
contact	Yosemite National Park, 209/372-8502

season, Hodgdon is a good choice for those who want to split their time between Yosemite Valley and the Tioga Road corridor, as you can do both from here without having to switch campgrounds. This part of Yosemite is characterized by its wide high country meadows and exposed granite peaks. Bird-watchers and wildflower admirers will be pleased with this area in spring.

Facilities: Each site has a picnic table and a fire grill. Running water and flush toilets are available nearby.

Getting there: From the Highway 120 entrance to Yosemite National Park at Oak Flat Road, drive a short distance to the campground access road, which is on the left side of the highway.

⑦ White Wolf Campground 🌲🌲🌲🌲

Those wishing to get a feel for the Yosemite National Park uplands will enjoy this quiet spot in the high country surrounded by little more than meadows, lakes,

sites	90

No hookups, RVs to 33 feet

open	June through October
reservations	None
contact	Yosemite National Park, 209/372-8502

rock outcroppings, wild streams, and a lot of silence. White Wolf is buried in snow most of the year, but the few months that it is open provide a great staging area for day hikes to some of Yosemite's hidden lakes, or longer backpacking trips toward Hetch Hetchy Lake and the Grand Canyon of the Tuolumne River. Lukens Lake and Harden Lake make great day trips from White Wolf. This is one of four campgrounds located along this stretch of the Tioga Pass but by far the most interesting because of its location in the far north reaches of the pass area. Keep in mind that in unusual circumstances Tioga Pass is closed to vehicle traffic well into the summer—it all depends how much snow comes down during the winter, and sometimes it can be an incredible amount.

Facilities: Each site has a picnic table and a fire grill. Running water and flush toilets are available nearby. The nearest services are in Groveland or Lee Vining.

Getting there: From Groveland drive east on Highway 120 for 19 miles to the Highway 41 junction. Turn left at White Wolf Road and continue to the campground entrance, which is a short distance up the road.

⑧ Tuolumne Meadows Campground 🌲🌲🌲

Tuolumne Meadows is one of the most strikingly lush high mountain wetland areas in the Southern Sierra. Socked in by snow for much of the year, the summertime is a highly productive period at Tuolumne, as plant and animal life flourish quickly. Students of ecology enjoy seeing the life web here moving at what seems like an accelerated pace; within a few weeks of snowmelt the fields are teeming with summer wildflowers, rare butterflies, and small animals. This recedes and changes after just a few months. Snows can return as soon as October. The Tuolumne Meadows Campground is among the largest in the entire Sierra Nevada and for that reason it can

sites	*314*
🏕️ 🚐	*No hookups, RVs to 33 feet*
open	*July to September*
reservations	*Up to 5 months in advance beginning the 15th of each month; National Park Service, 800/436-PARK, or http://reservations.nps.gov; 25 sites are drop-in only*
contact	*Yosemite National Park, 209/372-8502*

Sprawling grasslands against a big sky make up the Tuolumne Meadows region of Yosemite National Park.

seem more like a parking lot than a pristine setting in a unique and ecologically complex area. Those looking for a less busy and crowded camp spot may want to consider continuing west on Tioga Road to one of the four smaller campgrounds in the area. Another alternative is to hike to one of five backpacker camps nearby, those being at May Lake, Glen Auilin, on the Pacific Crest Trail, Sunrise, Merced Lake, and Vogelsang Lake. Information about the backpacking camps and necessary permits are available at the Tuolumne Meadows Visitor Center near the campground.

Facilities: Each site has a picnic table and a fire pit. Running water, flush toilets, and an RV sanitary dump station are available nearby.

Getting there: From Groveland, drive west on Highway 120 for 45 miles. At Highway 41, turn right and enter the campground.

⑨ Crane Flat Campground 🌲🌲🌲🌲

The main attractions in this part of Yosemite National Park are two impressive groves of giant Sequoia redwoods, at Tuolumne Grove and Merced Grove. Trail connections are made from Crane Flat to the Arch Rock area and to Inspiration Point overlooking Yosemite Valley. It's a long day hike, but worth the walk, as the view from up here is spectacular. There is a pretty little cascade on Crane Creek that we hesitate to call a waterfall (especially since there are real waterfalls here), but it's a pleasant find nonetheless. Escape the hustle and bustle of Yosemite Valley and admire it from afar instead by camping out here. The campsites are well situated, spacious, and private enough, but those wishing for real serenity should probably delve deeper into the park or head out east on Tioga Road.

sites	*166*
🏕️🚐	*No hookups, RVs to 32 feet*
open	*June to September*
reservations	*Up to 5 months in advance beginning the 15th of each month; National Park Service, 800/436-PARK, or http://reservations.nps.gov*
contact	*Yosemite National Park, 209/372-8502*

Facilities: Each site has a picnic table and a fire grill. Running water and flush toilets are available nearby. There is a general store in Crane Flat, the nearest town.

Getting there: From Groveland drive west on Highway 120 for 45 miles and turn right at Highway 41. Continue forward to the Crane Flat Ranger Station and the campground entrance, which is on your left.

⑩ Tamarack Flat Campground 🌲🌲🌲

Looking for one of those "ooh" and "ah" views? So are those who seek out this campground in the northern highlands of Yosemite National Park. While the high mountain meadows, pine forest groves, granite outcroppings, and wild creeks alone are enough to make Tamarack Flat a fantastic camp spot, the real draw is the easy trail access from the campground to El Capitan and Yosemite Falls, with spectacular views of the valley below. With the valley as crowded as it is during the peak outdoor season, Tamarack is a good alternative for many who do not mind a more primitive camping experience. Instead of hiking up from the valley, from here it is possible to enjoy it from afar. Cascade and Tamarack Creeks are a good source of running water, but be sure to filter it anyway.

sites	52
open	July to September
reservations	None
contact	Yosemite National Park, 209/372-8502

Facilities: Each site has a picnic table and a fire pit. Pit toilets are available nearby. There is no running water.

Getting there: From Groveland drive west on Highway 21 for 42 miles. Turn right on Old Big Flat Road. The campground is straight ahead.

Yosemite's Northern Uplands

⑪ Yosemite Creek Campground 🌲🌲🌲🌲🌲

Ever look at a raging waterfall and wonder where that endless supply of water actually comes from? Camp at Yosemite Creek Campground and you'll have an idea of the answer. The campground, a quiet spot with few amenities, is nestled in an area of high mountain meadows and forested knolls containing the streams of creeks feeding Yosemite Falls. It is possible to hike from the campground to the falls and down into Yosemite Valley in one day. Alternatively, just do the waterfall hike and enjoy the valley from above.

sites	75
open	July to September
reservations	None
contact	Yosemite National Park, 209/372-8502

The tufa surrounding Mono Lake is truly a geologic oddity.

Tourists tend to avoid this campground because it has few amenities; that's good news for those of us trying to find a bit of peace in one of the nation's most popular outdoor destinations. Bird-watchers and those who enjoy wildflowers will be especially fond of this area during the summer, which is springlike for the duration because of the odd seasons this far up in the high country. The elevation is 8,000 feet.

Facilities: Each site has a picnic table and a fire pit. Pit toilets are available nearby. There is no running water.

Getting there: From Groveland, drive west on Highway 120 for 64 miles to White Wolf Road. After White Wolf there is an access road to Yosemite Creek on the right side of the highway. Turn right and follow the road to the end.

⑫ Bridalveil Creek Campground ♠♠♠♠♠

Another smart alternative to camping in the crowded Yosemite Valley during the peak season is to retreat to the one developed campground in the high country south of the valley. Bridalveil Creek Campground is located in an area of marshes, meadows, and creeks feeding Bridalveil Falls in Yosemite Valley. Nearby Glacier Point offers spectacular views of the valley and its many geologic wonders. The campground is quiet and has plenty of room for everyone, but at the height of the summer madness it fills up easily. Be sure to arrive early if you want to be sure you secure a site. In addition to the easy access from here to Glacier Point by car in the summer, there is trail access to Cathedral Rocks and Inspiration Point; both offer great vistas of the valley and surrounding high country.

sites	*115*
🏕️ 🚐	*No hookups, RVs to 24 feet*
open	*June through September*
reservations	*None*
contact	*Yosemite National Park, 209/372-8502*

Facilities: Each site has a picnic table and a fire grill. Running water and flush toilets are available nearby. There is a general store in the nearby Badger Pass ski area.

Getting there: From the Highway 41 junction out of Yosemite Valley, go south 10 miles on Wawona Road to Glacier Point Road. Turn east and follow the road 25 miles, past the Badger Pass ski area, to the campground on the right side of the road. Glacier Point is another 10 miles ahead.

Southern Yosemite and the Eastern Sierras / Mono Lake Area

⑬ Big Bend Campground 🌲🌲🌲🌲

Welcome to the high country. This is one of a half dozen small campgrounds located along Highway 120 between Mono Lake and the Tuolumne Meadows entrance to Yosemite National Park. While the campground serves mostly as an overflow for Yosemite, it is actually much nicer than some of the Tuolumne area campgrounds within the park boundaries, particularly the main Tuolumne Meadows Campground itself (page 229). In addition to being set in on a lovely creekside in a lush forested area, the campgrounds along this stretch of Highway 120 also provide easy access to the Ansel Adams Wilderness area, which has some of the best day hiking and longer backpacking trips in the region. The John Muir Trail and the Pacific Crest Trail each pass through this section of forest. Those wishing to see both the Yosemite backcountry and Mono Lake can make good use of this campground and those nearby. This is also a suitable location from which to stage longer backpacking trips into the wilderness areas and forest. Note that the Yosemite access is not usually open until the late spring, as the Mono basin receives tremendous snowfall. On rare occasion, access is closed well into late May or even early June. Be sure to check on snow conditions before planning your itinerary.

sites	17
🏕️ 🚐	No hookups, RVs to 28 feet
open	May to October
reservations	Up to 240 days in advance; Forest Service Reservations, 800/280-2267
contact	Mono Lake Ranger District, 760/647-3044

Facilities: Each site has a picnic table and a fire grill. Running water and vault toilets are available nearby. The nearest services are in Lee Vining.

Getting there: From Lee Vining, go south on US 395 for 2 miles. At Horse Meadows Road, turn right. The campground is straight ahead.

⑭ Saddlebag Lake Campground 🌲🌲🌲🌲

This small, pretty lake set in the high mountains east of Yosemite National Park is a little-known place to hide from the summer crowds. Because it is in the 10,000-foot range, be prepared for cold nights here even during the summer. The

The Mono Lake shore is a briny place brimming with unique wildlife; in the background are the snowcapped peaks of the eastern Sierra.

sites	*21*
	No hookups, RVs to 21 feet
open	*May to October*
reservations	*Up to 240 days in advance; Forest Service Reservations, 800/280-2267*
contact	*Mono Lake Ranger District, 760/647-3044*

surrounding terrain, however, is so crisp and pristine that you will hardly mind having to bundle up a little to deal with the elements. Golden trout occupy the lake and adjoining creeks. The higher peaks surrounding the lake hold snow year round. Don't count on swimming here unless you're a polar bear.

Facilities: Each site has a picnic table and a fire grill. Running water and vault toilets are available nearby. The nearest store is in Lee Vining.

Getting there: From Lee Vining, go south on US 395 for 1 mile to Highway 120. From Highway 120 go west 7 miles. Turn right on Saddlebag Lake Road and go to the end of the road to the campground.

⑮ Tioga Lake Campground 🌲🌲🌲🌲

Since the National Park Service strictly regulates and controls fishing within Yosemite National Park, those who want to combine a trip to Yosemite with a fishing expedition camp at places like this—a beautiful high mountain lake just outside the national park borders where the fish stocks are healthy enough and the rules lenient enough that everybody is happy. The lake is one of those heavenly spots, a cup-shaped bowl with granite walls filled with the most pristine blue waters imaginable. The slate-gray granite and the cobalt blue waters of the lake are mesmerizing. There is no RV access here, making it ideal for those who are desperate for a prime nature setting with the flavor of Yosemite but who don't care for the noise that often accompanies RV camping. While the lake and its campground are looked upon as an overflow spot for when Tuolumne Meadows campgrounds fill up during the summer, this spot is actually much nicer and much more peaceful than most of those found within park boundaries. Keep it a secret and you will be enjoying it for years to come. The elevation is 9,700 feet.

sites	13
open	May to October
reservations	Up to 240 days in advance; Forest Service Reservations, 800/280-2267
contact	Mono Lake Ranger District, 760/647-3044

Facilities: Each site has a picnic table and a fire grill. Running water and vault toilets are available nearby. The nearest store is in Lee Vining.

Getting there: From Lee Vining, go south on US 395 for 1 mile and turn west on Highway 120. Continue 11 miles west to the campground entrance, which you will see just after Ellery Lake.

⑯ Junction Campground 🌲🌲🌲🌲

Nestled in the shadows of 11,513-foot Tioga Peak, this small, quiet, peaceful campground is located halfway between Ellery Lake and Saddlebag Lake, and well enough away from the Highway 120 corridor that it is not easily found by stray Yosemite visitors who couldn't find a campsite. There is also easy access from here to not only Yosemite but to the Hoover Wilderness section of Toiyabe National Forest. A great day hike is to venture up to the falls on Lundy Creek, just north of Sad-

sites	13
	No hookups, RVs to 21 feet
open	May to October
reservations	Up to 240 days in advance; Forest Service Reservations, 800/280-2267
contact	Mono Lake Ranger District, 760/647-3044

dlebag. Because all of this is set at 10,000 feet, brace yourself for weather extremes even during the summer.

Facilities: Each site has a picnic table and a fire grill. Running water and vault toilets are available nearby. The nearest services are found in Lee Vining.

Getting there: From Lee Vining, go south on US 395 1 mile to the Highway 120 exit. Head west 12 miles and then turn right on Saddlebag Lake Road. Proceed a short distance to the campground access road, which is on the left side of Saddlebag Lake Road.

⑰ Ellery Lake Campground 🌲🌲🌲🌲

Dig out the nightcrawlers. It's fishin' time. Just like its neighbor Tioga Lake (see above), Ellery Lake is a lifesaver for those wishing to experience the Yosemite high country without having to forgo a little bit of fishing action because of National

sites	*13*
🏕️🚐	*No hookups, RVs to 21 feet*
open	*May to October*
reservations	*Up to 240 days in advance; Forest Service Reservations, 800/280-2267*
contact	*Mono Lake Ranger District, 760/647-3044*

Park Service restrictions within Yosemite National Park boundaries. Located just outside the Tuolumne Meadows entrance to Yosemite on Highway 120, the lake and its crystal clear blue waters with granite walls are a breathtaking sight. The campground is small, private, reasonably quiet, and allows small RVs only. Do not bank on launching motorboats here, as they are not allowed. But a small aluminum fishing boat is all you will need to take advantage of the Department of Fish and Game's aggressive rainbow trout stocking program. This is a great spot to cast a line during the summer and just be plain lazy. Bring the kids, too. The elevation is 9,500 feet.

Facilities: Each site has a picnic table and a fire grill. Running water and vault toilets are available nearby. The nearest store is in Lee Vining.

Getting there: From Lee Vining, go south on US 395 south to the Highway 120 crossing. Head west on Highway 120 and go 10 miles. Ellery Lake is on the right side of the road. If you reach adjacent Tioga Lake, you have gone too far.

⑱ Minaret Falls Campground 🌲🌲🌲🌲

Everything runs downhill from here. Literally. This pretty spot near the headwaters of the San Joaquin River is a prime staging point for backpackers looking for a jump-on point for the Pacific Crest Trail sections entering Devil's Postpile National Monument. The forested canyons are within walking distance of several waterfalls on the river, which supplies irrigation water for much of the Central Valley. This is another very secluded and quiet spot, but it can overload during the height of the summer outdoor season when Yosemite is packed. There are a number of other small campgrounds along the Mammoth Scenic Loop; those who shop around are sure to find one that suits their needs. The elevation is 7,800 feet.

sites	30
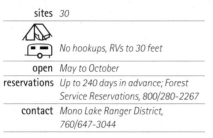	No hookups, RVs to 30 feet
open	May to October
reservations	Up to 240 days in advance; Forest Service Reservations, 800/280-2267
contact	Mono Lake Ranger District, 760/647-3044

Facilities: Each site has a picnic table and a fire grill. Running water and vault toilets are available nearby. The closest store is found in Lee Vining.

Getting there: From Lee Vining, go south on US 395 for 18 miles to Highway 203, otherwise known as the Mammoth Scenic Loop. Turn right and follow 203 for 13 miles, passing the Devil's Postpile National Monument entrance, to the campground entrance, which is on the left side of the road.

19 Sonora Bridge Campground

Once Sonora Pass opens to traffic following the snowmelt each year, it becomes a favorite backroad route connecting the Mono Lake basin with the Sierra foothills and Yosemite National Park. Sonora Bridge Campground is in a virtual no-man's-land between gold country and the main attractions of the eastern Sierra, but there is a lot to be said for these well-hidden and little-traveled cubbyholes found all over the state's national forests. The small, quiet campground is set on the banks of the West Walker River, which provides anglers with good rainbow trout action during the summer. More than anything, though, it's a lazy spot away from the hustle of the more popular tourist spots. The elevation is 7,000 feet.

sites	25
	No hookups, RVs to 36 feet
open	May to October
reservations	Up to 240 days in advance; Forest Service Reservations, 800/280-2267
contact	Bridgeport Ranger District, 760/932-7070

Facilities: Each site has a picnic table and a fire grill. Running water and vault toilets are available nearby. The nearest store is in Bridgeport.

Getting there: This section of Sonora Pass is often closed well into the late spring and early summer, so be sure to check on road conditions before heading up. It is most easily approached from US 395. From Bridgeport, drive north on US 395 for 10 miles to the Highway 108 junction. Head west 2.5 miles. The campground is on the right side of the highway.

Mono Lake is the center attraction for those visiting the eastern Sierra region.

⑳ Obsidian Campground 🌲🌲🌲

In that stretch of high country stranded between the Tahoe and Mono basins are 48,000 acres of rugged, seldom-visited wilderness pockmarked with hundreds of subalpine lakes, glacial steams, meadows, stunning granite rock formations, and endless forested canyons. Obsidian Campground is at a prime staging point for all of this, right on the back door of the Hoover Wilderness area of Toiyabe National Forest. Hikers have four nearby trailheads to choose from, and most veterans to this spot know to take their fishing gear with them, as the streams and creeks are teeming with rainbow and brook trout. Among wildlife found in these higher reaches are bear, deer, mountain lions, and small game. In wildflower season, in midsummer because of the snow pack, rare butterflies and plants are a delight. Because of its size, this campground remains quite peaceful even during the height of the tourist season; most of the road war-

sites	*15*
🏕️ 🚐	*No hookups, RVs to 30 feet*
open	*May to October*
reservations	*Up to 240 days in advance; Forest Service Reservations, 800/280-2267*
contact	*Bridgeport Ranger District, 760/932-7070*

riors are headed to big-name spots and pass this one by, luckily. The region contains countless waterfalls, deep river canyons, and numerous peaks topping 10,000 feet. The campground elevation is 8,000 feet.

Facilities: Each site has a picnic table and a fire grill. Vault toilets are available nearby. There is no running water. The nearest store is in Bridgeport.

Getting there: From Bridgeport, take US 395 north and drive 11 miles to the campground access road, which is on the left side of the road. Continue another 3.5 miles to the campground.

㉑ Robinson Creek Campground 🌲🌲🌲🌲🌲

What a set of gems. Twin Lakes is a set of adjoined alpine lakes nestled at around 7,000 feet in the high country between Sonora Pass and Mono Lake, with Hoover Wilderness adjacent. This is a great staging spot for day hikes or longer backpacking trips into the Cattle Creek watershed and adjoining areas. Hundreds of smaller lakes and fish streams dominate the wooded canyons and wide high mountain meadows here. At Twin Lakes, low-impact water sports such as kayaking and canoeing are popular during the summer. Watch for bears, bobcats, and mule deer.

sites	55
🏕️ 🚐	No hookups, RVs to 43 feet
open	May to October
reservations	Up to 240 days in advance; Forest Service Reservations, 800/280-2267
contact	Bridgeport Ranger District, 760/932-7070

Facilities: Each site has a picnic table and a fire grill. Running water and vault toilets are provided. The nearest store is in Bridgeport.

Getting there: From Bridgeport, drive west on Twin Lakes Road for 10 miles to the campground entrance, which is on the right side of the road.

㉒ Bootleg Campground 🌲

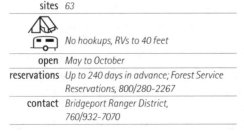

sites	63
🏕️ 🚐	No hookups, RVs to 40 feet
open	May to October
reservations	Up to 240 days in advance; Forest Service Reservations, 800/280-2267
contact	Bridgeport Ranger District, 760/932-7070

If you're just looking for a convenient place to park an RV, this will suffice. If you're looking for a quiet, out-of-the-way, pristine, natural setting where you can pitch a tent and be free of highway noise and diesel fumes, keep looking. The campground is big, crowded, noisy, too close to the highway, and too full of concrete slabs.

Facilities: Each site has a picnic table and a fire grill. Running water and vault toilets are available nearby. The nearest store is found in Bridgeport.

Getting there: From Bridgeport, go a 10 miles north on US 395. After passing the Highway 108 junction at Sonora Pass, look for the campground on the right side off the road.

㉓ Buckeye Campground 🌲🌲🌲

While the stats may make this place seem like a busy, crowded campground, it's actually quite nice, since most people are reluctant to drive on the poorly maintained dirt access road. As a result, the campground is often half empty even when the tourist areas are filled to the brim. There is good fishing in surrounding lakes and streams for brook trout and rainbow. Twin Lakes are close enough by for a day visit.

sites	65
🏕️🚐	No hookups, RVs to 28 feet
open	May to October
reservations	Up to 240 days in advance; Forest Service Reservations, 800/280-2267
contact	Bridgeport Ranger District, 760/932-7070

Facilities: Each site has a picnic table and a fire grill. Running water and vault toilets are available nearby. The closest store is found in Bridgeport.

Getting there: From Bridgeport, drive west on Twin Lakes Road for 7 miles. Turn right and continue another 4 miles to the campground.

㉔ Lower Twin Lakes Campground 🌲🌲🌲🌲

Don't be disappointed if you can't get a spot in this small, popular camping and boating location. There are several alternative campsites nearby, and access to the lake is easy enough that you can launch your boat and the hike a short distance from wherever your tent is pitched. People come to Twin Lakes for one thing: the water. The high reaches of the eastern Sierra are buried in snow for much of the year, but come late spring and early summer spots like these

sites	15
🏕️🚐	No hookups, RVs to 38 feet
open	May to October
reservations	Up to 240 days in advance; Forest Service Reservations, 800/280-2267
contact	Bridgeport Ranger District, 760/932-7070

start opening up to the Baywatch crowd. Look for beaches, bikinis, boats, and barbecues through the summer. A great place to swing from a rope swing, but to enjoy a quiet moment you'll have to hike out a little ways. The elevation is 7,800 feet.

Facilities: Each site has a picnic table and a fire grill. Running water and flush toilets are available nearby. There is a public boat ramp nearby. The closest store is found in Bridgeport.

Getting there: From Bridgeport, go west on Twin Lakes Road for 12 miles to the lake and campground entrance.

㉕ Summit Campground 🌲🌲🌲🌲🌲

Those wishing to escape the insanity of Yosemite's summer tourist season without having to forgo the wonder of sleeping under the stars in this geologic wonderland breathe a long sigh of relief when they find out places like Summit Campground exist. You know who you are: You've got a road-worthy vehicle and aren't afraid to take a few oddball turns on seldom-visited Forest Service roads. The payoff for your sense of adventure is this: shallow high mountain lakes trickling with the purest mountain waters, vast forests of Jeffrey pines and fir trees that seem undisturbed, hidden rivers and creeks just waiting for you to lower a kayak in and go for a high-speed adventure—no RVs, no barking dogs, no hotel, general store, or pizza stand. This section of Sierra National Forest contains the 584,000-acre John Muir Wilderness Area, whose snowcapped mountains, high-country glaciers and forests of pine, cedar, and fir were such and inspiration to the mountain man who dubbed the Sierra Nevada "the Range of Light." The wise and road-worn know to rest here while enjoying Yosemite Valley from afar. The elevation is 6,300 feet.

sites	6
open	May to October
reservations	Up to 240 days in advance; Forest Service Reservations, 800/280-2267
contact	Mariposa Ranger District, 559/683-4665

Facilities: Each site has a picnic table and a fire grill. Running water and vault toilets are available nearby. The nearest store is found in Fish Camp.

Getting there: From Fish Camp, go east on Highway 41 for 17 miles. Turn right on Forest Road N1402 and continue for 7 miles. At Chowchilla Mountain Road, turn left and continue another 4 miles to the campground, which is on the left side of the road.

㉖ Summerdale Campground 🌲🌲🌲🌲

If you want to be within a stone's throw of Yosemite National Park and the ever-popular Mariposa Grove of giant Sequoias, this small, pleasant campground just

sites	30
🏕️🚐	No hookups, RVs to 21 feet
open	May to October
reservations	Up to 240 days in advance; Forest Service Reservations, 800/280-2267
contact	Mariposa Ranger District, 559/683-4665

outside the town of Fish Camp may be just what you're looking for. While Summerdale could stand to be at least a little ways more off the busy Highway 41 corridor, its modest size keeps it from being overrun with the unpleasantries found in Yosemite Valley and other national park campgrounds. A lot of people bound for Yosemite pass this one by, so you shouldn't. The elevation is 4,900 feet.

Facilities: Each site has a picnic table and a fire grill. Running water and vault toilets are available nearby. The nearest store is found in Fish Camp.

Getting there: From Fish Camp, head east on Highway 41. The campground entrance is half a mile outside of town on the left.

㉗ Jerseydale Campground 🌲🌲🌲

Like Summerdale (above), this small and little-known campground outside Yosemite National Park's south entrance is a suitable alternative to the national

sites	10
🏕️🚐	No hookups, RVs to 21 feet
open	May to October
reservations	Up to 240 days in advance; Forest Service Reservations, 800/280-2267
contact	Mariposa Ranger District, 559/683-4665

park's crowded and exceedingly popular campgrounds. Set in a pretty grove of mixed pine, fir, and cedar forest, Jerseydale is a short drive from both the Mariposa Grove at Yosemite and the Wawona corridor along the south fork of the Merced River. Bring your fishing gear, kayak, birding scope, and telescope—the wildlife and bird life and big sky moments in these parts exceed expectation. The elevation is 5,200 feet.

Facilities: Each site has a picnic table and a fire grill. Running water and vault toilets are available nearby.

Getting there: From Mariposa, drive north on Highway 140 for 5 miles to Triangle Road. Turn left and continue another 3 miles to Jerseydale Road. Turn left again and proceed straight ahead to the campground.

28 Tuttletown Campground 🌲

If you didn't know you were at a federal water project campsite, you'd swear you were either at an RV dealership parking lot or a truck pull. The campgrounds are all concrete slab, and while there is greenery in the surroundings, the activities here are geared almost exclusively toward speeding around the lake in really fast boats. Oh, a bit of fishing goes on here too, as the lake is stocked with bass and rainbow trout. If you're not a big boater or fisher, skip this one, as the campground itself is dreary, unkempt, and noisy.

sites	160
🏕️ 🚐	No hookups, RVs to 40 feet
open	All year
reservations	None
contact	U.S. Bureau of Reclamation, 209/536-9004

Facilities: Each sit has a picnic table and a fire ring. Running water, flush toilets, showers, a full-service marina, public boat launch, and a sanitary disposal station for RVs are available nearby. The nearest full services are in Sonora.

Getting there: From Sonora, go north on Highway 49 for 12 miles to the small hamlet of Tuttletown. Turn left on Reynolds Ferry Road and continue a short distance to the campground and reservoir.

Other Eastern and Southern Sierra Campgrounds

There are numerous other campgrounds in the Mono Lake area. Contact the Mono Lake Ranger District office, 760/647-3044, and Forest Service Reservations, 800/280-2267, for information. Silver Lake Campground (62 sites for tents or RVs, no hookups, RVs to 30 feet) is on the banks of Silver Lake south of Mono Lake. June Lake Campground (28 sites for tents or RVs, no hookups, RVs to 30 feet) is on the banks of June Lake south of Mono Lake. Harley Springs Campground (20 sites for tents or RVs, no hookups, RVs to 22 feet) is in a pretty meadow area southeast of June Mountain.

In the Mammoth Mountain area, call the Mono Lake Ranger District as well, 760/647-3044. Other campgrounds in this region include Reas Meadows (56 sites for tents or RVs, no hookups, RVs to 30 feet), south of the Pumice Flat/Scotcher Lake complexes. Another is Lake George Campground (16 sites for tents or RVs, no hookups, RVs to 22 feet) on the banks of Lake George just southeast of Mammoth Pass. Convict Lake Campground (88 sites for tents or RVs, no hookups, RVs to 35 feet) is a popular boating area east of the Mammoth Lakes facilities near the Sierra Nevada Aquatic Research Laboratory and due north of Mammoth Mountain.

In the Sonora Pass area, call the Bridgeport Ranger District, 760/932-7070. Among choices here is Spicer Reservoir Campground (50 sites for tents or RVs, no hookups, RVs to 30 feet), in a pretty canyon flooded by a narrow lake and popular for boating. Fence Creek Campground (34 sites for tents or RVs, no hookups, RVs to 30 feet) is on a fishing creek in the high mountains near the Carson-Iceberg Wilderness. Dardanelle Campground (30 sites for tents or RVs, no hookups, RVs to 22 feet) is a more secluded choice on the middle fork of the Stanislaus River.

South of Yosemite, the Sierra National Forest Mariposa Ranger District is the contact, 559/683-4665. Choices include McCabe Flat Campground (10 sites for tents only) on the banks of the Merced River near Briceburg, a great spot for rafters. Grey's Mountain Campground (25 sites for tents or RVs, no hookups, RVs to 24 feet) is on Willow Creek and popular among visitors to Bass Lake. Fresno Dome Campground (15 sites for tents or RVs, no hookups, RVs to 22 feet) is on Big Creek near several popular trailheads to the summit of the peak for which it is named.

The nature walk along the Mono Lake shore is marked by interpretive plaques explaining the lake's complicated ecological makeup.

Southern Gold Rush Region

29 Woodward Reservoir Campground ♣ ♣ ♣

This small, pleasant, well-hidden reservoir in the Sierra foothills west of Yosemite National Park can be a pleasant stopover for outdoor travelers looking for a place

sites	155
	No hookups, RVs to 40 feet
open	All year
reservations	Up to 4 weeks in advance; Stanislaus County Department of Parks and Recreation, 209/847-3334
contact	Woodward Reservoir, 209/847-3304

to cool off at the water's edge. The lake has excellent swimming and fishing for largemouth bass and rainbow trout. The campground spaces are well-appointed and spacious. The county does a good job of managing the place and keeping the undesirable elements found at other Sierra range reservoir camp areas under control. This is still little more than a place to launch a fishing boat and park an RV, but it's at least clean and orderly.

Facilities: Each site has a picnic table and a fire ring. Running water, flush toilets, showers, a public boat ramp, and a sanitary dump station for RVs are available nearby. The nearest services are in the town of Oakdale.

Getting there: From Oakdale, take County Road J14 east for 3 miles to 26 Mile Road. Turn right and continue another 200 feet to the campground entrance.

30 Moccasin Point Campground ♣ ♣ ♣

This spot on Moccasin Lake is a quiet and peaceful setting surrounded by pretty forested areas of pine, fir, and cedar in the foothills below Yosemite National

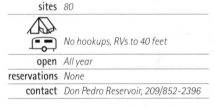

sites	80
	No hookups, RVs to 40 feet
open	All year
reservations	None
contact	Don Pedro Reservoir, 209/852-2396

Park. The lake is a holding area for water used by the city of San Francisco. One curiosity found nearby is the abandoned town of Moccasin. Once thriving as a company town occupied by water department employees, its clapboard wood-framed houses and community buildings are now abandoned. The pristine, glassy-topped lake has good bass and rainbow trout fishing during the summer. Motorboats are not allowed.

Facilities: Each site has a picnic table and a fire ring. Running water, flush toilets, showers, a public boat ramp, and a sanitary dump station for RVs are available. The nearest store is in Coulterville.

Getting there: From Coulterville, go north on Highway 49 for 3 miles to Jacksonville Road. Turn right and continue forward a short distance to the campground, which is situated on the west banks of the reservoir.

③① Horseshoe Bend Campground

We've said it before and we'll say it again: This is just another place to park your RV or pitch your tent for a few desperate hours in the middle of the night. The lake attracts a rough and rowdy type of camper. Should you take a wrong turn somewhere on your way to Yosemite or a real campground, this could very well be where you might end up. But if at all possible, skip this one.

sites	*110*
	Electrical hookups, RVs to 42 feet
open	*All year*
reservations	*Lake McClure office, 209/878-3452*
contact	*Lake McClure office, 209/878-3452*

Facilities: Each site has a picnic table and a fire ring. Running water, flush toilets, showers, a public boat ramp, a full-service marina, a general store, and a sanitary disposal station are available nearby.

Getting there: Drive Highway 132 west from Coulterville and drive 3.5 miles. Look for the campground entrance on your left.

③② Big Sandy Campground 🌲🌲🌲

This small, little-known campground very near the south entrance to Yosemite National Park is set in a pretty section of pine and fir forest in the shadows of the 7,500-foot Speckerman Mountain, on the banks of Big Creek. This campground, because of its limited size and the difficult roads leading to it, is a great place to hide out from the Yosemite tourist crowds. While it is just under 10 miles from the Yosemite entrance and the Mariposa Grove, it has the feeling of being out in the middle of nowhere. Even at the height of the tourist season, it is not uncommon to find this particular camp half empty. Those who brave it tend to be the more savvy among us; RVs tend to stay away. Steelhead fishing on Big Creek is a winner; watch out for hungry bears, as they are familiar with the camp and know how to peel apart a subcompact in search of grub. The elevation is 5,800 feet.

sites	*14*
	No hookups, RVs to 20 feet
open	*All year*
reservations	*Up to 240 days in advance; Forest Service Reservations, 800/280-2267*
contact	*Mariposa Ranger District, 559/683-4665*

Facilities: Each site has a picnic table and a fire ring. Running water and vault toilets are available nearby. The nearest store is in Fish Camp.

Getting there: From Oakhurst, go 14 miles north on Highway 41 to Fish Camp. Turn right on Jackson Road and go 5 miles to County Road 632. Turn right and continue 19 miles to the campground.

33 Chilkot Campground 🌲🌲🌲🌲

Nestled between Sivels Mountain and Graham Mountain, and set on the banks of Chilkot Creek just north of the ever popular Bass Lake, this quiet, out-of-the-way campground is a pleasant alternative not only to the more rambunctious lakeside camps but also to the crowded campgrounds within nearby Yosemite National Park.

sites	15
🏕️🚐	No hookups, RVs to 22 feet
open	All year
reservations	Up to 240 days in advance; Forest Service Reservations, 800/280-2267
contact	Mariposa Ranger District, 559/683-4665

The creek makes a nice wading area during summers when there are high enough flows. Day hikes to either mountain are a favorite activity among those who choose Chilkot, but the campground is also a great staging area for days-long backpacking trips into the wilderness. The elevation is 4,600 feet.

Facilities: Each site has a picnic table and a fire ring. There is no running water. Pit toilets are available. The nearest store is in Oakhurst.

Getting there: From Oakhurst, take Highway 41 north and go 3 miles. Turn right on Bass Lake Road. Continue another 6 miles to Beasore Road and continue forward, veering right where the road splits, to the campground.

34 Forks Campground 🌲🌲🌲

This popular boating and fishing spot, in a pretty canyon near Yosemite, is superior to most of your run-of-the mill reservoir campgrounds found throughout the Sierra Nevada. Because the lake and the campground are reasonably small, Skeeter and the "boys" are unlikely to show up with the ice chest full of beer, ready to party. Because it is a quiet spot offering easy access to the water, high-end water-skiers and bass fishers are attracted to this spot, but not in numbers large enough to spoil the ambience.

sites	30
🏕️🚐	No hookups, RVs to 22 feet.
open	May to October
reservations	Up to 240 days in advance; Forest Service Reservations, 800/280-2267
contact	Mariposa Ranger District, 559/683-4665

The creeks feeding Bass Lake all are ripe for exploration, drawing a wide variety of animals, including mule deer, coyotes, and more than 200 varieties of birds.

Facilities: Each site has a picnic table and a fire ring. Running water and vault toilets are available nearby. The nearest store is in Oakhurst.

Getting there: From Oakhurst, go 3 miles north on Highway 41 to Bass Lake Road. Turn right and proceed another 4 miles to South Shore Road. Turn right and proceed to the campground.

Other Southern Gold Rush Region Campgrounds

In the Highway 49 corridor, other campgrounds in addition to those fully profiled above include Glory Hole Campground (145 sites for tents or RVs, no hookups, RVs to 40 feet) on the banks of New Melones Reservoir, contact 209/536-9094; Horseshoe Bend Recreation Area (110 sites for tents or RVs, no hookups, RVs to 40 feet) near Lake McClure, contact 209/878-3452; Turlock Lake State Recreation Area (60 sites for tents or RVs, no hookups, RVs to 27 feet) on the banks of Turlock Lake, contact 800/444-7275; and Barrett Cove Recreation Area (275 sites for tents or RVs, no hookups, RVs to 40 feet) at Lake McClure, contact 800/486-8889.

In the Highway 41 corridor, contact the Mariposa Ranger District, 559/683-4665. Campgrounds include Millerton Lake Campground (130 sites for tents or RVs, no hookups, RVs to 32 feet) on the banks of Millerton Reservoir, contact 800/444-7275; Soquel Campground (10 sites for tents or RVs, no hookups, RVs to 22 feet) on Willow Creek in the forest; Nelder Grove Campground (10 sites for tents or RVs, no hookups, RVs to 22 feet) in a grove of Sequoia Redwoods near Oakhurst; and Clover Meadow Campground (10 sites for tents or RVs, no hookups, RVs to 22 feet) near the Ansel Adams Wilderness area.

Yosemite / Mammoth Region

㉟ Lupine-Cedar Campground 🌲🌲

For those who can't get into the smaller and much more peaceful Forks Campground (page 249), this large but nicely appointed alternative will have to do. While Lupine-Cedar is much more crowded and noisy than Forks, the lake's beauty and charm quickly make up for that if you've got the right attitude. That said, if you're looking for something smaller and more quiet, there is plenty to choose from nearby. Just keep looking.

sites	115
	No hookups, RVs to 43 feet
open	All year
reservations	Up to 240 days in advance; Forest Service Reservations, 800/280-2267
contact	Mariposa Ranger District, 559/683-4665

Facilities: Each site has a picnic table and a fire ring. Piped water and flush toilets are available nearby, as is a public boat ramp.

Getting there: From Oakhurst, go 3 miles north on Highway 41 to Bass Lake Road. Turn right and proceed another 4 miles to South Shore Road. Turn right and proceed to the campground.

㊱ Upper Highland Lake Campground 🌲🌲🌲

This is one of two nice, quiet campgrounds on the banks of Highland Lake, a well-hidden water sports spot in the foothills north of Yosemite National Park. The campgrounds rarely fill unless it's a holiday weekend during the summer, meaning you not only have a spread of prime waterfront real estate almost exclusively for your own use, but you might also even be able to get away with skinny dipping at night without shocking your neighbors (if there are families and others around, just hike into the adjacent forestlands and choose any one of dozens of smaller lakes instead). The lake is stocked with rainbow and golden trout.

sites	35
	No hookups, RVs to 40 feet
open	All year
reservations	Up to 240 days in advance; Forest Service Reservations, 800/280-2267
contact	Calaveras Ranger District, 209/795-1381

Facilities: Each site has a picnic table and a fire ring. Running water, flush toilets, and a public boat launch are nearby. There are stores in both Markleeville and Sonora.

Getting there: From Markleeville, go south on Highway 89 for 2 miles to the Highway 4 intersection. Turn right and continue 14 miles to Highland Lake Road. Turn left and continue a short distance more to the lake and campground.

37 Union Reservoir Campground 🌲🌲🌲

You won't find screaming ski boats or RVs at this small, pretty, quiet lake in the Stanislaus National Forest near Alpine Lake. The pretty walk-in sites are at the water's edge. Fishing is allowed, but local custom mandates that you avoid putting a motorboat into the water. This glassy, calm lake is best suited for rowboats and kayaks; regular customers simply will not put up with the noise of a motor. While reservations are taken, the campground is typically not full, as most boaters head for the easier-to-reach lakes with amenities for RVs. The elevation is 6,600 feet.

This knoll at Lupine-Cedar Camp has a terrific vista overlooking Sierra National Forest.

sites	15

open	All year
reservations	Up to 240 days in advance; Forest Service Reservations, 800/280-2267
contact	Calaveras Ranger District, 209/795-1381

Facilities: Each site has a picnic table and a fire ring. There is no running water. Pit toilets and a boat ramp are found nearby.

Getting there: From Markleeville, take Highway 89 and go south for 2 miles to Highway 4. Turn west and continue 27 miles to Forest Road 7N75. Turn left and go another 3 miles to the campground.

⓷ Alpine Lake 🌲🌲🌲🌲🌲

Sometimes it all just comes together: the granite walls, the rolling pine-forested foothills, the soft mountain breezes in the afternoon, and the friendly small-town manner of people who have found contentment. All of this—and some great boating, swimming, fishing, hiking, winter snowplay, and more—are found at Alpine Lake, on the Highway 4 route near Ebbett's Pass in Stanislaus National Forest. The campsites are scattered around the lake's east and south shores, in small enough clusters that there is no chance of feeling crowded in by camping rigs and boat trailers, as is the case at so many other Sierra Nevada lakes. The lake is stocked with brown trout, rainbows, catfish, and crappie. Fishing is best during the summer. In winter, this area is a good staging point for the Badger Pass ski area, but camping is not sanctioned by the Forest Service out of season. The elevation is 7,300 feet.

sites	77

	No hookups, RVs to 22 feet
open	May through October
reservations	Up to 240 days in advance; Forest Service Reservations, 800/280-2267
contact	Calaveras Ranger District, (209) 795-1381

Facilities: Each site has a picnic table and a fire grill. Running water and flush toilets are available. A public boat ramp and a general store are nearby.

Getting there: From Markleeville, take Highway 89 south for 2 miles to Highway 4. Turn right and continue 21 miles to Lake Alpine village. Follow the signs to the Lake Alpine access road, turn left, and continue forward a short distance to the lake and camping facilities.

39 Mill Creek Campground 🌲🌲🌲🌲

While you could be waiting a long time for a fish to go by while you're camping out on the banks of Mill Creek, anglers enjoy this small, quiet, secluded campground because it is equal distance between three good fishing spots: Donnell Lake, Beardsley Lake, and Pinecrest Lake. Nestled in a pretty canyon of pine forests, Mill Creek Campground is also a favorite among day hikers who want a base of operation for expeditions into the rugged Dardanelle region of the Carson–Iceberg Wilderness, located just a few miles to the north. During hunting season, this small camp is often crowded in by game hunters using the state refuge on the other side of the Stanislaus River—so if you don't like rifles, stay away toward the end of the outdoor season and during the winter. The elevation is 6,312 feet.

sites	18
🏕️🚐	No hookups, RVs to 32 feet
open	All year
reservations	Up to 240 days in advance; Forest Service Reservations, 800/280-2267
contact	Summit Ranger District, 209/965-3434

Facilities: Each site has a picnic table and a fire ring. There is no running water. Vault toilets are available nearby. The nearest store is in Hot Springs.

Getting there: From Hot Springs on Highway 108 go 12 miles west to Forest Road 5N21. Turn left and continue 200 feet to the campground entrance.

40 Niagara Creek Campground 🌲🌲🌲🌲

Safely out of reach of the nearby water sports areas of Donnell Lake and the busy highway traffic along Highway 108, this small, well-hidden campground on the banks of Niagra Creek resembles a backcountry setting you'd normally have to hike for days to reach. The short hike to Double Dome Rock is an easy way to get a grand vista of the surrounding foothills, including a sweeping view of the Stanislaus River drainage and the Emigrant Wilderness off to the southwest. While the creek is not much of a fishing spot, Donnell Lake is just a stone's throw away. Hikers will enjoy the easy access from here to the Carson–Iceberg Wilderness and Emigrant Wilderness. Black Hawk Mountain and Three Chimneys in Emigrant Wilderness make great day hikes, but they require a drive from camp to stage at the appropriate trailheads. Note that of the dozen sites found here, three are reserved for hike-in campers only. If you can manage to score one of these, your experience will be twice as nice. The elevation is 6,400 feet.

sites	12
🏕️🚐	3 tent-only / No hookups, RVs to 21 feet.
open	All year
reservations	Up to 240 days in advance; Forest Service Reservations, 800/280-2267
contact	Summit Ranger District, 209/965-3434

Facilities: Each site has a picnic table and a fire ring. There is no running water. Vault toilets are available nearby. The nearest store is in Hot Springs.

Getting there: From Hot Springs, go west on Highway 108 for 17 miles to Forest Road 6N24. Turn left and continue half a mile to the campground.

④ Pigeon Flat Campground 🌲🌲🌲🌲

This small walk-in campground is a great spot to introduce children to the concepts of backpacking while staying close enough to civilization to run for cover if it becomes necessary. The setting is a pretty forested flat in the shadows of Bald Peak and Red Peak in the Carson–Iceberg Wilderness. A small creek flows nearby. Note that while this is a private and quiet setting on the balance of things, there is a YMCA camp right next door and a highway not far away. We suggest it mostly to provide the illusion of primitive camping and seclusion without having to push a stroller up 20 miles of switchbacks. The elevation is 6,700 feet.

sites	7
open	All year
reservations	Up to 240 days in advance; Forest Service Reservations, 800/280-2267
contact	Summit Ranger District, 209/965-3434

Facilities: Each site has a picnic table and a fire grill. There is no running water. Vault toilets are available nearby. The nearest store is in Dardanelle.

Getting there: From Hot Springs, drive west on Highway 108 west for 24 miles to Dardanelle. The campground is on the left side of the highway near the Columns of the Giants.

④ Lumsden Campground 🌲🌲🌲🌲

San Francisco residents who want to see where their drinking water comes from can pitch a tent here, on the banks of the Tuolumne River, and do just that. And before they go home to drink some of that water, they can lower a raft into the source and have a little bit of fun. Word has it that rafters outnumber the number of people who come to Lumsden just to admire a good drinking water source. The other obvious reason to camp out here is that there is easy access to the Highway 120 entrance to Yosemite National Park. In fact, those who have several days to make of it can hike from a base camp here on the river over Pilot Ridge

sites	11
open	All year
reservations	Up to 240 days in advance; Forest Service Reservations, 800/280-2267
contact	Groveland Ranger District, 209/962-7825

and Pilot Peak to Crane Flat in Yosemite and ultimately down into Yosemite Valley. The campground elevation is 1,500 feet.

Facilities: Each site has a picnic table and a fire pit. There is no running water. Vault toilets are available nearby. The nearest store is in Groveland.

Getting there: From Groveland, go east on Highway 120 for 7.5 miles to Forest Road 1S23. Turn left and follow the road to a parking area for the campground. The camp itself is half a mile from the parking area.

④③ Cherry Lake Campground

This very well-managed campground on the banks of Cherry Lake, an irrigation dam on Cherry Creek, is a great spot for boaters and RV campers looking for an out-of-the way enough spot that they can enjoy what they enjoy without having to put up with the crowds found at larger, easier-to-reach facilities. While hikers will enjoy the easy access to Cherry Ridge and Hells Mountain, this is primarily a camping, fishing, and swimming spot during the summer. Lake Eleanor, within the Yosemite boundaries, is nearby also. The elevation is 5,000 feet.

sites	46
	No hookups, RVs to 40 feet
open	All year
reservations	Up to 240 days in advance; Forest Service Reservations, 800/280-2267
contact	Groveland Ranger District, 209/962-7825

Facilities: Each site has a picnic table and a fire ring. Running water and vault toilets are available nearby. There is a public boat ramp nearby also.

Getting there: From Groveland, take Highway 120 east and drive 12 miles to Forest Road N107. Turn left and continue another 24 miles, along a number of treacherous twists and turns, to the lake.

④④ Lost Claim Campground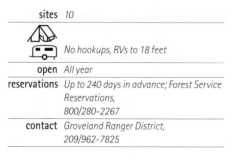

sites	10
	No hookups, RVs to 18 feet
open	All year
reservations	Up to 240 days in advance; Forest Service Reservations, 800/280-2267
contact	Groveland Ranger District, 209/962-7825

Ever pack the car for Yosemite on a busy summer weekend and then chicken out half way there? Lost Claim, then, is the perfect escape for you. Just a few miles from the Highway 120 entrance to Yosemite, this small, well-managed campground has all of the privacy and quiet that Yosemite Valley doesn't—and yet is conveniently located enough that day visits to the popular tourist areas are indeed still possible. When not visiting Yosemite, instead enjoy the small creeks and forested canyons of the Tuolumne River canyon. Lost Claim is a great place for fishing, hiking, swimming, and staging longer backpacking trips, even into Yosemite itself. The elevation is 3,000 feet.

Facilities: Each site has a picnic table and a fire ring. Running water and vault toilets are available nearby. There is a general store in Groveland.

Getting there: From Groveland, drive east on Highway 120 east for 14 miles. The campground is on the left side of the road.

45 Sweetwater Campground ▲▲▲

In the mood to climb a mountain? Or sneak into Yosemite National Park without paying the $20? Then camp out at Sweetwater. This small campground on the banks of the Tuolumne River's south fork is more than just an overflow camp for those spots in Yosemite Valley that tend to fill up too quickly. There is good trail access for backpackers and day hikers to Saw Mountain, Ascension Mountain, Ackerson Mountain, Bear Mountain, and Pilot Ridge, which is one of the most popular hiking routes into Yosemite National Park from Stanislaus National Forest. The elevation is 6,300 feet.

sites	13
	No hookups, RVs to 21 feet
open	All year
reservations	Up to 240 days in advance; Forest Service Reservations, 800/280-2267
contact	Groveland Ranger District, 209/962-7825

Facilities: Each site has a picnic table and a fire pit. Running water and vault toilets are available nearby. There is a store in Groveland.

Getting there: From Groveland, go 25 miles east on Highway 120. The campground is on the left side of the road.

Ratings Index

Campground Index

D

E

F

M

N